THE MORAL PHILOSOPHERS

THE MORAL PHILOSOPHERS

An Introduction to Ethics

RICHARD NORMAN

CLARENDON PRESS · OXFORD

Oxford University Press, Great Clarendon Street, Oxford OX2 6DP
Oxford New York
Athens Auckland Bangkok Bogota Bombay
Buenos Aires Calcutta Cape Town Dar es Salaam
Delhi Florence Hong Kong Istanbul Karachi
Kuala Lumpur Madras Madrid Melbourne
Mexico City Nairobi Paris Singapore
Taipei Tokyo Toronto
and associated companies in
Berlin Ibadan

Oxford is a trade mark of Oxford University Press

Published in the United States by
Oxford University Press Inc., New York

British Library Cataloguing in Publication Data
Norman, Richard
The moral philosophers.
1. Ethics—History
I. Title
170'.9 BƷ71
ISBN 0-19-875059-5 Pbk

10

Printed in Great Britain
on acid-free paper by
Biddles Ltd, Guildford and King's Lynn

Preface

A book such as this, aiming to cover a large area of philosophy, is bound to involve many intellectual debts. To those who taught me moral philosophy, those with whom I have taught moral philosophy, and those to whom I have taught moral philosophy, I am most grateful for all that I have learned from them and all the stimulation I have gained from them.

More specifically I should like to thank Chris Cherry, Bruce Landesman, Sean Sayers, and Tony Skillen for reading all or part of the first draft and making valuable comments, Karen Jones for all her help with the process of revision, and Sue Macdonald, Eileen Barker, Pat Evans, Yvonne Latham, and Jane Neame for their help with the typing.

When a previous book of mine on ethics was published, my landlady, to whom I gave a copy, commented 'It must be very good—I can't understand a word of it.' My hope is that, in this respect at least, the present book is less good.

Contents

1 Introduction
Ethics and its History

The area of philosophy traditionally known as 'ethics' or 'moral philosophy' is the attempt to arrive at an understanding of the nature of human values, of how we ought to live, and of what constitutes right conduct. The present book is intended as an introduction to ethics. I shall present some of the main positions in ethics which have been advocated by different philosophers, and convey some idea of the variety of these and the disagreements between them. I shall not, however, be neutral. In part this is inevitable; one cannot escape judgements about which positions are important enough to be taken seriously and to be worth discussing, and about how much attention they merit. My non-neutrality will not end there, however. I shall attempt a critical assessment of the different positions, and thereby work towards some conclusions about what a correct ethical theory would look like.

'Ethics' or 'moral philosophy' (I use the terms interchangeably) is not concerned solely with the elucidation and justification of 'morality' in the narrow sense. What precisely that narrow sense is, we shall have to consider in due course. However, it is clear that to assess people's conduct as immoral or as morally admirable is to consider it from only one point of view, and not the only possible one. In the study of moral philosophy we are concerned more generally with questions about how one ought to live, about what could count as good reasons for acting in one way rather than another, and about what constitutes a good life for human beings, meaning thereby not necessarily 'morally good', but treating as an open question, where would be the proper place for morality in the good life, and whether indeed it has any place there at all.

Many contemporary philosophers distinguish between

'substantive ethics' or 'normative ethics' on the one hand, and what they call 'meta-ethics' on the other. Substantive ethics, they say, is concerned with the question, 'What kinds of action are good or right?', whereas meta-ethics is concerned with the question, 'What is it to say of an action that it is good or right?' That is to say, the second question is a question about the correct analysis of the *language* used in the first question. The aim of meta-ethics is to discover not what is good, or what is right, but what we *mean* when we say of something that it is 'good' or 'right'. To put it another way, it is concerned with an examination of *concepts*—with analysing concepts such as 'good' and 'right', rather than with actually using the concepts to talk about human conduct. Or again, meta-ethics is concerned with examining the *logic* of ethical discourse—with questions such as, 'How do we *know* that one course of action is better than another?', 'Can we ever really be said to *know* such a thing?', 'What kinds of *argument*, if any, could support such a claim?' The difference between substantive ethics and meta-ethics can be summarized as a difference between 'first-order' and 'second-order' discussions. At the first level, that of substantive ethics, our discussions are directly concerned with practical questions of conduct, but we can then move the discussion to a second level, from which we look back at the first level, and raise questions about what it was that we were doing at that first level.

That distinction is a useful one. It becomes suspect, however, when it is accompanied by the further suggestion that the proper concern of philosophy is solely with meta-ethics, and not at all with substantive ethics. That is what many contemporary philosophers would assert. It is not the business of the philosopher, they say, to tell people how to live. People can, and should, make such decisions for themselves. The only contribution which the philosopher can usefully make is to help them to clarify the terms which they use, and the arguments which they employ, in making such decisions.

Why this philosophical modesty? Part of what is involved here is a desire on the part of philosophers not to set themselves up as preachers, a desire that people should decide for themselves how to live instead of being told by self-appointed experts. These liberal attitudes are ones which I would share. It does not follow, however, that a philosophical engagement in substantive ethics is bound to take the form of preaching. It does so only if we think of philosophers as a race apart, and assume that when they set out their views about the nature of human good, they are implying that no one else is capable of having such views. We do not have to accept these assumptions. Philosophy as I understand it is, on the contrary, a shared enterprise in which everyone is, at least potentially, a participant, and when I, as a professional teacher of philosophy, set out certain theories of substantive ethics, I do so not in order to preach, but in order to contribute to that common enterprise.

There is a second factor which helps to explain the prevalent philosophical modesty. Many philosophers would say that they cannot establish correct theories about how one ought to live, because *no one* can do so. There is, they would say, no such thing as a 'correct' view about how one ought to live, since beliefs about such matters cannot properly be said to be either true or false. Rather, they should be understood as expressions of feelings or attitudes, choices or commitments, and if people differ from one another in their basic attitudes about what is good or right, there is in principle no way of resolving the disagreement, no 'correct' answer to be arrived at.

This is a doctrine, known as ethical subjectivism or ethical scepticism, which we shall have to consider in due course. It is itself a meta-ethical doctrine. Clearly, if correct, it sets severe limits on what can be done in the way of substantive ethics. It does not rule out substantive ethics entirely, for it is still open to the ethical subjectivist to try to set out in a systematic and coherent way his own ethical attitudes, in the hope that they will appeal to others also. The great ethical philosophers of the past have all aimed to do at least this. But most of them have aimed at more. They have assumed that by the use of philosophical argument, and by appealing to shared human experience, they can provide a rational justification for a systematic theory of what would constitute right conduct or a good life for human beings.

For the purposes of this book, at any rate, I want to suggest that we cannot decide whether ethical subjectivism is or is not inescapable until we have made the attempt to work out a substantive ethical theory. The only way to find out whether reason and experience can objectively establish a view of the good life is to trust to them and see how far they will take us. This brings me to my own view of the relation between substantive ethics and meta-ethics. I have said that the distinction is a useful one. I also believe, however, that each enterprise can be properly carried out only in close conjunction with the other. Again, this has been the practice of the great philosophers of the past. In aiming to give a rational account of the good life, they have also been self-conscious about the nature of their procedures, their terminology and their modes of argument. In other words, they have been engaged in substantive ethics but have combined this with meta-ethical reflections on the status of their own substantive ethics. By contrast, many modern philosophers isolate meta-ethics from substantive ethics. As a result they not only produce extremely arid and dissatisfying moral philosophy, but also produce meta-ethics which is bad even as meta-ethics, just because it is isolated from substantive considerations and is therefore based on artificial and over-simplified examples of ethical beliefs.

I have said that I intend to examine the ethical theories proposed by some of the great philosophers of the past. This procedure needs some defending. When we contemplate the history of philosophy and find a succession of theories, each of which has been refuted by subsequent philosophers, and none of which has survived criticism intact, we may feel that the best thing to do with this history is to turn our backs on it. This tends to be the reaction of newcomers to the study of philosophy, who are likely to feel that they should waste no time on past theories which everyone now agrees to be untenable. Perhaps then we should dispense with the history, and concentrate on developing those approaches on which contemporary philosophers agree—although this resolve may itself succumb to a historically-induced scepticism, in view of the frequency with which philosophers have turned away from the past, declared a fresh start, and claimed that now at last they have found the correct approach, only to be superseded by the next such claim.

The one philosopher who has attempted to work through this scepticism, and to arrive at some positive response to it, is the nineteenth-century German philosopher Hegel. In his *Lectures on the History of Philosophy* he notes how, faced with the diversity of past philosophies, and the fact that they all seem to refute one another, we may feel

the necessity for applying to philosophy the words of Christ, 'Let the dead bury their dead; arise, and follow me.' The whole of the history of philosophy becomes a battlefield covered with the bones of the dead; it is a kingdom not merely formed of dead and lifeless individuals, but of refuted and spiritually dead systems, since each has killed and buried the other.[1]

For all that, Hegel wants to place the study of the history of philosophy at the centre of his philosophical method, and to insist that 'no philosophy has ever been refuted'. What have been refuted are the claims of particular philosophical systems to be final and complete in themselves. Past philosophies have typically erred by being partial and one-sided, treating as all-embracing a certain explanatory principle which has an appropriate application within its own proper philosophical sphere. The task of the history of philosophy is, therefore, to identify the important principle to be retained from each of the major philosophies of the past, to allot to it its appropriate place as an element within the whole, and to identify its proper relations to the other necessary philosophical principles.[2]

The method must not be misunderstood. It is not simply a matter of mixing together all past philosophies in the hope that the resulting pot-pourri will contain something to satisfy everyone. As Hegel insists, the history of philosophy is as much a negative as a positive enterprise. It is essentially a critical activity. Only through the criticism of past philosophies can one determine the positive form in which each is to be retained, its appropriate limits and its appropriate place within the whole. None of them can be accepted as it stands; the transforming role of criticism is essential.

We may indeed feel that we need to go even further than

Hegel in emphasizing the role of negative criticism. He perhaps fails to recognize sufficiently the way in which the positive contributions of past philosophies coexist with distortions arising from the limited social perspective of the philosopher in question. Every philosophy contains an ideological component—an element which is to be explained as a rationalization of the limited interests and perspective of the philosopher's own social class. Part of the task of examining the history of ethical theories is therefore to distinguish the ideological components from the contributions to a shared understanding of the human good. There can, of course, be no guarantee that our own ethical discussions will not contain their elements of class ideology, but if we are aware of the danger we can, at least to some extent, guard against it.

To the idea that one can simply and indiscriminately lump together all previous ethical philosophies a further corrective must be mentioned. What are we to count as 'past philosophies'? Not every single recorded instance of human reflection on the nature of the good life. Quite apart from the inconceivability of ever completing such a survey, the very idea of a *history* of philosophy involves the discrimination of the significant from the insignificant and, beyond that, the identification of those major contributions which should form the core of the historical tradition. We need to recognize here the operation of what Raymond Williams has called 'the selective tradition'.[3] Any cultural tradition (not only philosophical but literary, artistic, or scientific) is formed and defined by a process of selection. When we speak, for example, of 'the nineteenth-century English novel', we are talking not of every novel written in England during that period, but of certain general lines of development exemplified by what have come to be seen as the most significant contributions to the genre. Nor is the process of selection ever completed once and for all. Each new generation offers its own re-definition of the tradition. 'In a society as a whole, and in all its particular activities, the cultural tradition can be seen as a continual selection and re-selection of ancestors. Particular lines will be drawn, often for as long as a century, and then suddenly, with some new stage in growth, these will be cancelled or weakened, and new lines drawn.'[4]

So it is also in moral philosophy, and one of the aims of this book is to propose a re-defining of the tradition. In a very broad sense my approach in the book is a Hegelian one. Through a critique of some major ethical theories I work towards a positive position which retains what is valid in them. However, though my approach is historical, what I have to offer is not a history of ethics. It is *too* selective for that. I have not attempted a general interpretation of the tradition, but rather have picked out what I take to be a few of the major contributions to Western ethical thought. I begin with the two great philosophers of Greek antiquity, Plato and Aristotle. I then leap two thousand years to some representative philosophers of the eighteenth and nineteenth centuries, who continue many of the themes and preoccupations of the Greeks, but within a Christian culture which also produces significant differences in their thought. I shall look at the ethical philosophies of David Hume, Immanuel Kant, and John Stuart Mill, and at Hegelian ethics as represented by the British Hegelian philosopher F. H. Bradley. So far, I trace a fairly orthodox lineage, though my inclusion of Bradley and Hegelianism may be thought to be somewhat deviant. At this point, however, I depart from the orthodox definition of the tradition. In my view its most important continuation is not to be found in the work of the professional academic philosophers. They do indeed constitute one line of development from Bradley. It would be foolish to deny that they have raised significant issues, and I shall pay some attention to them in my final chapter. But if we are to look for that intellectual work which substantially extends the Western tradition of ethical thought, which raises the most significant problems in relation to contemporary experience, and which has had the greatest impact on popular consciousness, I suggest that we shall find it in the ideas stemming from Karl Marx and Sigmund Freud. Neither of them is primarily an ethical philosopher, but that is one aspect of their importance, for what their work does above all is to render problematic the whole status of ethical thought. In what they have to say about the relation of ethics to politics and to psychology respectively, they force us to ask whether the very idea of ethics, with its focus on the voluntary actions of the individual agent, may not be radically misconceived.

One further word about the organization of this book. It is not complete in itself. I do not provide a comprehensive paraphrase of the major writers whom I discuss. There is no substitute for reading their own words. At the beginning of each chapter I suggest a basic text, which I assume that the reader will look at in conjunction with my own chapter. All of them are readily available. My own discussions will include suggestions about how to read the texts, as well as critical comments on them, but I do not aim to take the place of the texts themselves.

I begin, then, with the Greeks. Why choose such a remote starting-point? The simple answer is that the work of Plato and Aristotle remains unsurpassed. We can learn as much about ethics from them as from any of their successors, and although, from a contemporary vantage-point, it is unlikely that any philosopher would describe himself unqualifiedly as a Platonist or as an Aristotelian, the position towards which I shall work in this book is closer to them than to anyone else.

There is another reason for starting with the Greeks. Ethics itself, as a form of intellectual enquiry, at least in the West, begins with them. In the thought of the Greek philosophers we can trace the beginnings of philosophical reflection on the nature of the good life and right conduct. Although the philosophies of Plato and Aristotle contain the first comprehensive and systematic ethical theories, it is among their predecessors that we find the origins of ethical thought, and in the remainder of this chapter I shall sketch these beginnings before turning to Plato and Aristotle themselves.

The emergence of critical philosophical thought about ethics can be traced to the ideas of the Sophists, a group of thinkers active in the Greek world of the fifth century BC. The Sophists were not primarily philosophers. They were itinerant teachers who travelled from city-state to city-state offering, for a fee, all manner of teaching—in mathematics, music, astronomy, and language, but above all in rhetoric. It was their ability to teach the art of rhetoric that gave the Sophists their popularity, for in the political life of the time, and especially in a democracy like Athens, the key to political success lay in the ability to persuade with a speech in the assembly or the lawcourts, and ambitious young men were eager to acquire this skill.

Although the Sophists were not primarily philosophers, certain philosophical ideas came to be associated with them, largely because of their need to justify their own activity. The accusation to which they were obviously exposed was that in teaching people the art of persuasion they were enabling them to make others believe what was in fact false. If the Sophists' pupils in rhetoric were concerned only to propagate those beliefs which happened to suit their own convenience, then all concern for truth seemed to have vanished. A typical response on the part of the Sophists was to question the very ideas of truth and falsity. Thus Protagoras, the most famous of the Sophists, held that 'man is the measure of all things, of what is, that it is, and of what is not, that it is not'. Whatever seems to me to be the case, is true for me, and whatever seems to you to be the case, is true for you. No belief can be said to be true or false in itself, for there is no objective truth. In this way Protagoras and other Sophists hoped to evade the criticism that they encouraged a contempt for truth.

This line of thought was applied also to morality. According to Protagoras, moral ideas are a matter of convention. 'Convention' is here contrasted with 'nature', and the distinction between nature and convention is perhaps the most important philosophical idea associated with the Sophists. In asserting moral laws to be human conventions they were influenced especially by the growing awareness of cultural diversity. With the growth of trade over the previous two centuries, leading to greater contact with other peoples, the Greeks had become increasingly aware of the ways in which customs vary from society to society. The historian Herodotus delights in listing such differences: the Egyptians do this, the Thracians do that, here they cremate their dead and there they embalm them, in this society they practise polygamy and in that one they practise incest. From this awareness of diversity it is a short step to the philosophical claim that what we call morality, justice, virtue, and the like is nothing other than a set of humanly created conventions.

The view that morality is conventional rather than natural does not necessarily entail a rejection of morality. On the contrary, among the more conservative Sophists it led to a stress on the importance of conventions. Protagoras' moral relativism took the form of asserting that whatever is thought right in a particular society *is* right for that society. Every society needs a set of moral conventions simply in order to function as a community. Without it the community would disintegrate as its members all went their separate ways. Although some conventions may be more effective than others, what matters most is not their precise content but the fact that they are shared and adhered to.

Among the younger Sophists and their more radical followers, however, the nature/convention contrast was put to a very different use. The conclusion was drawn that if moral constraints are mere conventions, they should be cast aside. What was rational was to live according to nature rather than according to convention. The idea of acting in accordance with nature was variously interpreted, but a common interpretation was that it meant pursuing one's own self-interest, and refusing to be tied down in this pursuit by moral inhibitions.

The more conservative and the more radical Sophists both recognize that standards of right and wrong can be questioned. Their response is either to deny them the status of truth, or to reject them altogether. In so doing they inaugurate the activity of ethical philosophy. What they do is to make human conduct problematic. Questions about how to act can no longer be answered by an automatic appeal to accepted norms. It becomes necessary to face the question, '*Why* should I act in this way rather than that?', to look for acceptable *reasons* for different kinds of actions, and to consider whether such reasons are in fact ever obtainable.

Plato and Aristotle take up this challenge. They retain many of the values of traditional morality, but they do not retain them uncritically. They attempt to place them on a rational foundation. In particular, both of them retain the traditional Greek conception of the virtues—qualities such as courage, moderation, wisdom, piety, and justice. The core of the ethical systems of both Plato and Aristotle is the attempt to justify the virtues in terms of human happiness, to show that they are good qualities to possess, because a life lived in accordance with the virtues is the happiest and most rewarding kind of life. If they can do this, they will have shown that nature and convention are not antithetical, that conventional values have their basis in nature. In the next three chapters we shall consider how successful Plato and Aristotle are in this enterprise.

Notes

1 G. W. F. Hegel: *Lectures on the History of Philosophy*, trans. E. S. Haldane and Frances H. Simson (London, 1894), p. 17.
2 Ibid., pp. 36-9.
3 Raymond Williams: *The Long Revolution* (Harmondsworth, 1965), pp. 66-70.
4 Ibid., p. 69.

PART I

The Ancients

2 Plato
The Health of the Personality

Reading: Plato: *The Republic*

Numerous translations are available. I shall quote from the translation by H. D. P. Lee in the Penguin Classics series. Page numbers refer to the marginal numbering which is standard in all texts and translations of *The Republic*. With the possible exception of Book X, *The Republic* is a unity and should be read as a whole. However, for our present purposes the most important sections are 327a–367e (the preliminary discussion), 434d–445e (definition of justice in the individual), 474b–480a (the theory of forms), 504a–521b (analogies of the sun, divided line, and cave), and 543a–592a (the various kinds of injustice).

Socrates

Almost all of Plato's philosophical writings take the form of dramatized discussions, and in most of them the main participant is Socrates. The life and thought of Socrates exercised an enormous influence on Plato. In the minds of many of his contemporaries Socrates was identified with the Sophists. He was not, however, a professional teacher, indeed he claimed he had nothing to teach. He simply questioned people. He would engage in discussion those of his fellow citizens who had a reputation for piety, courage, moderation, or some other virtue; he would ask them 'What is piety?', 'What is courage?', or 'What is moderation?', and by following up their answers with further persistent questioning, would reveal that they could give no satisfactory account of the virtues they were supposed to possess.

Like the Sophists, Socrates thereby raises the basic questions of ethics. What is the good life, and why should we live it? But in contrast to the Sophists, Socrates' intent was much less negative and much more serious. He was not concerned to dismiss the possibility of ethical knowledge. On the contrary, he maintained that though he himself did not possess it, such knowledge was attainable, and was by far the most important thing to strive for.

Nevertheless, one can see how Socrates could have come to be linked with the Sophists, and how his activities would have been resented as disruptive by the conventionally upright citizens of Athens. In 399 BC he was brought to trial on a charge of corrupting the young and introducing new divinities. He was found guilty, and put to death. The manner of his death, as that of his life, remained for Plato an enduring inspiration.

The form of Plato's dialogues presents us with a problem. In a work like *The Republic* all the important philosophical ideas are put into the mouth of Socrates. Do these ideas represent the philosophy of the historical Socrates, or the philosophy of Plato? The question is a vexed one, which we cannot deal with here. I shall simply assume what is at present the most widely accepted view, that, though in some of his earlier and shorter dialogues Plato may give us a fairly accurate picture of the historical Socrates, in major works like *The Republic* the philosophy presented is Plato's own, using Socrates as his mouthpiece.

Plato's Aims in *The Republic*

The theme of *The Republic* is the nature of justice. The Greek word is *dikaiosuné*. In English versions of Plato the term is standardly translated as 'justice', but the Greek concept is somewhat wider than that. The English word 'justice' primarily refers to ethical principles regulating the distribution of social benefits and burdens. It suggests the idea of people receiving their fair share or their appropriate deserts, and is closely linked also with the idea of law. *Dikaiosuné* sometimes carries similarly specific connotations, but is also used more widely so that it almost amounts to something like 'the disposition to act rightly'—to act rightly, that is, in one's dealings with other people, for *dikaiosuné* is the social virtue *par excellence*. Often we could translate it as 'morality' and not be far off the mark. As Plato says, typical manifestations of injustice would be committing sacrilege or theft, betraying one's friends or one's country, breaking promises, committing adultery, and neglecting one's duties to one's parents and to the gods. I shall abide by the standard translation 'justice', but the reader should bear in mind the wider connotations.

The account of justice in *The Republic* is built upon a comparison between the just individual and the just society. The work therefore deals not only with ethics or moral philosophy in the strict sense, but also with social and political philosophy (and indeed with metaphysics, the theory of knowledge, the theory of art—it is Plato's most comprehensive treatment of all his various philosophical interests). Much of the work is taken up with Plato's account of the organization of his ideal society, and with a discussion of how the existing societies of his day deviated from this ideal. How successfully Plato integrates his moral philosophy with his social philosophy is a matter for debate, to which I shall return. For the time being I shall concentrate on the more specifically ethical parts of *The Republic*.

The preliminary discussion of justice can be related to the Sophists' contrast between 'nature' and 'convention'. The old man Cephalus and his son Polemarchus are the spokesmen of convention. They can define justice only in terms of conventional examples: telling the truth and paying one's debts (Cephalus); or, at a slightly more theoretical level, giving everyone his due, benefiting one's friends and harming one's enemies, or perhaps benefiting the good and harming the bad (Polemarchus). When Thrasymachus impatiently bursts into the discussion, it is as the advocate of nature against convention. His views are typical of the more radical Sophists. He thinks that conventional justice and morality consist of rules promulgated by the ruling group in society, to keep everyone else in check and to promote the rulers' own interests. The conclusion which he draws is: don't be fooled, disregard justice whenever you can get away with it, pursue your own interests and not those of other people. He believes that the only rational and natural mode of conduct is the pursuit of self-interest, and that this requires a rejection of conventional justice.

The position subsequently put forward by Glaucon, and elaborated by his brother Adeimantus, can usefully be seen as a compromise between nature and convention. They present it not as their own view, but as one which is very widely held. (For brevity's sake, however, I shall refer to it as 'Glaucon's view'.) According to this common opinion, they say, the way of life advocated by Thrasymachus would be. the best if one could get away with it. If one possessed the mythical ring of Gyges, which could render one invisible, this would be possible. But as things are, if you simply pursue your own interests and entirely disregard the interests of others, inflicting harm and injury on them whenever it suits you, then others will act in the same way towards you, and you are likely to end up the loser. When people realize this, they come to an understanding with one another that each will as far as possible refrain from inflicting harm on others, provided everyone else likewise refrains. Justice, then, is indeed a convention, but it is the best available approximation to that 'self-interest which all nature naturally pursues as good'. Adeimantus adds that conventional justice has the further advantage of securing the favour of the gods as well as that of our fellow humans. Again this is an unfortunate but inescapable fact of life; if we could manage without the favour of the gods we would do so, and would then not need justice.

These ethical positions, put forward by Thrasymachus and by Glaucon and Adeimantus, set the scene for the dialogue. Socrates will confront them and attempt to refute them. It cannot be emphasized too strongly that they are not merely 'straw men'. Commentators on *The Republic* are tempted to treat Thrasymachus, in particular, as someone who is quite obviously wrong. We should, on the contrary, take very seriously the possibility that he may be right. Certainly the position presented by Glaucon as the popular view is as widely held in our own day as it was in his. The question, 'Why should I pursue my own interests?' seems redundant; such action has an obvious rationality. On the other hand the question, 'Why should I heed other people's interests?' does seem to require an answer. And in view of the obvious rationality of pursuing my own interests, the most plausible answer would seem to be that it is rational for me to heed other people's interests, just in so far as I need to do so for the sake of my own interests. This is the plausibility in Glaucon's view. And if there is that degree of truth in it, then there may be an equal degree of truth in Thrasymachus' view. For, though there are some cases where we cannot get away with injustice, there are surely other cases where we can, and is it not then rational to do so? We do not have to choose between total justice and total injustice. If the only test of rationality is self-interest, then it must be rational to lie or cheat or steal or harm others, when no one else will know and one can save one's reputation—in a shady business deal, perhaps, or minor pilfering from one's place of work, or a host of other everyday situations where a little bit of injustice would come in handy.

Can Thrasymachus be answered? Should we want to answer him? Plato, through Socrates, intends to do so. His response to Thrasymachus, and to the Sophists generally, is threefold.

1. He rejects the antithesis of nature and convention. He wishes to link the two more closely than Glaucon does. Conventional justice is not simply the best available approximation to the dictates of nature. It is itself grounded in nature, that is, in human nature. If we understand our own nature as human beings, we shall see that the life of conventional justice is thoroughly in accordance with that nature.
2. He rejects the opposition between conventional justice and personal benefit. A life lived in accordance with conventional justice will itself be the happiest and most worthwhile kind of life. Again the link between justice and well-being is closer than that posited by Glaucon. For Glaucon the relation between justice and happiness is that of means and ends; justice is not desirable in itself, but it secures happiness as a *consequence*, because it ensures that other people will be just towards oneself. For Plato the life of justice is *by its very nature* the happiest life.
3. He rejects Protagoras' view that there are no objective ethical truths or values. Since justice is grounded in human

nature, we can establish as an objective truth that there are good reasons for living the life of justice.

In Plato's attempted refutation of the Sophists, the crucial role is played by the definition of justice at 434d–445e. Justice in society has been defined as a harmonious relation between the three main social classes: the guardians, the auxiliaries, and the economic class. When each class performs its proper function—when the guardians rule, the auxiliaries defend the society against its enemies, and the economic class engages in production and exchange—the society as a whole will be a harmonious unity and will be perfectly just. Socrates now suggests that to these social classes there correspond three parts of the soul, three aspects of the human personality. These are reason, spirit, and desire. By 'spirit' is meant those emotional capacities which variously express themselves in such phenomena as anger, strength of will, conscience, and shame. Though the noun 'spirit' may have misleading connotations, the adjective 'spirited' captures something of the right meaning. 'Desire' seems to mean primarily the physical appetites, the desires for food and drink and sexual satisfaction, but this raises questions of interpretation which we shall have to look at later.

Socrates proposes that, as justice in society is a harmonious relation between classes, so justice in the individual consists in a harmonious relation between the different aspects of the personality. Reason must rule, spirit must assist reason by providing the required emotional qualities of self-control and strength of will, and through their combined efforts desire must be inhibited so that it seeks no more than the satisfaction of essential physical needs. And just as bodily health exists when the different physical organs are all in a state to perform their proper function (heart, lungs, sense organs, etc., all functioning properly), so also we can say that when the three parts of the self are performing their proper functions this will constitute mental health. Goodness, then, is the health and harmony of the personality.

How does this enable Plato to answer the Sophists? Consider the three tasks which we identified for him.

1. *The reconciliation of nature and convention* Here, I think, Plato is weakest. If human goodness or justice is analogous to health, this will indeed serve to ground it in nature. Moral goodness will be something which human beings need in the way that they need physical health, as a requirement of their very nature. What is more questionable is the claim that this 'natural' justice will coincide with justice as conventionally understood. Plato claims that it will. At 442e–443b he takes it to be simply obvious that the person who is just, in the sense of having a properly harmonized soul, will not embezzle money, commit sacrilege or theft, betray his friends or his country, break promises, commit adultery, dishonour his parents, or be irreligious. At 589c–590c slightly more elaboration is provided. There it is said that, 'the things that are conventionally dishonourable', such as getting money unjustly, self-indulgence, obstinacy and bad temper, luxury and effeminacy, flattery and meanness, are so regarded because they involve subservience to physical appetites. One might doubt, however, whether injustice always stems from such a source, and we shall have to consider later whether Plato adequately establishes the link between typically unjust actions and his own psychological analysis.

2. *The linking of justice and benefit* Here the appeal of the analogy with health is obvious. Physical health is quite clearly advantageous to its possessor, and preferable to illness. The proper functioning of his or her physical organs is something which any human being needs, and is intrinsically pleasurable. So if justice can be equated with psychic health, we can see how this will help Plato to establish that the just life is intrinsically happy and desirable.

3. *The objectivity of values* We can see too how the analogy with health will help Plato to assert the objective character of ethical values. What counts as health or illness seems to be objectively determinable, and it seems plausible too to maintain that the desirability of health is not merely a matter of subjective preference.

A great deal, therefore, hangs on whether Plato can successfully maintain the analogy with physical health. I want now to examine this analogy in more detail.

Justice as Mental Health

Anthony Kenny has pointed out interesting similarities between Plato's theory and Freudian psychology.[1] Both of them offer an account of mental health in terms of a harmony between the three parts of the personality. Freud, in his later works, divided the psyche into the ego, the super-ego, and the id. The ego and the id correspond very closely to Plato's reason and desire. What Freud understands by 'the super-ego' is rather narrower than Plato's 'spirit'. The super-ego is a specifically moral phenomenon. It is, in effect, the conscience created by the internalization of parental and social authority. It is akin to Plato's 'spirit', however, in that its characteristic function is to assist the ego (reason), by providing the emotional force which will keep in check the id (desire).

In a later chapter I shall discuss Freud in his own right. At this point the comparison between him and Plato is useful because it alerts us to the general significance of Plato's theory. As Kenny says, 'the concept of mental health was Plato's invention',[2] and in introducing it into ethical theory, Plato was the forerunner of those who in our own day have suggested that ethical questions can be illuminated by a psychology of mental health and illness. Kenny himself is deeply suspicious of the whole enterprise. He says:

It is characteristic of our age to endeavour to replace virtues by technology. That is to say, wherever possible we strive to use methods of physical or social engineering to achieve goals which our ancestors thought attainable only by the training of character ... The moralistic concept of mental health incorporates the technological dream: it looks towards the day when virtue is superseded by medical know-how. But we are no more able than Plato was to make ourselves virtuous by prescription or pharmacology: and renaming virtue 'mental health' takes us no further than it took Plato in the direction of that chimeric goal.[3]

Why should the assimilation of moral virtue to mental health be thought objectionable? It may firstly seem simply implausible to suppose that someone who behaves immorally or unjustly must therefore be mentally sick or insane. Do we not know all too many people who, though ruthlessly unjust, seem also to be quite disconcertingly free of mental disharmony or disturbance, and whose mental faculties function all too effectively? Here we have to recognize, however, that we are not dealing with a simple dichotomy between total insanity on the one hand and total psychic health on the other. The comparison of Plato with Freud should remind us of Freud's insistence on the continuous spectrum that extends from psychic harmony to mental breakdown. The analogy with physical health should point us towards the same recognition. Most of us are neither sick nor perfectly healthy. We are healthy enough to function at a basic level, but not fully fit, and we can recognize the desirability of improving our health to the level of positive physical harmony and well-being. Similarly with psychic health. Plato's account attempts to establish, on the continuum between health and insanity, a close affinity between the thoroughly unjust person and the madman, and then to locate lesser degrees of injustice as intermediate points on the spectrum. This is done in the survey of unjust societies and individuals in Books VIII and IX, and especially in the discussion of the tyrannical character-type at 571a–576b. The latter discussion begins with a striking concurrence with Freudian theory —the assertion of the existence of a class of 'lawless desires', such as inclinations to incest, sadism, or bestiality, which are normally repressed but tend to manifest themselves in dreams. In the tyrannical person, who corresponds to the society ruled by a tyrant and is the extreme of injustice, these desires are no longer repressed but acted out, and one of them is set up as 'a master passion in him to control the idle desires that divide his time between them'. This master passion acquires a total dominance over the mind, and the other desires subserve it like worker bees feeding and fattening a drone, until 'the master passion runs wild and takes madness into its service, . . . all discipline is swept away and madness usurps its place'. The reference to madness is then supported by a comparison between the tyrannical character of sexual desire, the behaviour of one who is drunk, and the fantasies of omnipotence typical of the madman.

For Plato, then, the main similarity between injustice and insanity lies in the *obsessive* or *compulsive* nature of the desire which dominates such a person. A particular desire has grown out of all proportion, and lost touch with reality. If Plato can indeed establish that this is the typical feature of injustice, the continuity with insanity will be clear, and especially with that form of mental illness known as obsessional neurosis, which consists precisely in a person's behaviour being dominated by a compulsive wish, fear, or belief whose expressions are wildly irrational. To substantiate the relevance of this to injustice (in the wider sense), think of the way in which our relations to others are distorted by our own obsessions, so that we cannot respond objectively to the other person's needs and desires, or treat the other as a person in his or her own right. Take, for example, the case of racial prejudice, and think of the way in which racist attitudes are typically grounded, not in any real features of the denigrated race, but in the insecurities and frustrations of the racist himself, leading him to project on to a scapegoat emotions and fears which have no rational foundation. Or think of the nature of possessive jealousy or infatuation in sexual relations, and of how in such cases the supposed 'love' takes on an exploitative character because it is a fantasy emotion, out of touch with any rational or objective awareness of the 'loved' one's real qualities. In both cases our description draws on Plato's notion of psychic imbalance, on the idea of reason, emotion, and desires having their proper roles, and of their becoming distorted and destructive when they cease to be in harmony with one another, when emotions and desires become irrational, fantasy-ridden, and obsessive.

These examples may prompt a second objection. It may be said that the analogy between physical and mental health is misleading because, whereas what we count as physical health or illness can be determined simply by the physical facts, what we count as mental health or illness will be determined by our prior evaluations. We regard the racist as 'sick' only because we already, on independent grounds, morally object to racism—so the objection would run. And this would be an objection both to the idea of mental health in general, and in particular to the idea that it can provide an objective foundation for ethical theory.

In response to this objection we should look more closely

at the status of the concept of physical health. For here too what we count as health will to some extent vary with prior values. What counts as physical health for an Olympic swimmer will differ from what counts as health for a university lecturer. The latter would be delighted with a physical condition which the former would call being hopelessly unfit. Again, what counts as physical health will vary not only in relation to different values and tasks, but also in relation to different social and physical environments. A different kind and degree of physical fitness would be needed in a pre-industrial and an industrial society, for instance, or in an Arctic climate and a temperate climate. Nevertheless there remains a central core of objectivity to the concept of physical health, and it seems plausible to suppose, as Plato does, that this objective core is provided by the notion of 'function'. A person is in a state of physical health when his or her physical organs perform their proper functions, and these 'proper functions' are determined by what it is for the person as a whole to function effectively. A hunter will need to be more fleet of foot and possess more acute vision than an office worker, but any human being needs to be able to walk and needs to be able to see. Underlying the notions of what it is to function effectively in this or that particular context or role, we have a general notion of what it is to function effectively as a human being.

The Platonic claim would be that a notion of mental health can be built on the same foundation. A certain basic harmony between the different aspects of the personality is likewise needed, if one is to function effectively as a human being. If one's emotions and desires are not guided by reason, one lives in a fantasy world. If one's rational capacities are not motivated by emotions and desires, one lapses into a state of meaninglessness. These, then, are requirements for *any* meaningful and effective human life, whatever more particular values a person may happen to live by. And they are requirements which are satisfied to different degrees, so that a person may, without being mentally ill, nevertheless fall short of real psychic harmony.

A third objection to the ethical employment of the concept of mental health might be that it attempts to make morality a matter for experts, just as questions of physical health are entrusted to the expertise of qualified doctors. Many of us would find this repellent, as Kenny does when he comments that, 'if every vicious man is really a sick man, then the virtuous philosopher can claim over him the type of control which a doctor has over his patients'.[4] There can be no doubt that Plato would welcome this implication. His justification for the role of the philosopher-kings in his ideal society is precisely that they need to act as physicians to the souls of those who cannot cure themselves.

All the same, we do not necessarily have to accept this implication, and we can reject it without having to abandon the concept of mental health. We can separate the question of whether that concept is a useful one in ethics from the question of whether it would commit us to the rule of experts. One way in which we might try to sever the two claims is by questioning the status of experts even in matters of physical health. Of course, there exists an objective body of knowledge about the causes of illness and the means to health, and of course doctors are better qualified than lay-men. But we may also feel that in our own society medical knowledge has become too much the prerogative of experts, that it carries with it too much of an assumption of authority, and that the result is that ordinary people feel intimidated and incapable of acting for themselves in the matter of their own physical well-being. Thus the inference that, if goodness is a kind of mental health, it must become the business of experts, can be blocked at this first step. But we could also block it by stressing the differences between physical and mental health. We can retain the central features of the comparison between physical and mental health while recognizing that there are also differences, and that these differences may make it even more dangerous to entrust mental health than physical health to experts. For example, a supposed expert's assessment of the mental health of others, though it may in principle be capable of objective determination, is in practice much more likely to be distorted by biases and privileged interests. Or again it could be argued that the capacity to direct one's own life is itself an essential component of full psychic health, and that the notion of having such a condition provided for one by experts is a contradiction in terms—a claim which could not be made in the same way about physical health. We could, then, accept Plato's assertion of the importance of mental health for the good life, while rejecting the further inference about the need to entrust such matters to experts. It should also be added, however, that *in particular cases* that inference *may* be valid; the compulsive sadist or the compulsive rapist, for example, may need not moral guidance but expert treatment by a psychotherapist.

The point made in the last paragraph can be generalized further. We can and should distinguish between the general claim that moral goodness is a kind of psychic health and harmony, and Plato's particular version of what this health and harmony consists in. Plato's psychology, like his politics, has an authoritarian cast. He believes that, for the proper inner harmony to be achieved, reason, in alliance with spirit, must exercise a strict control over the desires, inhibiting some, and eliminating others. Just as we might question Plato's authoritarian politics from a democratic standpoint, so also we might question Plato's authoritarian conception of psychic health, and attempt to make a case for what might be called a more 'democratic' character-structure.

The reference to Freud could again help us here. Freud's account of mental health and illness exhibits a much greater ambivalence about the repression of desires. Like Plato, Freud sees such repression as inescapable, both within society and within the individual, if civilized human life is to be viable. However, Freud also recognizes that, beyond a certain point, excessive repression becomes harmful and self-defeating. Desires which are repressed do not simply disappear, they continue to exist, but remain unconscious. If the repression is too severe, the thwarted desires find expression in substitute satisfactions. Just because their activity is unconscious, they become all the more difficult to control, and the ways in which they find expression, and resist the attempts to block them, may well give rise to mental illness. Thus the control of the desires which Plato equates with mental health can, on Freud's account, itself be a cause of mental illness, and conversely mental health may actually require the gratification of those instinctual desires which Plato wants to inhibit.

It is not entirely clear what Plato means by 'desire' in his partition of the self. Sometimes, and especially when the division is first introduced at 437d–439e, it seems to include all the desires, hunger and thirst simply being the most conspicuous. Plato's scheme would then embody a classic opposition of reason and emotion ('spirit' and 'desire' together constituting 'emotion'), of a kind which I shall consider in the next chapter. Subsequently, however, what seems more likely is that Plato wants to confine 'desire' to only certain desires. Reason has its own characteristic emotions and desires, aiming at their own special pleasures (580d–581c), and 'desire' so-called is limited to the instinctual physical desires for food and drink and sex. On this interpretation, Plato's assumption is that it is these physical desires which are essentially opposed to reason.

We might, however, question this assumption. The physical desires do not have to be irrational. Sexual desire, for example, need not be a blind and uncontrollable craving. Such desires can have their own rationality, they can be discriminating, directed at their appropriate objects. We might therefore retain from Plato the conception of goodness as psychic health, and retain also the analysis of this health as a harmony between the parts of the personality, but look for a less authoritarian, less repressive conception of what this harmony would consist in.

Further discussion of the place of 'mental health' in ethics must await our consideration of Freud in a later chapter. So far I have been concerned to lend an initial plausibility to Plato's use of the concept. We now need to look further at how it helps him to answer the Sophists.

Justice and Happiness

We saw that Plato wishes to meet Thrasymachus' challenge by showing that the just life is the happiest and most fulfilling. Initially this is held to have been demonstrated at 445a, as a direct consequence of a definition of justice as mental health. For 'men don't reckon that life is worth living when their physical health breaks down, even though they have all the food and drink and wealth and power in the world. So we can hardly reckon it worth living when the principle of life breaks down in confusion, and a man wilfully avoids the one thing that will rid him of vice and crime, the acquisition of justice and virtue in the sense which we have shown them to bear.'

The claim is further substantiated in Book IX (from 576b), where three arguments are offered.

(i) The first is a further elaboration of the appeal to the idea of mental health. Plato has suggested that the tyrannical personality is one which is dominated by a single obsessive and compulsive desire. It follows, he claims, that though such a person may appear to be happy when that desire is gratified, he is in reality enslaved to the desire. The crucial point here is that satisfaction of the desire does not necessarily mean satisfaction of the person, as a whole self. Plato is appealing to the idea of the self as a unity, not just a bundle of desires, and consequently whether a person is happy must be determined by considering not his or her superficial satisfactions, but the deeper harmony that underlies them.

(ii) The second argument appeals to the idea that each of the three parts of the personality has its own characteristic pleasures. There are the pleasures of reason, of spirit, and of desire. Persons in whom reason is the dominant faculty (who will be those who live the just life) will value most highly the pleasures of reason, and likewise those dominated by spirit or desire will value their own respective pleasures. The question, then, is how to decide between these three estimates of the value of the different kinds of pleasure. Plato argues that the person dominated by reason possesses in the greatest measure the very qualities of knowledge and rationality which are needed to make a correct estimate. Moreover, only such persons have fully experienced all three kinds of pleasure and are in a position to judge between them, whereas the person dominated by desire knows only his own kinds of pleasures, and cannot appreciate the value of higher kinds. Therefore, when the person dominated by reason asserts from his experience that his own kind of life, the life of justice, is the happiest, he must be right. Plato's important insight here is that, in considering the quality of a person's life, we have to ask not only whether he or she is happy in the sense of being satisfied with his or her existing experiences, but also whether that person could be happier if his or her life were enriched by new kinds of experience.

(iii) Plato's final argument is that our pleasures are unreal when we take pleasure in things which are themselves unreal. For Plato it follows that physical pleasures, the pleasures of food and drink and sex, are unreal, since the physical world is unreal. The only fully real world is the world of ideal forms known by the intellect, and therefore the only true pleasures are the pleasures of reason. Here we are entering Plato's metaphysics, to which I will turn in a moment. However, there is a more general question which Plato's argument poses, separable from the metaphysical issues. What is the status of pleasures which are based on illusion? Suppose that I am sustained in my life by a belief that I am widely respected by my colleagues and acquaintances, and this belief is essential to my happiness, and suppose that the belief is quite false—that I am in fact regarded by people with contempt, although they carefully shield me from a knowledge of it. Can I really be said to be happy, if my happiness depends on this illusion? Plato's answer is un-equivocal: if my happiness is based on a false belief, it is a false happiness, that is, it is not really happiness at all. Can we accept such a simple answer? There are problems in doing so, for against Plato one is inclined to say that if a person really does *feel* happy, then as a matter of plain psychological fact that person surely *is* happy, whether or not he or she ought to be. And yet one is also inclined to agree with Plato, at least to the extent that there is something defective or degenerate about a happiness based on illusions, however secure those illusions are from being shattered.

In general, this section of *The Republic* offers a subtle and complex conception of happiness, which is clearly distin-guished from the mere satisfaction of immediate desires. We have seen that, according to Plato, whether one is truly and fully happy will depend not only on the degree of immediate satisfaction, but on the degree of unity and harmony in one's life, on the range of one's experience, and the extent to which one has acquaintance with different possibilities, and on the depth and veracity of one's knowledge of oneself and one's world. For Plato, the mindless pleasures of the media-drugged zombie (like the prisoners in the cave at the beginning of Book VII, sitting and watching the flickering images on the wall) are not true happiness. We shall appreciate more fully the richness of Plato's account of happiness when we come to compare it with other accounts, such as those of some Utilitarian philosophers, but in the meantime we can also see that it stands in marked contrast to the conceptions of happiness invoked by Thrasymachus, by Glaucon and Adeimantus, and by many of the Sophists.

Objective Values and the Theory of Forms

As the third of Plato's responses to the Sophists I listed his assertion of the objectivity of ethical values. Implicitly this is embodied in Plato's account of justice as mental health. When articulated as an explicit theory, it becomes Plato's famous 'theory of forms' or 'theory of ideas'. What does this theory assert?

To begin with let us take it that among these 'forms' or 'ideas' Plato includes values such as goodness, justice, and beauty. Minimally, then, the theory is the assertion that there *are* such things as goodness, justice, and beauty. More substantially, what Plato maintains is that goodness itself is something *distinct* and *separate* from the many individual things which are good, that in addition to all the various just individuals and just acts and just societies, and in addition to all the various beautiful sights and sounds, there are also justice itself and beauty itself. This *separation* of the one quality from its many exemplifications is understood by Plato in a strong sense. It amounts to a separation between two distinct worlds, the everyday physical world and the world of the forms. The language of 'two worlds' is to be found especially in the analogy of the cave (514a–521b), where the interior of the cave represents the everyday physical world, and only the enlightened few can ascend to the world of true reality outside the cave, which is the world of the forms.

This talk of the separation of two worlds should not be understood too crudely. It is not a spatial separation between two different locations—the world of the forms is not literally 'up there' above the heavens. This would be too crude, because the forms, not being physical things, are not in space at all. This indeed is the real nature of the separation. The many good things exist in the physical world of space and time, whereas goodness itself is not a physical thing, and does not exist in space or time. It makes no sense to say of it that it exists 'here' or 'there', that it existed or will exist at this or that time.

This, then, is one aspect of the separation, a distinction between a spatio-temporal existence and a non-spatio-temporal existence. But Plato also has other reasons for emphasizing the separateness of the forms. In the first place, it indicates the contrast between the perfection of the forms and the imperfection of their exemplifications. Justice itself cannot be equated with the sum of individual just persons and societies, because none of these are ever fully and perfectly just. Even the best of them fall short of the ideal in some respect.

Plato regularly puts this in terms of a contrast between 'being' and 'becoming'. The world of forms is the world of being, the world of physical exemplifications is the world of becoming. In part, 'becoming' signifies literal change. Individual good things come into existence at a certain time and cease to exist at a later time, and their goodness is therefore transitory. But their instability is also a matter of changes of aspect. Any particular good thing will also, *at the same time*, be bad in some respect, that is to say, it changes according to how you look at it. To say that it 'becomes' is therefore to say that it is never fully and completely good in all respects, and in that sense is variable. The 'being'/'becoming' contrast also serves to indicate that *objectivity* of the forms which was our starting-point. Any particular good thing is subject to becoming, not only in the sense that it is good in some respects and not others, but also in the sense that it will seem good to some people and not others. Goodness itself, however, cannot vary. It is what it is, independent of the beliefs of individual human beings. Presented with the adage that 'beauty is in the eye of the beholder', Plato would say that this may be true of the beauty of individual things, but cannot be true of beauty itself. Accordingly Protagoras' dictum that 'man is the measure of all things' is the reverse of the truth.

A further aspect of the separation of forms and their exemplifications is the contrast between the kinds of knowledge we have of each. Individual good things, since they exist in the physical world, must be known by the senses. However, since their goodness is necessarily an imperfect approximation to an ideal, we could not recognize them as good unless we already had a (perhaps unconscious) prior knowledge of the ideal itself. We could not derive our knowledge of goodness itself from our sensory experience of its instances, just because these are all imperfect. Sense-experience can awaken our knowledge of goodness, but that knowledge must be something which we already possessed prior to all sense-experience. Strictly speaking, therefore, when we speak of 'coming to know' goodness through our acquaintance with individual good things, this 'coming to know' must really be a kind of 'recollection', a re-awakening of that innate knowledge of goodness which we already possessed at birth, before all our sensory experience, and which has lain dormant in us since then. This innate knowledge, since it is not sensory perceptual knowledge, must be what we know by pure reason, by thought, by the intellect alone. In modern philosophical terminology, it is *a priori* knowledge, as contrasted with the empirical knowledge acquired through sense-experience. The forms are therefore objects of pure thought, and in that respect the modern English word 'idea' (which derives directly from one of Plato's own Greek terms for 'form') is an appropriate one by which to refer to them. In calling goodness, justice, and the rest 'ideas', however, we should not give the impression that they exist only 'in the mind'. They are known by the mind, but can exist quite independently of any mind. Goodness would be what it is, even though no human minds had ever existed or had ever thought about it.

I have referred to two kinds of knowledge. According to Plato, however, the so-called knowledge acquired through sense-experience is not genuine knowledge at all. Knowledge can never be false, and therefore beliefs cannot count as knowledge if it is possible for them to be false. Sense perception fails to meet this requirement, for our senses often deceive us. Therefore, if perception can turn out to be erroneous, it cannot be knowledge. It is merely *belief*. The only real knowledge is knowledge of the forms, purely rational knowledge which, when we have it, is direct and indubitable.

The 'separation' of forms from their instances amounts, then, to this. The forms are not physical things and do not exist in space or time. They are perfect, as contrasted with the imperfection of their instances. And they are apprehended not by the senses but by rational thought, which provides our only genuine knowledge rather than mere belief.

So far I have presented the theory of forms simply as a theory of ideal values. However, Plato also recognizes other kinds of forms. There are mathematical forms—for example, forms of geometrical entities such as 'triangle', 'circle', and 'straight line', and of mathematical relations such as 'equality'. There are forms of so-called 'natural kinds', and especially of biological species and genera such as 'man', or 'horse', or 'oak-tree'. The theory of forms is therefore not just a theory of ethical knowledge, but a theory of knowledge in general, and it is elaborated as such in the analogy of the divided line (509d–511e). Plato there distinguishes between four stages of awareness: (i) the use of images as a way of apprehending physical things; (ii) direct empirical acquaintance with physical things; (iii) the use of physical things as images of the forms; (iv) direct intellectual knowledge of the forms.

Rather than discuss further Plato's theory of knowledge in general, I want now to raise some doubts about it as a theory of *ethical* knowledge. This can be done by asking: what kind of ethical knowledge does Plato himself provide in *The Republic*? Into which of the four sections of the divided line does it fall? What about the account of justice, for example, in terms of the parts of the soul? Is this to count as direct intellectual knowledge of the form of justice, or is it the use of a physical image as a means of knowing the form? Does it belong in the third or the fourth section of the line? The question is difficult partly because Plato was unsure where to locate the soul in his metaphysical scheme. He sees the soul as akin to the forms and the intelligible world, and yet individual souls cannot themselves be forms, since they are all imperfect exemplifications of the general form 'soul'.

However, if we look at what is actually going on in Plato's account of justice in the soul, we must surely conclude that it belongs in the third rather than the fourth stage of the line. It involves constant reference to the facts of the empirical, physical world. The division into the parts of the soul is established by appeal to the observed facts of mental conflict. The proper relationship between the parts of the soul is presented through an analogy with physical health. The connection with justice is supported by descriptions of the kinds of observable actions in the physical world which would be produced by a condition of psychic harmony or conflict. All of this must presumably count as appealing to physical images of justice. We may well conclude that nowhere in *The Republic* does Plato himself go further than the third stage of the line.

What I now want to ask is whether he could ever conceivably do so. What would an account of justice be like which made no reference to the physical world? How could one possibly define justice or any other ethical quality, except in terms of the kinds of actions it involves and how it requires us to live in the world of our perceptual experience? It is difficult to see what could possibly count as knowledge of the form all by itself, and Plato is able to offer us nothing other than the idea of some kind of mystic vision, about which nothing can be said. This, then, is the consequence of Plato's radical separation of forms from their exemplifications. If justice or goodness really were quite separate from their instances, we could have no knowledge of them.

The conclusion which I propose is that when Plato's view of the objectivity of values is elaborated as the fully-fledged theory of forms, it leads us ultimately to a dead end. When it is presented as a thesis about the objective desirability of a healthy and harmonious state of the personality, it is much more fruitful. The most valuable parts of *The Republic* are those which lead in the direction of what is known as ethical *naturalism*—the view that a knowledge of how human beings can best live can be derived from the empirical facts of human nature and the human situation. These are the parts of *The Republic* which deal with the relationship between justice, happiness, and mental health. I have tried in this chapter to exhibit what is plausible and attractive in these ideas. There remain more fundamental questions which we need to ask about the whole enterprise, and I shall consider these in Chapter 4. But since they are questions which arise also for Aristotle's ethical theory, I turn first to Aristotle.

Notes

1   Anthony Kenny: 'Mental Health in Plato's Republic', in *The Anatomy of the Soul* (Oxford, 1973), reprinted from the *Proceedings of the British Academy*, 1969.
2   Ibid., p. 1.
3   Ibid., pp. 26–7.
4   Ibid., pp. 23f.

3 Aristotle
The Rationality of the Emotions

Reading: Aristotle: *The Nicomachean Ethics*

I shall concentrate especially on Books I–IV and X. The translation to which I shall refer is Aristotle: *Ethics*, translated by Hugh Tredennick and introduced by Jonathan Barnes, in the Penguin Classics series.

Aristotle and Plato

Aristotle's *Nicomachean Ethics* was not a work written for publication. He did write such works, but none of them have survived. All of his philosophical works which have come down to us, including the *Nicomachean Ethics*, are in the form of lecture notes, simply for Aristotle's own use when he gave his lectures in his school, the Lyceum, and arranged and organized by later editors after Aristotle's death. Two versions of his course of lectures on ethics have survived, the other version being known as the *Eudemian Ethics*. The *Nicomachean Ethics* seems to have been the later and more definitive version, and is usually referred to simply as the *Ethics*.

Aristotle was for twenty years a pupil of Plato, from the time when at the age of seventeen he entered Plato's teaching establishment, the Academy, until his departure after the death of Plato in 347 BC. This apprenticeship shaped Aristotle's preoccupations, in respect both of his intellectual debts to Plato, and his divergences from him. As a rough guide, we can say that Aristotle's substantive ethics continues in a broadly Platonic direction, but that his meta-ethics takes a radically different turn. His disagreements with Plato stem from his rejection of the theory of forms. He developed a number of critical arguments against the theory, including the criticism to which I subscribed in my previous chapter, that Plato's radical separation of forms from particulars makes it difficult to see how we could ever have knowledge of them. Aristotle adds that even if such knowledge could be obtained, it could have no relevance for ethics. Knowledge of the Platonic forms would be knowledge of something eternal and unchanging, whereas ethical knowledge would have to be a kind of knowledge which could guide our *actions*, and would therefore have to be a knowledge of things that can be changed. Again, knowledge of the forms would be a knowledge of universals, whereas in ethics what we need is a knowledge of particulars, since it is in particular situations that we have to decide how to act. Of course, in ethical philosophy we aim at more than just a knowledge of particulars, but any universal claims which we try to produce will be generalizations from our experience of particular situations. As such they will be rough and ready approximations, and in ethics we must not look for a greater degree of accuracy and exactness than is appropriate to the subject. Every discipline has its appropriate standards of precision; the carpenter, for example, does not measure a right angle with the same accuracy as a geometrician. Accordingly in ethics we can expect generalizations which are true only for the most part, and which derive from the accumulated experience which we have built up from everyday life and particular situations. Ethical philosophy presupposes this shared experience, and is therefore not a fit subject for the young and inexperienced. This conception of ethical knowledge is stressed especially in a number of digressions and asides in Book I of the *Ethics*, and is linked with the criticisms of the Platonic theory of forms in Ch. 6 of Book I.

What Aristotle retains from Plato is the general nature of the enterprise in substantive ethics. Like Plato, Artistotle wants to show that there are objectively valid reasons for living in accordance with the traditional virtues, and like Plato, he attempts to justify the virtues by examining the nature of human beings, in order to argue that a life lived in accordance with the virtues will be the happiest life. In Aristotle's version of the argument there are three main steps:

(i) The ultimate end of human action is happiness.

(ii) Happiness consists in acting in accordance with reason.

(iii) Acting according to reason is the distinguishing feature of all the traditional virtues.

The first two steps are to be found in Book I of the *Ethics*, and the third step is the theme of Books II to IV. I shall examine in turn each of the three steps.

Happiness

The first stage of Aristotle's argument, then, is the claim that the ultimate end of human action is happiness. The Greek term conventionally translated as 'happiness' in the *Ethics* is *eudaimonia*, but this is another case where we should note differences of nuance between Greek and English terms. The English word 'happiness' refers primarily to a psychological state, a state of feeling. Whether one *is* happy is largely (though not entirely) a question of whether one *feels* happy. *Eudaimonia*, on the other hand, is more an objective condition of a person, and there is more room for a contrast between *feeling* happy and genuinely *being* happy. *Eudaimonia* thus has some of the connotations of 'well-being' or 'flourishing'. It is easier, too, for Aristotle to distinguish between 'happiness' and 'pleasure'. We should not, however, exaggerate the differences between the Greek and English vocabularies. On the one hand, there have been plenty of English philosophers who have asserted an important difference between 'happiness' and 'pleasure', and even, though less easily, between 'being happy' and 'feeling happy' (where locutions such as 'true happiness' may help). On the other hand, there were Greek philosophers ready enough to equate 'happiness' with 'pleasure' (such as some of the Sophists, and later the Epicureans).

Differences between Greek and English, then, cannot by themselves account for Aristotle's position. Equally important is the influence of Plato. Like Plato, Aristotle accepts that happiness cannot be divorced from pleasure. One who is happy will necessarily find pleasure in his way of life. The converse however is not true, and here too, Aristotle follows

Plato. The fact that a person experiences pleasure does not entail that the person is happy. According to Aristotle's account in Book X, pleasure is a state of mind which supervenes upon human activities. When we are fully committed to and involved in an activity, we take pleasure in it. 'The pleasure perfects the activity' (1174b 23). From this it follows that pleasures take their character from the activities which they complete, and the value of the pleasure will be determined by the value of the activity. If we take pleasure in good activities, the pleasure is good pleasure, but if the activity is bad, the pleasure is bad also. If a person takes pleasure in corrupt and perverse activities (e.g. the infliction of wanton cruelty) the existence of the pleasure is not an element of positive value in the situation, which could be set against the negative value of the activity. Rather, the very fact that the person takes pleasure in the activity is a measure of how corrupt he or she is, and the pleasure is itself a corrupt pleasure. Therefore pleasure cannot itself function as a criterion of value. We need an independent criterion to determine the value of different kinds of life, and to determine which constitutes genuine happiness, and this criterion can then serve to determine also the value of different kinds of pleasure.

Aristotle, then, shares with Plato a rich conception of happiness, which is distinguished from mere immediate satisfaction of desires. This, and the wider connotations of *eudaimonia*, help Aristotle to treat almost as a truism the claim that the ultimate end of human action is happiness. At I.4 (1095a 17) he says that there is 'pretty general agreement' that the highest good is happiness, and at I.7 (1097b 22) he says that this may look like a platitude. We can appreciate his point, if we think of the assertion as having some of the obviousness of the statement that the ultimate end is well-being.

The crucial step, then, is not the introduction of happiness as the ultimate end, but the assumption which is prior to this and which Aristotle does not even question—the assumption that human action is to be understood in terms of ends and means. This is baldly stated in the first sentence of the *Ethics*: 'Every art and every investigation, and similarly every action and pursuit, is considered to aim at some good.' No argument is offered. And once this framework of ends and means is presupposed, the stage is already set for the idea that if we want to know what the highest *good* is, we have to ask, 'What is the ultimate *end* of human action, what is it that all our actions finally *aim* at?'

There are two aspects of the relation between happiness and the ends/means framework which need to be clarified, both because Aristotle is liable to misrepresentation on these two points and because he is himself somewhat confused on them. In the first place, it is important to notice that Aristotle is *not* saying that happiness is the *only* thing which is an end in itself, and that everything else which human beings desire is desired as a means to happiness. That thesis has been maintained by other philosophers and is therefore easily read into the *Ethics*, but is not Aristotle's position. In I.7, at 1097b1, he says of happiness that

we always choose it for itself, and never for any other reason. It is different with honour, pleasure, intelligence and good qualities generally. We do choose them partly for themselves (because we should choose each one of them irrespectively of any consequences); but we choose them also for the sake of our happiness, in the belief that they will be instrumental in promoting it.

Here it is quite clear that, according to Aristotle, honour, pleasure, intelligence, and the virtues are all aimed at for their own sake, and that he therefore recognizes a plurality of things which are all good in themselves.

What is also clear from the passage, however, is that he wants to give happiness a special status within this plurality. What are his grounds for doing so? Honour, pleasure, intelligence, and the virtues are, he says, not only aimed at as ends in themselves, but are also aimed at for the sake of happiness, whereas happiness is never pursued for the sake of anything else. And because these other things are both ends and means, whereas happiness is never a means to anything else, Aristotle claims that this makes it a 'more final' end (1097a 30), and thus the supreme good.

The argument is, however, a *non sequitur*. The fact that intelligence, for instance, *can* be desired as a means to happiness, in no way shows that when it *is* desired as an end in itself, it is at all inferior to happiness as an end. This would be equivalent to saying that because people enjoy drinking both milk and Coca Cola, and also drink milk (but not Coca Cola) for its additional nutritional benefits, it follows that they enjoy milk less than Coca Cola. That would be nonsense, but Aristotle's own argument is no more respectable than that. So far, then, he has not shown that honour, pleasure, intelligence, and the virtues are at all inferior or subordinate to happiness. If he had recognized this, and had given all these things a place in the good life in their own right, independent of happiness, he might have ended up with a significantly different account of the good life.

To deal with this difficulty, Aristotle could perhaps invoke another remark which he makes in the same chapter —and this is the second point that needs to be clarified. Still speaking of happiness, he says: 'What is more, we regard it as the most desirable of all things, not reckoned as one item among many; if it were so reckoned, happiness would obviously be more desirable by the addition of even the least good, because the addition makes the sum of goods greater . . .' (1097b 16–19). The key phrase here is 'not reckoned as one item among many'. This seems to mean that happiness is not to be regarded as one more good thing in the same list as honour, pleasure, intelligence, and the various virtues. Rather, happiness is a good in so far as it is that of which all the other goods are constituents. It is not a separate good from them; they are the things which go to make up happiness. This would provide a way of making sense of the claim that happiness is 'more final', and is therefore the 'supreme' good. The idea would be that happiness is more basic than the other goods, not as being something better of the same kind, but as being the framework into which the various particular goods fit.

To illustrate the point further, compare the case of having or lacking a meaning in one's life. Suppose someone says, 'I thought I had everything I wanted—a well-paid job, a lovely family, a nice house—but none of it seems to make sense, it all seems meaningless'. In wanting to have a meaning in his life, such a person is not looking for one more item of the same order as all the others, as though he should say

'I've got the job, I've got the family, I've got the house, all I need now is the meaning.' What he wants is that all the other things should add up to something, that they should fit together in a coherent way which would endow them all with real value. And this, perhaps, is how Aristotle likewise sees happiness, as the shape or pattern into which the various items fall.

Such an idea might also assist Aristotle in a further respect. When he says that happiness is the highest good, he means, of course, *one's own* happiness. For any human agent, the ultimate end must necessarily be that person's own happiness. This presents Aristotle with the problem of what significance to give to our relations to other people. Is the fulfilment of our obligations to others, or the exhibiting of concern for others, not a good in itself? I shall look more closely at this question in the next chapter, but for the moment we can simply note that the concept of happiness as an overall framework might help. It would enable Aristotle to say that our relations to others are *constituents* of our own happiness, and this might seem more satisfactory than saying that our relations to others are merely *means* to our own happiness.

The Human Function

We have seen that for Aristotle the identification of happiness as the highest good is something of a truism. The more important task, he thinks, is to find out what happiness consists in, and his answer forms the second step in the three-stage argument. He sets out to show that happiness consists in acting in accordance with reason, and he does so by appealing to the idea of the *function* of a human being. Just as a good sculptor or a good carpenter is one who succeeds in performing the proper function of a sculptor or carpenter, so also we can determine what a good human life is by looking for the function of a human being. Do human beings, then, have a function? Yes, says Aristotle, for 'just as we can see that eye and hand and foot and every one of our members has some function, should we not assume that in like manner a human being has a function over and above these particular functions?' (1097b 30.) To determine what this function is, we have to look at what is *distinctive* of human beings. Life is something shared by all plants and animals, so the proper function of a human being cannot be mere biological survival and growth. Nor can it be a mere life of sensations, for this is shared by animals of all kinds. What is distinctive of the human species is the possession of reason, and the exercise of this must therefore be the proper function of a human being.

To many of Aristotle's modern readers, the idea of a 'human function' has seemed very implausible. His analogies fail to convince. Sculptors or carpenters have a function because they are the occupants of social roles, and the functions which attach to these roles are defined by the institutional arrangements of an organized society. Being a human being, however, is not just a matter of filling a social role, nor is the human race an organized society. It may be that we all fill social roles, but we are not, as human beings, fully defined by them. The analogy with bodily organs fares no better. An eye or a hand or a foot has a function because it belongs within a system of interdependent parts, which is the human organism. There is, however, no corresponding organism of which human beings are all parts. The only plausible candidate for such an organism would be a human society, considered as a system of interdependent roles. That, however, simply takes us back to the previous analogy. It might help to strengthen the view that as members of society we have functions, but not that as human beings we have functions.

A third possible analogy which Aristotle could have utilized would be the analogy with artefacts. A knife or a chair has a function, a good knife is one which cuts, and a good chair is one which is comfortable to sit in. Again, however, the analogy with a human being fails. The counter-argument has been forcibly stated by the modern French philosopher Jean-Paul Sartre, in his lecture 'Existentialism and Humanism'. 'If', says Sartre, 'one considers an article of manufacture—as, for example, a book or a paper-knife—one sees that it has been made by an artisan who had a conception of it . . . Thus the paper-knife is at the same time an article producible in a certain manner and one which, on the other hand, serves a definite purpose, for one cannot suppose that a man would produce a paper-knife without knowing what it was for.'[1]

Now a human being, Sartre thinks, can analogously be thought of as existing for a purpose only if he is likewise the product of a divine artisan. If that were the case, God as artisan would define the purpose and create human beings to serve it. If, on the other hand, there is no God, the analogy is no longer available. Human beings are then free to choose what they will be and what purposes they will recognize. There can be no pre-given purpose which human beings exist to serve.

Sartre here implies that within a theistic context the notion of a human function or purpose might indeed make sense. This possible development of Aristotelian ethics was in fact taken up by Catholic theology, most notably by the medieval philosopher Thomas Aquinas. It then becomes the basis of a so-called 'natural law' morality. Two examples will illustrate the role of 'function' in Catholic morality. Since human beings have been created by God to live and to perpetuate their own being, suicide is wrong. And since human beings have been given sexuality in order to reproduce and perpetuate the species, contraception, frustrating this proper purpose of sexuality, is wrong. In each of these examples, the appeal is to a purpose with which human beings have been endowed by God, and the violation of which is therefore held to be morally wrong.

The Christian version, then, is a possible way of retaining Aristotle's notion of a human function. Even then, however, there are problems. It is not clear how we are to identify, from among all the possible purposes which human beings and their capacities can serve, those which are their proper and natural purposes. No doubt the proper purposes of human beings are those for which they are intended by God, but how do we tell which those are (other than by appealing to revelation)? To take the case of sexuality, human beings undeniably *can* employ sexuality for purposes of sheer pleasure; why then is not that, but reproduction, held to be the 'natural' purpose of sexuality?

Some philosophers have defended Aristotle by suggesting

that the word 'function' is not the appropriate translation of the Greek term *ergon*. The latter means literally 'work' or 'task'. Therefore, it has been said, Aristotle is not claiming that human beings have a 'function' (which would require the improper analogy with social roles, or organs, or artefacts), but simply that they have something like a 'characteristic activity'. This, however, will not suffice as a defence, for the difficulty lies not just in the concept of 'function', but in the general pattern of argument which underlies it. The premiss of that argument is that a certain kind of activity is *distinctive* of the human species, and the conclusion of the argument is that that kind of activity is the *best* for human beings. We may doubt whether Aristotle can infer the conclusion from the premiss via the concept of 'function', but if we deprive him of that concept, the problem still remains whether there is any other way in which he can get from the premiss to the conclusion. Replacing the concept of 'function' with that of 'characteristic activity' is no solution; indeed it leaves the argument even more obviously incomplete, for the problem is precisely that of showing why the fact that an activity is 'distinctively' or 'characteristically' human is any reason for engaging in it. It is distinctive of us as human beings that we are the only species capable of destroying all life on this planet, by means of a nuclear war, but that is no reason why we should do it. Why, then, from the fact that rational activity is distinctively human, should it follow that we ought to live according to reason?

I want to mention one other criticism which has been directed at Aristotle's concept of the 'human function'. In this case, however, not only do I consider the criticism invalid, but I think that by looking at it we can begin to discover what is of positive value in Aristotle's position. The criticism is an *ad hominem* one. It points to the fact that Aristotle, as well as recognizing a human function, ascribes a characteristic function also to women and to slaves. In his *Politics* (Book I Ch. 5) he claims that some human beings are slaves by nature. Rationality is distinctive of all human beings, but natural slaves possess it in a lesser degree, and so likewise do women, since their distinctive functions also are different. The proper function of women is to obey men. And the proper function of natural slaves is to obey those who are by nature masters, since the former possess sufficient reason to understand rational principles, but not to formulate them for themselves. For Aristotle, then, the fully human life can be lived only by the free-born male citizen.

That is what the concept of a 'natural function' leads to— or so, at least, Aristotle's critics would claim. From these examples, they would say, we can see that the concept serves to legitimate the functions assigned to human beings, and to particular groups of human beings, in particular societies. The so-called natural function is really a specific social role, treated as though it were sacrosanct and eternal.

Does Aristotle's idea of a human function, however, inevitably have to commit him to such a view of women and of slaves? I think not. The very same concept could have been used by him to criticize the existing roles of these groups. Women and slaves, he could have said, are human beings with distinctively human capacities. It is therefore quite wrong that they should be assigned to roles which prevent them from realizing these capacities. In treating them as fit only to obey, we are treating human beings as less than fully human. Now of course, Aristotle does not say this. The point is, however, that his ethical vocabulary could lend itself as readily to this as to what he in fact does say. The concept of a fully and distinctively human life does not have to legitimate existing social roles, it can equally well serve as a socially critical concept.

Moreover, not only is it the case that Aristotle *could* have argued in this way. It is also the case that we might well *want* to argue in this way. The fact that a certain kind of life is 'less than fully human' might well be a valid reason for criticizing the fact that people either choose or are compelled to live such a life. The idea at work here is that if people are unable to make full use of their distinctively human capacities, their lives are thereby impoverished. Notice further that the critical force of this idea may hold good, even if the person concerned is content with such a life. If someone's life is taken up with the menial tasks of a slave, or with the mindless and mechanical operations of the modern production line, or the kitchen sink, then although he or she may acquiesce in or even have come to enjoy such a life, we might still want to describe it as dehumanized. The concept of a fully human life is, therefore, closely bound up with the Platonic and Aristotelian conception of genuine happiness as more than a sum of immediate satisfactions.

I do not think that Aristotle has adequately worked out such a concept. In due course we shall have to consider what more can be made of it, and we shall look at alternative versions offered by Mill and by Marx. Something more is needed than the bald Aristotelian argument that because a certain activity is distinctively human, it is therefore constitutive of a good human life; nor does the concept of 'function' render the argument any more valid. What more is needed, we shall have to decide.

The Doctrine of the Mean

I turn now to the third stage in Aristotle's overall argument. Having claimed that the highest good is happiness, and having attempted to link happiness with the idea of acting in accordance with reason, Aristotle now has to analyse the traditional virtues, such as courage and moderation, as various forms of action in accordance with reason. With this step he will have completed his attempt to show that the life of the traditional virtues is the best kind of life.

This third step takes the form of Aristotle's celebrated 'doctrine of the mean'. Virtue, he says, consists in observing the mean between excess and deficiency, and this idea of 'following the mean' is the particular sense which we should give to the requirement of acting in accordance with reason. The doctrine is introduced in Book II, in a preliminary way in chapter 2, and then more substantially in chapters 6–9. It is applied to the analysis of the particular moral virtues in Books III 6–IV, and a cursory attempt is also made to apply it to the virtues of justice in V 5 (at 1133b 30).

The doctrine of the mean has been popularly and superficially understood as a counsel of moderation. It is supposed that the people who observe the mean are the people who never exhibit strong emotions and who never go to extremes.

They will never be greatly elated, nor greatly dejected. They will never fall violently in love nor out of love. They will never show great enthusiasm for any object or enterprise, but neither will they show any great aversion. In political life they will define their position as midway between the main contending parties. In everything they will observe a sober caution.

Many of Aristotle's more philosophical commentators have protested against this popular reading. The doctrine of the mean is not, they say, a doctrine of moderation, and Aristotle is not saying that we should never feel anything strongly. They would point especially to II.6, at 1106a 26, where Aristotle distinguishes between 'the mean in relation to the thing' and 'the mean in relation to us'. The 'mean in relation to the thing' would be a mid-point between the available extremes. If, for example, we had to choose a portion of food, and the biggest portion available was ten pounds, and the smallest was two pounds, then to aim at the mean in relation to the thing would be to choose a six pound portion. Therefore if Aristotle were advocating that we should always observe the mean in relation to the thing, the popular reading would be correct. However, Aristotle is emphatic that this is not what he is advocating. He is saying that we should observe the mean in relation to us. How, then, are we to understand this? Aristotle explains:

It is possible, for example, to feel fear, confidence, desire, anger, pity, and pleasure and pain generally, too much or too little; and both of these are wrong. But to have these feelings at the right times on the right grounds towards the right people for the right motive and in the right way is to feel them to an intermediate, that is to the best, degree; and this is the mark of virtue. (1106b 18–23.)

To observe the mean in this sense will not necessarily involve always choosing a mid-point, for sometimes the right way to feel anger, or fear, or whatever will be to feel it very strongly. In some circumstances, feeling a moderate degree of anger, to the extent that one is moved to raise one's voice, may be to feel too much anger, but in other circumstances the same degree of anger may be too little. It all depends on the circumstances, and all that the principle of 'the mean in relation to us' requires us to do is to exhibit the degree of anger appropriate to the circumstances.

The trouble is that the doctrine now begins to seem vacuous. When, we might ask Aristotle, should I feel fear? His answer is: at the right time. For what reasons? On the right grounds. Towards whom? Towards the right people. The principle of 'the mean in relation to the thing', as a principle of moderation, would at least have given us a significant answer to the questions. We therefore have the following dilemma. The doctrine of moderation seems unattractive and implausible, but it is at least a substantial doctrine, and we know what it would be to follow it. On the other hand the doctrine of the mean, in its proper Aristotelian sense, may appear to be acceptable only at the cost of saying nothing substantial at all. Let us therefore see if we can, after all, give rather more substance to it.

I take the doctrine to be a thesis about the proper relation between reason and feeling. I use the word 'feeling' widely, to include emotions, desires, and inclinations in general. In concentrating on feelings I may seem to be misrepresenting Aristotle, who says that the mean applies to both feelings and actions (1106b 16–17). His subsequent discussion, however, suggests that it is intended to apply to actions in so far as they are themselves expressions of feelings. That, at any rate, I regard as the most fruitful way of interpreting him. On this interpretation, then, an action which accords with the mean will be an action which is an expression of feelings which accord with the mean.

Now, the first and most basic point which Aristotle is making is that in so far as our actions are expressions of our feelings, the difference between right and wrong actions is very much a matter of degree. The judgement that an action is wrong will not typically be a qualitative judgement, to the effect that the action expresses a wholly improper kind of feeling. Rather, it will be a quantitative judgement, to the effect that the action expresses a feeling which, though acceptable enough if felt to the right degree, is in the present context excessive or deficient. Basic human feelings such as fear, pleasure, generosity, pride, ambition, and anger cannot, according to Aristotle, be called wrong in themselves, but only if they are felt to the wrong degree. Thus to say that, in the matter of actions and feelings, what is right is the mean, is, at the very least, to make the negative point that what is wrong is excess and deficiency.

To indicate the fuller significance of Aristotle's position, however, I want to contrast it with two other views of the relation between feeling and reason. The first of these is Plato's discussion of the relations between the parts of the soul. I say 'Plato's', but in fact his position is ambiguous. In general, as we have seen, Plato thinks that the proper relation between reason and feeling is that reason should rule, and the feelings should obey. Aristotle says the same (at the end of Book I, at 1102b 30-1). To bring out the contrast between them, therefore, we need to clarify what each of them means by this formulation. The general picture we get from Plato is that the rule of reason consists in reason checking and inhibiting the feelings. This, however, is where the ambiguity emerges, for it is not clear whether he wants to urge the inhibition of *all* the feelings by reason, and certainly, as we saw, he sometimes recognizes that reason has its own characteristic emotions and desires. But the physical desires, at any rate, need to be firmly repressed, and the overall impression we obtain from the *Republic* is of a fundamental opposition between reason and feeling. They are, respectively, the man and the beast in us, and the man must tame and control the beast.

As a contrast with Plato, consider the views of D. H. Lawrence. Lawrence is even more wayward and ambiguous than Plato, and I shall have to over-simplify again. But at least sometimes, Lawrence presents the proper relation between reason and feeling as this: that reason should keep out of the way, and leave room for the free and entirely spontaneous expression of the feelings.

Let us call these two views the 'Platonic' position and the 'Lawrentian' position, and let us retain the inverted commas to signal that we may not be doing justice to Plato or to Lawrence. Plato may not have been 'Platonic' and Lawrence may not have been 'Lawrentian', but other people have been, and the two positions are recognizable ones. Common to them both is the idea of a necessary antagonism between reason and feeling. Either reason must check the feelings, or it must yield to them; one or the other must give way. I want to suggest that we can usefully see Aristotle as questioning the necessity of this antagonism. For Aristotle, feelings can themselves be the embodiment of reason. It is not just a matter of reason controlling and guiding the feelings. Rather, the feelings can *themselves* be more or less rational. Reason can *be present in them*.

What does it mean to say that feelings can be more or less rational? Essentially it is a matter of their being more or less appropriate to the situation. Take the case of anger. Suppose I become furious because someone fails to say hello to me. I fly off the handle, in a way which is quite inappropriate, and entirely out of keeping with such a cause. Here my anger is irrational. Suppose, in another case, that I become furious because I see a gang of children heartlessly taunting and bullying a younger child. Here my anger may be quite appropriate; the cause may be genuinely appalling. In these two cases, then, my anger is irrational and rational respectively.

To speak of, and to advocate 'rational anger' may sound excessively intellectualist. Notice carefully, however, what is meant here. It is not that my anger is the product of an independent rational decision. I do not first ask myself what my response should be, reflect on and assess the situation, and then decide to become angry. My anger may be entirely immediate and automatic. Nevertheless, my feelings may be rational in the sense that they are sensitive to the real nature of the situation. They are not, for instance, distorted by extraneous considerations, as they might have been in the first example. It might have happened, perhaps, that I had had a row with my family before leaving home, and that this was why I vented my anger on the poor unfortunate who failed to greet me. I would then be insensitive to the real nature of the occurrence, in treating it as an occasion for anger. In contrast, it is when my feelings are not blinded and distorted in this sort of way that they can be said to be sensitive to the situation. And it is in this sense that they are rationally appropriate.

This, I think, is what Aristotle is referring to when he says that observing the mean is having feelings on the right occasion, for the right reason, to the right degree, and towards the right person. Aristotle's ideal is that of the rational emotional life. And we can perhaps accept a limited sense in which it is a doctrine of moderation. Not only does it involve the avoidance of whatever would on the particular occasion be an excess or a deficiency. It could also, at the general level, be described as a position intermediate between the 'Platonic' ideal of reason inhibiting and checking the feelings and the 'Lawrentian' ideal of non-rational emotional spontaneity. In another sense, however, it is not a mid-point between these two positions, but is fundamentally opposed to both of them, since it rejects their shared assumption of a necessary antagonism between reason and feeling.

This still leaves the problem: how are we to tell where the mean lies? How can we know when, and to what degree, and on what grounds to feel anger, or fear, or pleasure, or whatever? Aristotle's only answer appears to be: we should feel these things as and when a good person would feel them. He says: 'So virtue is a purposive disposition, lying in a mean that is relative to us and determined by a rational principle, and by that which a prudent man would use to determine it' (1106b 36—the word 'prudent' here translates the Greek *phronimos*, meaning a possessor of practical wisdom). This does not look much more helpful. It seems open to an obvious circularity, since the *phronimos* is the person who gives the right answers, and the right answers are those which are given by the *phronimos*. Why does Aristotle nevertheless think that this is sufficient, and that we neither need nor can say more than this?

For answer we must look to his theory of moral knowledge. Practical wisdom or moral knowledge is what Aristotle calls *phronesis*, the kind of knowledge possessed by the *phronimos*. We have previously seen that Aristotle emphasizes the difference between practical and theoretical knowledge. The essential feature of practical knowledge is that it is concerned with particulars, not with universals. To possess it is to know what to do here and now. It is not a matter of appealing to rules and general principles, not a matter of logical argument or intellectual ability. It consists simply in knowing, in a particular situation: this is what I should do.

How is this knowledge acquired? From practical experience and by habituation (II.1). What Aristotle means, I think, is this. One's moral education consists in being told in particular situations that one's behaviour is appropriate or inappropriate. On one occasion one may be told 'You lost your temper too easily, your anger was out of all proportion to the situation'. On another occasion one may be told 'You reacted much too meekly, you shouldn't take things lying down'. In this way one builds up an intuitive sense of when, and to what extent, anger is appropriate. Now, a crucial point is that the matters about which one acquires this sense are very much matters of degree. This is why one cannot formulate any precise rules about them. It is impossible to say in any very informative way what the different degrees of anger are, and how severe a situation has to be to warrant them. (The impossibility will, I think, be apparent to anyone who tries to do it.) The same goes for the other emotions. Nevertheless, one can come to know when and how far to feel anger, or fear, or pleasure, or pride. This is why Aristotle thinks it impossible and unnecessary to say any more than that the mean is 'at the right time, to the right degree, on the right grounds and towards the right person', and that the standard is fixed by the *phronimos*. The knowledge which enables us to understand this is acquired not by learning theoretical principles, but by moral training, by being properly brought up in a morally civilized community.

This, then, is Aristotle's picture of the life of reason. However, I should add that at the very end of the *Ethics* a completely new picture suddenly emerges. Throughout most of the work we are given the impression that the life of reason is what I have called 'the rational emotional life', the life guided by *phronesis*. Then, at X.7, we are abruptly told that the highest happiness will consist in rational activity in a quite different sense, namely the activity of intellectual contemplation. This ability does not belong in the everyday social world where the moral virtues have their place. It is pursued in retreat from that world, in the lonely splendour of the philosopher. The two pictures can, if we wish, be made formally consistent with one another. The life of the moral virtues is the fully human life, and that is why Aristotle devotes most of his attention to it, whereas the contemplative life is more properly divine than human, and only a few can attain to it. Nevertheless the switch is disconcerting.

I believe that the strength of both Plato and Aristotle lies in their attempt to work out a naturalistic ethics, based on an understanding of human nature. This leads them both to offer an account of the psychological foundations of the traditional virtues, and to formulate this in terms of the relations between the different aspects of the personality. Aristotle's version I take to be the more acceptable, incorporating as it does a more satisfactory understanding of the relation between reason and feeling. Each of them uses his psychological theory to forge a link between the virtues and happiness, and each of them produces a subtle and suggestive account of what constitutes happiness.

This whole approach common to Plato and Aristotle has nevertheless met with certain fundamental criticisms. I shall consider these in the next chapter.

Notes

1 Jean-Paul Sartre: *Existentialism and Humanism*, trans. Philip Mairet (London, 1948), p. 26.

4 The Problem of Egoism and Altruism

Prichard's Objection

The central enterprise upon which Plato and Aristotle are engaged is the attempt to show that the traditionally good and virtuous way of life is one which we have reason to follow, since it is the happiest and most fulfilling. It has been argued by some philosophers that the whole enterprise is in fact radically misconceived. A classic statement of this criticism can be found in H. A. Prichard's 1928 lecture, 'Duty and Interest'.[1] Prichard's central argument is this: if justice is advocated on the grounds that it is advantageous to the just person, it is thereby reduced to a form of self-interest. In that case it will not really be *justice* that we are advocating. The just person—the morally good person as conventionally understood—is someone who keeps his promise simply because he has promised, who pays his debt simply because he owes it, who refrains from lying simply because it would be dishonest. He is essentially different from someone who does these things because it will make him happier or better off. Therefore, if Plato or Aristotle were to succeed in persuading someone to be 'just' or 'virtuous' because he would thereby be happier, he might induce him to perform the appropriate actions, but would not really have made him into a morally good and just person.

Prichard's argument is formulated in terms of the concept of 'duty'. For Prichard, duty is not really duty unless it is done for duty's sake. The same criticism could be reformulated, just as powerfully, in terms not of 'duty' but of 'altruism'. Within our own moral culture, largely as a product of the Christian tradition, an altruistic concern for others is widely held to be a, or even the, supreme value. If, however, in caring for other people, I do so because I think that it will make my own life happier, then it would seem that it is not really a concern for others which motivates me, but a concern for myself. From the above standpoint, the action then ceases to be morally admirable.

Notice exactly what is being claimed here. It is not being suggested that Plato and Aristotle exclude altruistic qualities from the good life, and advocate a selfish disregard for the interests of others. That would be the position of someone like Thrasymachus. We have seen that, for Plato, justice is essentially an altruistic virtue requiring respect for others' interests, loyalty to one's parents and friends and country, the honouring of one's promises and agreements, and so forth. Justice likewise figures in Aristotle's list of the virtues, as does generosity. Aristotle also has a lengthy discussion of friendship, and gives concern for one's friends a central place in the good life. So the criticism is not that Plato and Aristotle exclude altruisim. It is that, because they justify it by reference to the agent's own happiness, they reduce it to a kind of enlightened self-interest, and so deprive it of its moral value.

This is likely to be seen as a searching criticism. And yet it also seems very plausible to defend altruism in the manner of Plato and Aristotle. For, surely it just is the case that a life lived in harmony and co-operation with others, sharing sympathetically in their hopes and sorrows, is the most fulfilling and rewarding. Is it not a basic fact of human experience that a life of mutual aid and consideration is more satisfying than one of hostility and enmity? And if so, is this not as good a reason as one could require for living such a life? We are thus faced with a dilemma between what look like two equally persuasive positions, that of Prichard on the one hand and that of Plato and Aristotle on the other. Can the dilemma be resolved?

We might begin to resolve it by emphasizing how the Platonic and Aristotelian position differs from the view presented by Glaucon and Adeimantus in *The Republic*. Glaucon and Adeimantus, it will be recalled, suggest that most people regard justice as a sort of mutual insurance policy. In this view, to live justly is not advantageous *in itself*, but it does have desirable *consequences* for the agent, since he earns the goodwill of others (not to mention that of the gods). This, then, is the popular view, but Glaucon and Adeimantus are dissatisfied with it. They ask Socrates to demonstrate that justice is a good to the just person, not simply in virtue of the consequences, but in its very nature. This is what Socrates in *The Republic* proceeds to do. The position is, of course, Plato's own, and it is also in its broad character that of Aristotle, who likewise claims not that the virtues are *means* to happiness, but that 'happiness *is* an activity of the soul in accordance with perfect virtue' (*Ethics* I.13, my italics). I shall refer to the two opposed positions as 'Glaucon's view' (although Glaucon himself does not advocate it), and 'the Socratic view' (which is shared by Plato and Aristotle).

According to Glaucon, then, justice is a good to the just man, because if you act justly towards others they will act justly towards you, and so you will be better off. According to the Socratic view, justice does not simply have advantageous consequences, it is *itself* the greatest benefit. For Glaucon, justice is an *instrumental* good; it enables you to get what you need in order to live well. For the Socratic view, justice is an *intrinsic* good; it *is* living well. According to Glaucon, then, there is an *external* relation between justice and benefit. According to the Socratic view, the relation is an *internal* one.

A further important difference follows. In Glaucon's account, justice is recommended in the light of a preconceived idea of what happiness consists in, what the agent's proper interests are. We are presumed already to have an idea of what happiness is—it is, perhaps, the acquisition of wealth and the wielding of power, and the like—and the argument proceeds on that assumption. In the Socratic account, no such idea of happiness, of the agent's interests, is assumed. On the contrary, happiness is itself re-defined in the course of the argument. If we are convinced by the Socratic account, then, in the light of our understanding of justice, we are brought to change our idea of happiness. Thus, for Glaucon, we first know what our interests are, and then come to see how justice contributes to them. For Plato and Aristotle, we must first understand what justice is, and only then can we come to see what our true interests are.

Plato's own analysis of Glauconian virtue comes in Book VIII of the *Republic*, in the account of the oligarchic personality. The person who acts justly, as an external means to his own self-interest, is there said to be ruled by desire rather than by reason. The desires which would lead him to cheat and steal and harm others are simply held in check by other desires which are equally self-interested. His is the 'shopkeeper' morality, the ethic of 'Honesty is the best policy':

the high reputation for honesty which he has in other business transactions is due merely to a certain respectable constraint which he exercises over his evil impulses, for fear of their effect on his concerns as a whole. There's no moral conviction, no taming of desires by reason, but only the compulsion of fear. . . . This sort of man, then, is never at peace with himself, but has a kind of dual personality, in which the better desires on the whole master the worse. . . . He therefore has a certain degree of respectability, but comes nowhere near the real goodness of an integrated and united character. (554c–e.)

Aristotle does not employ the vocabulary of 'health' and 'illness', but he too appeals to the psychological facts. Like Plato, he analyses the virtues in terms of the right relation between reason and feeling. He argues that the happiest and most fulfilling life is that of the person in whom this right relation obtains, because he will be living the fully human life of reason.

I think that when the Platonic and Aristotelian position is properly spelled out in this way, and clearly distinguished from the Glauconian position, Prichard's criticism loses a good deal of its force. That objection seems persuasive largely because we feel that if someone treats others as *means* to his own happiness, then however much this may lead him to respect their interests, his attitude towards them can hardly be described as an altruistic one. Rather, it is an instrumental attitude to others. If Plato and Aristotle, however, are presenting a proper concern for others as *constitutive* of one's own happiness, their account of the altruistic virtues may appear no more suspect than the altruism of one who simply enjoys helping others.

Moral Egoism

Nevertheless there remain difficulties, and I think that they can be brought out if we consider the following example. Suppose that someone, perhaps a neighbour of mine, is in trouble and needs help; he needs, perhaps, someone to talk to, with whom to share his troubles, and from whom to ask advice. Suppose now that I put to myself the question: why should I help him? The Glauconian answer would be: 'By helping him, you will put him in your debt and increase the chances that he may help you some day, and you will improve your reputation in the eyes of others so that they too will be well disposed towards you.' Such an answer exhibits a purely instrumental attitude to the other person. It is not an attitude of genuine concern for him, but one which regards him simply as a means to one's own benefit. The Platonic and Aristotelian answer would be: 'I should help him because a life of sympathetic concern for others is the most rewarding and fulfilling kind of life.' This, as I have been stressing, is an importantly different answer. It does not represent, in the same kind of way, an instrumental attitude to the other person. But now contrast it with a third possible answer: 'Because he needs help'. This answer is different again. And when we compare it with the second answer, we must surely agree that it is this, the third answer, that represents most fully the attitude of genuine responsiveness to the other's needs. As such, it suggests that there is still something unsatisfactory about the Platonic and Aristotelian answer.

These remaining doubts may be strengthened if we look particularly at some of Aristotle's discussions of particular virtues. Consider this description of the person who exhibits liberality (i.e. generosity at the individual level):

He will avoid giving to any and everybody, so that he may have something to give to the right people at the right time and in circumstances in which it is a fine thing to do. (IV.1. 1120b 3–4.)

Clearly the motivation which Aristotle envisages in such a person is not that he wants to make sure that the right people get the help they need, but that he wants to ensure that he himself has the best opportunities to exhibit generosity.

We find something very similar in Aristotle's account of the so-called 'great-souled' or 'magnanimous' person, whose virtue has seemed peculiarly offensive to many modern readers.

> The magnanimous man does not take petty risks, nor does he court danger, because there are few things that he values highly; but he takes great risks, and when he faces danger he is unsparing of his life, because to him there are some circumstances in which it is not worth living. He is disposed to confer benefits, but is ashamed to accept them, because the one is the act of a superior, and the other the act of an inferior. When he repays a service he does so with interest, because in this way the original benefactor will become his debtor and beneficiary. (IV.3 1124b 6–12.)

It appears that he will reserve his courage not for when it is most needed but for when he can be most courageous, and he will regard the activities of giving and receiving, and of paying one's debts, as a veritable competition in virtue. Think back to our previous three-way comparison. Aristotle's virtuous individual does not cultivate the altruistic virtues as means to his own interests. He cultivates them for their own sake. But he cultivates them very much *as states of himself*, and in this he is in marked contrast with the third of the three individuals we imagined. He is preoccupied with himself, he focuses on the sort of person he wants to be, instead of focusing on the needs of the other person and responding to them in their own right. He is not an egoist in a straightforward sense, but he exhibits what we might call a kind of 'moral egoism'.

Part of the trouble here is Aristotle's emphasis on *ends*, which I noted in the previous chapter. This commits him to saying that, if virtuous activity is not wanted for the sake of further consequences, then it must itself be an end, something which we aim at. This already has the effect of detaching the virtuous activity from the circumstances (including other people's needs) which require it; the circumstances become an opportunity to achieve the end of performing the virtuous activity, instead of the activity being a response to the circumstances. The question then is: can either Plato or Aristotle avoid this, so long as they want to retain the link between virtue and individual happiness? Our own happiness is surely an end; therefore if virtuous activity is constitutive of happiness, and if this is a reason for performing it, do we not have to say of the virtuous activity also that it is an end in itself?——and does this not automatically put us in the position of 'moral egoism' which I have been ascribing to Aristotle?

There is one way in which we might try to avoid it, and might retain *both* the idea of one's own happiness *and* the idea of other people's needs as reasons for altruistic activity. We might do this by distinguishing between two levels of reason-giving. We could perhaps distinguish between the question, 'What action should I perform (here and now)?', and the question, 'What kind of life should I lead?' What makes these distinct? Consider the circumstances in which I might put the second question to myself. I might come to be struck by the narrowness of my life, by the extent to which I am preoccupied with myself, and to which my experience is thereby impoverished. I might decide that I need to think consciously about being more attentive to others, and giving more play to my own sympathetic responses. My reason for trying to change my life in this way might be that my life would thereby be enriched. But the change might involve precisely the cultivation of habits of thinking about others' needs as such, rather than about how my helping them can enrich my own life. In other words, I might become more the sort of person who, on particular occasions, helps others just because they need help.

This distinction between two levels of reasoning may help to make something like a Platonic or Aristotelian position more acceptable. I shall return to it later. For the time being, I want to leave the discussion in this inconclusive state. I have argued that Plato and Aristotle do not reduce the virtues to self-interest in any straightforward and obvious sense. I have also suggested that there is a more subtle and problematic form of egoism to be found in their ethics. Whether this is a ground for criticism of them, is a question which must now wait until we have worked out a clearer view of the whole problem of egoism and altruism, and this will require that in subsequent chapters we do two things.

The Social Dimension

First, we need to look more closely at the *social* dimension of human life. At this point I shall simply assert dogmatically that a satisfactory account of the ethical significance of altruism depends upon a satisfactory treatment of the role of social relations in the life of the individual. In saying this, I am implying that Plato and Aristotle do not provide an entirely adequate treatment. In the case of Plato, there is a profound ambivalence. On the one hand, *The Republic* combines moral philosophy and social philosophy to a quite unusual degree. The account of justice in the individual is paralleled by the account of justice in society, with its lengthy description of the ideal state. The problem, however, is whether the two accounts are ever really integrated with one another. The relation between them is basically one of *analogy*. The account of justice in the individual does not proceed by looking at the individual in a social context, but simply by arguing that, since justice in society must be harmony between the parts of the state, so by analogy justice in the individual must be a harmony between the parts of the personality. What we need to know, however, is not only how the justice of the individual is *analogous to* the structure of society, but how it is actually *affected by* the individual's existence in society. Plato says surprisingly little about this, but he does say something, and his answer would appear to be this. Ordinary people, in whom the rational part of the soul is not very strong or well developed, can in fact achieve justice only in a well-ordered society. In such a society they would make up the economic class, and presumably also the auxiliary class. At the end of Book IX Plato says of them:

To ensure that people of this type are under the same authority as the highest type, we have said that they should be subjected to that highest type, which is governed by its divine element; but this control is not exercised, as Thrasymachus thought, to the detriment of the subject, but because it is better for every creature to be under the control of divine wisdom. That wisdom and control should, if possible, come from within; failing that it must be imposed from without, in order that, being subject to the same guidance, we may all be brothers and equals. (590c–d.)

In other words, if justice means being under the control of reason, and if one's own reason is not strong enough, then the reason of the rulers must do the job instead. For such a person, therefore, justice is possible only in a just society.

What of those whose own reason is powerful enough to play the commanding role? They would, of course, be the guardians in a just society. Could they, however, achieve justice in themselves without filling that social role? Plato's answer is that they could, and that they most probably would have to do so. Book IX concludes with Glaucon suggesting that the good man is unlikely to enter politics, to which Socrates replies:

'Oh yes, he will, very much so, in the society where he really belongs; but not, I think, in the society where he's born, unless something very extraordinary happens.'

'I see what you mean,' he said. 'You mean that he will do so in the society which we have been describing and which we have theoretically founded; but I doubt if it will ever exist on earth.'

'Perhaps,' I said, 'it is laid up as a pattern in heaven, where those who wish can see it and found it in their own hearts. But it doesn't matter whether it exists or ever will exist; it's the only state in whose politics he can take part.' (592a–b.)

Plato is here expressing his doubts about the practical feasibility of the just society, and his confidence that even in its absence it is possible for some individuals to be just. He also thinks, however, that even if such a society could be created, it would add nothing to the justice of the just individuals. They would take on the role of guardians, not in order to complete their own justice, but with reluctance, and solely for the sake of the rest of society. When, in the analogy of the cave, Socrates says that the philosophers must return to the world of the cave, Glaucon protests:

'But surely that will not be fair. We shall be compelling them to live a poorer life than they might live.'

'The object of our legislation,' I reminded him again, 'is not the welfare of any particular class, but of the whole community. . . . You see, then, we shan't be unfair to our philosophers, but shall be quite justified in compelling them to have some care and responsibility for others. . . . But of course, unlike present rulers, they will approach the business of government as an unavoidable necessity.' (519d–520e.)

The implication is that the truly just individual does not need society; he can live a just life in any society or in none.

There is something of the same ambivalence in Aristotle. Although the bulk of the *Ethics* envisages the virtues being exercised in society, the introduction of the contemplative life at the end of Book X forms a kind of Platonic post-script. Despite his rejection of Plato's other-worldly meta-physics, Aristotle retained an attraction to the Platonic ideal of the self-sufficient philosopher living the life of the pure intellect. He concedes that:

the wise man, no less than the just one and all the rest, requires the necessaries of life; but, given an adequate supply of these, the just man also needs people with and towards whom he can perform just actions, and similarly with the temperate man, the brave man, and each of the others; but the wise man can practise contemplation by himself, and the wiser he is, the more he can do it. No doubt he does it better with the help of fellow-workers; but for all that he is the most self-sufficient of men. (1177a 28–b1.)

Neither Plato nor Aristotle, then, does full justice to the place of social relations in the good life. Until we have worked out a more satisfactory account of the nature of our relations with others, we cannot deal adequately with the question of the ethical significance of altruism. I shall return to this suggestion later in the book, and especially in Chapter 8.

The Christian Tradition

The other thing which we have to do in order to deal with the problem of egoism and altruism is to look at the alter-native to the Platonic and Aristotelian position, and that means looking at the Christian tradition, and at those ethical philosophies which have been influenced by it. I shall not in this book provide any substantial discussion of Christian ethics, nor indeed of the relation between ethics and religion in general. (My neglect of this area is to be explained partly by limitations of space, and partly by my own religious scepticism.) Nevertheless, it is clear that Christianity places altruism at the centre of the good life. This altruistic morality is formulated directly in, for example, the so-called Golden

Rule, 'All things whatsoever ye would that men should do
to you, do ye even so to them' (Matt. 7:12), or in Jesus'
commandment 'Thou shalt love thy neighbour as thyself'
(Matt. 22:39).

Even more striking, when seen against the background of
Greek ethics, is the positive value which Christianity places
on self-denial. This is a central theme of Jesus' Sermon on the
Mount, which begins with the Beatitudes: 'Blessed are the
poor in spirit . . . Blessed are they that mourn . . . Blessed are
the meek . . .' etc. There is some similarity with Plato here—
with the ascetic strand in Plato which advocates a turning
away from material goods and physical pleasures, for the
higher life of communion with the world of the forms.
Christianity and Plato share a 'two worlds' metaphysics,
a division between the world of the flesh and the world of
the spirit. The contrast with Aristotle, however, is absolute.
Consider Jesus' doctrine of non-resistance to evil: that if anyone strikes you on the right cheek you should turn to him
the other, and that if anyone would take your coat you
should give him your cloak as well (Matt. 5:38). Of these
examples Aristotle would say: here anger is appropriate.

Similarly, contrast the Christian praise of humility and
meekness with the qualities of Aristotle's 'great-souled'
or 'magnanimous' person. The virtue which the latter exhibits
is what we might call self-respect or self-esteem, taking a
pride in oneself and one's achievements. It is linked with the
virtue of 'truthfulness' (IV.7), by which Aristotle means
being honest and open about oneself, acknowledging one's
merits as well as one's faults. In Aristotle's ethics there is no
room for false modesty.

Which of these two contrasting ethical views is the more
acceptable? There is no immediate and obvious answer to
the question, and it is not enough simply to consult our
culturally-formed prejudices. We have to look at how the
two views can be defended, and consider whether those
defences can stand up to critical scrutiny. Now, in so far as
the Christian morality involves this positive valuing of self-
denial, I do not think it can be assessed without a consideration of the Christian metaphysics on which it depends, and
that is a task beyond the scope of this book. I do not see how

self-denial can be regarded as having any value in itself, except against the background of the sort of 'two worlds' view I have mentioned. Then, and only then, can one make sense of the idea that the things of this world are worthless, that they are devalued when set against a timeless spiritual world, and that our object must be to transcend all worldly aspirations, so as to bring the soul nearer to God. All I am able to say here is that I cannot accept the metaphysics, and therefore cannot accept the morality which goes with it.

What I do want to consider at length is the broader ethics of altruism which Christianity has fostered. I shall look at it not in a form which ties it to the Christian religion, but as it occurs in subsequent ethical philosophies which bear the imprint of the Christian tradition, and which take something like the Golden Rule, or 'Love thy neighbour as thyself', as the central principle of ethics. The claims of this altruistic morality have to be weighed against those of the Platonic and Aristotelian ethics which, though it does not exclude altruism, assigns the central place to the agent's own happiness. The philosophers whom we shall consider believe that the ethics of altruism can be defended. They defend it, not by appealing to divine revelation, or to a divine command which has to be accepted on authority, but by appealing to human reason and/or experience. Let us see whether they can make good their claim.

Note

1 Included in H. A. Prichard: *Moral Obligation and 'Duty and Interest'* (London, 1968).

PART II

The Moderns

5 Hume
Sympathy

Reading: David Hume: *Enquiry Concerning the Principles of Morals* (first published 1751). Since there is no uniform system of page numbering, references will be to paragraph numbers, and I suggest that the reader should number the paragraphs in his or her own copy. I shall use roman numerals to refer to Sections of the work, and arabic numerals to refer to the paragraphs within the Sections. For example, 'II.1' means paragraph 1 of Section II. The only Sections to which numbered paragraph references will be given are II, III, V, IX, and Appendices I and III.

An earlier and more difficult presentation of Hume's ethical theory is to be found in Book III of his *A Treatise of Human Nature* (1739), which I shall occasionally mention.

David Hume, the eighteenth-century Scottish philosopher, can hardly be enlisted in the Christian tradition. He was the author of one of the great works of religious scepticism, his *Dialogues Concerning Natural Religion*. We may, however, reasonably consider his ethical theory as an example of the ethics of altruism. Central to Hume's theory is the concept which he variously refers to as 'sympathy', or 'humanity', or 'fellow-feeling', and an examination of this concept will prove a useful point of entry into his moral philosophy.

Virtues and Vices

We need first to avoid certain misunderstandings. Hume does not use the term 'sympathy' in the narrow sense in which it is now commonly used, to mean something like 'compassion' or 'pity'. He means by it a capacity to be moved or affected by the happiness and suffering of others—to be pleased when others prosper, and distressed when others suffer. He insists that sympathy, thus understood, is an independent human tendency which exists in its own right.[1] Various of his philosophical predecessors had claimed that sympathy was analysable as a form of self-love, and had erected their ethical systems upon that claim.[2] Hume repudiates the claim.

Another possible misunderstanding should also be noted. When Hume discusses the role of sympathy, he is not talking about it as itself a morally admirable quality. He is not concerned to persuade us that we ought to exhibit sympathy or humanity, or even to claim that we do in fact admire it. He is not entirely consistent in his vocabulary, but on the whole when he wants to talk about altruistic qualities as virtues, he uses the term 'benevolence'. 'Sympathy' is not itself the name of a virtue. The terms 'sympathy' and 'humanity' denote not an *object* of moral approval, but the *source* of moral approval. Hume's central claim is that when we ascribe moral praise or blame, that praise or blame derives from an attitude of sympathy. The fact that we feel sympathy towards others is what explains why we judge as we do.

Like Plato and Aristotle, Hume assumes that moral judgements are primarily judgements about virtues and vices. We morally praise people in so far as they exhibit virtues, and blame them in so far as they exhibit vices. Only secondarily are our moral judgements concerned with individual actions. We praise or blame actions because they reveal morally admirable qualities in the agent. The difference from Plato and Aristotle emerges when we look at what Hume counts as virtues. According to Hume, what makes various qualities 'virtues' is that they are useful or agreeable, either to their possessor or to others. He agrees with Plato and Aristotle to this extent, then, that the virtues would not be virtues unless possession of them were in some sense an advantage. It may be a direct advantage—that is, possession of such qualities may be immediately pleasing, in which case he describes the qualities as 'aggreable'; or it may be an indirect advantage—that is, possession of such qualities may help to promote states of affairs which in their turn are pleasurable, and these are the qualities which Hume describes as 'useful'. He parts company from Plato and

Aristotle, however, in that he thinks that not only qualities useful or agreeable to their possessor, but also qualities useful or agreeable to others, are regarded as virtues.

Typical examples in Hume's list of virtues are:

Qualities useful to others: benevolence, justice, fidelity.
Qualities useful to their possessor: discretion, industry, frugality, strength of mind, good sense.
Qualities agreeable to their possessor: cheerfulness, magnanimity, courage, tranquillity.
Qualities agreeable to others: politeness, modesty, decency.

Such a list has much in common with those of Plato and Aristotle, but the prominent place given to benevolence marks a decisive shift from the standpoint of the Greeks. Benevolence is given a chapter to itself in the *Enquiry*, and in that chapter Hume remarks that 'the epithets *sociable, good-natured, humane, merciful, grateful, friendly, generous, beneficent,* or their equivalents . . . universally express the highest merit which *human nature* is capable of attaining'. (II.1.) It may be doubted whether Plato and Aristotle would concur with the phrase 'highest merit', and they would certainly disagree with Hume about *why* we regard such qualities as virtues.

Hume, then, thinks that we admire the virtues because we feel sympathy and humanity. Benevolence, for example, is a quality the exercise of which promotes the happiness or well-being of people in general, and because, through sympathy, we take pleasure in this general happiness or well-being, we are led to admire the quality which promotes it. Similarly, industry is a quality which makes for happiness on the part of its possessor, and it is through sympathy with that happiness that we admire industry in those who possess it. The relationship between sympathy and the virtues is, however, not quite as simple as this, and Hume proceeds to add complications. He recognizes that the strength of people's sympathy varies according to circumstances, whereas moral judgements are made (or at least purport to be made) in accordance with fixed and unvarying standards. The same qualities ought to call forth the same judgements of praise and blame, though our level of sympathy may rise or fall.

When we contemplate the virtues of someone in a remote time or place, for example, we may be pleased at the thought of the happiness which these virtues helped to produce among his or her fellows, but our sympathy will be much weaker than it would be if we were contemplating the happiness of those close to us. Hume deals with this problem by suggesting that our immediate feelings are 'corrected' by general standards. He sees this adoption of a general point of view as a practical contrivance, whereby human beings are able to communicate more effectively, and introduce a greater degree of uniformity into their judgements.

> Sympathy, we shall allow, is much fainter than our concern for ourselves, and sympathy with persons remote from us much fainter than that with persons near and contiguous; but for this very reason it is necessary for us, in our calm judgments and discourse concerning the characters of men, to neglect all these differences and render our sentiments more public and social . . . The intercourse of sentiments, therefore, in society and conversation, makes us form some general unalterable standard by which we may approve or disapprove of characters and manners. (V.42.)

We might reformulate Hume's position as follows. Moral judgements are not a *direct* expression of our feelings of sympathy. Rather, the operation of sympathy enables us to adopt certain *criteria* for the ascription of moral praise and blame, and moral judgements are then made by the application of these criteria.

A further complication is introduced in the case of certain of the virtues, and again the complication involves the further extension of our judgements by general rules. Of the virtues in question, the most important is justice, which Hume discusses in Section III and Appendix III of the *Enquiry*. By 'justice' we are to understand a set of social rules which govern the distribution of the goods which society makes available. Hume assumes that the most effective way of distributing such benefits is to protect all members of society in the enjoyment of whatever property they happen to possess. To act justly, in short, is to respect the property rights of others. In the *Treatise*, Hume had *simply* assumed this. In the *Enquiry* he sees the need to argue against alternative conceptions of justice. It might be felt that justice requires more than the maintenance of property rights, since the existing distribution of property may itself be unjust. Some members of society may own vastly more than others, simply because they happen to have inherited it, or because their property has been augmented by the vagaries of the market. Is this not unjust? Would it not be more just if property were apportioned to people according to what they deserve, or alternatively if it were distributed equally among all the members of a society?

Hume rejects both the idea of 'justice as desert' and that of 'justice as equality' on the grounds of their disutility. Attractive though it may be to reward people as they deserve, 'so great is the uncertainty of merit, both from its natural obscurity and from the self-conceit of each individual, that no determinate rule of conduct would ever result' (III.23). People would never agree about what they deserved, and the result would be chaos. Likewise the pursuit of equality is 'at bottom impracticable', and persistence in it against the odds 'would be extremely pernicious to human society' (III.26). People differ in their talents and abilities. Consequently, they naturally tend towards inequality, and any attempt to obstruct the tendency will either prove futile, or require extremely authoritarian measures to prevent people rising above others. Unjust though it may appear, therefore, the most useful conception of justice is that which guarantees to people what they already have.[3]

What all these conceptions of justice have in common, nevertheless, is that they generate a system of rules for the distribution of social goods. And it is their connection with a system of social rules that gives justice and other similar virtues a special status in Hume's theory. A particular act of justice, taken in isolation, may well have harmful consequences, and a particular act of injustice may have beneficial consequences. If I were to rob the rich and give to the poor, for instance, the rich would scarcely miss what I took from them, and the poor would gain far more than the rich would lose. Nevertheless, though the individual act of theft may be useful, the act is of a kind which, if generally practised, would be extremely harmful. What has to be assessed, according to Hume, is not the individual act but the system as a whole. When we make this assessment we find, according to Hume, that a system of rules which guarantees everyone security of possession is more useful than any alternative system. And this is what entitles us to say that justice, understood as a disposition to respect people's property, is a virtue. In the *Treatise*, Hume had described justice and similar virtues as 'artificial virtues' (in contrast to 'natural virtues') because they presupposed the existence of a set of social conventions. He abandoned this terminology in the *Enquiry*, in order to avoid the other associations which might be invited by a description of justice as 'artificial' or 'unnatural'. Nevertheless, the distinction between 'natural virtues' and 'artificial virtues' remains a useful way of marking the special status which Hume ascribes to the latter.

Hume, then, envisages three stages by which our judgements are extended:

Stage 1. Sympathy induces us to take account of the happiness and suffering of others as well as our own.

Stage 2. General standards correct the operation of sympathy, so that we attach the same moral importance to the happiness or suffering of anyone, ourselves or others, close to us or remote from us.

Stage 3. In some cases we need to take into account not merely the utility of particular acts, but the usefulness to society of a whole system of general rules and conventions.

Each of these three is a move from a limited to a more generalized standpoint. Together they challenge the Platonic-Aristotelian view that one's moral assessments are necessarily made from the standpoint of a concern for one's own well-being. How successful are they? I shall now examine each of them in turn, taking them in the reverse order.

Justice

Hume's account of justice is an example of a position often referred to as 'rule-utilitarianism'. Utilitarianism in general will be the subject of Chapter 7. For the moment it will be sufficient to define utilitarianism as the theory which states that actions are right in so far as they produce happiness or prevent suffering, wrong in so far as they produce suffering or prevent happiness. It differs from Hume's overall ethical theory in applying the utility-test to actions rather than to qualities of the agent.

Utilitarianism itself, however, has its variants, and some utilitarians have wanted to defend the variant known as 'rule-utilitarianism' in contrast to 'act-utilitarianism'. The utilitarian assessment, they say, should be applied not to individual actions but to moral rules. We should ask not 'Which actions will produce the greatest happiness?' but 'What are the moral rules, observance of which would produce the greatest happiness?' We then have a two-tier system of moral justification. Individual actions are to be assessed by asking, 'Is this action in accordance with an acceptable moral rule?' Moral rules in turn are to be assessed by asking, 'Will the observance of this rule produce more happiness than the observance of any alternative rule?' Hume, then, is putting forward essentially the same position when he suggests that the utility of justice resides not in the utility of individual just acts but in the utility of the general system of property-rules.

The question which arises for any two-tier system of moral justification is: can the two tiers really be kept separate? Critics of rule-utilitarianism have argued that they cannot, and the same criticism may, I think, be applied to Hume's account of justice. Consider his admission that someone who stole from the rich in order to give to the poor could, in the particular case, do more good than harm. Hume thinks that the rules of property ought nevertheless to be observed because of the utility of the overall scheme. How might our benevolent thief take issue with Hume?

He might first accuse Hume of assuming that rules must always be very simple and general. Simple rules, he may say, cannot do justice to the complexity of particular situations. If it is normally in the interests of society that property should be respected, but if there are also exceptional circumstances where one can do more good than harm by stealing, then the rules of justice should incorporate the exceptional circumstances as well as the normal case. In place of the simple rule, 'Do not steal', we may need the more complex rule, 'Do not steal unless you are stealing from very rich people who do not need what you take from them, and giving it to poor people who can make much better use of it.' And once we make our moral rules more complex, the gap between general rules and individual acts disappears. However detailed the relevant features of the individual act may be, they can always be incorporated into a rule, albeit a highly complex one. Thus rule-utilitarianism turns out to be indistinguishable from ordinary 'act-utilitarianism', and the two-tier structure collapses.

Hume may reply that our moral rules *ought* to be kept simple and general, and that the reasons for doing so are themselves reasons of utility. If the rules for the protection of property have all sorts of exceptions built into them, the security which they are supposed to provide will vanish. Everyone will regard his or her own case as exceptional, and the discretion which the rules allow will be exploited to the point of chaos.

But now, our objector may say, this argument for keeping rules clear and simple is itself an act-utilitarian one. What is being claimed is that, if the rule against stealing allows for exceptions, any particular agent who is contemplating an act of theft will be biased in his or her own favour, will be incapable of reviewing the consequences accurately and objectively, and will probably end up doing more harm than good. But that is a claim about the consequences of an individual act. Moreover, if it is recognized as such, it may in some circumstances become a debatable claim. There is indeed a risk that people will make exceptions in their own favour, and this is a risk of which I ought to be conscious when I am inclined to regard my own case as exceptional, but if, in a particular case, I can be confident that I have reviewed the circumstances objectively, and that I really will do more good by stealing, ought I not to make the exception and commit the act of theft, even though the necessarily simple rules forbid me to do so?

Not so, Hume will reply, for the question you should put to yourself is not 'What will happen if *I* keep or break the rule?' but, 'What will happen if *people in general* keep or break the rule?' 'The benefit resulting from [virtues such as justice] is not the consequence of every individual single act, but arises from the whole scheme or system concurred in by the whole or the greater part of society' (Appendix III.3). General rules safeguarding property are morally desirable, because if everyone abides by them this will be highly useful to society, and though the consequences of someone's breaking them on a particular occasion might be good, the consequences of a general infraction of them would be disastrous.

If general rules are regarded in this way as rules whose *general* observance would be beneficial, a gap really does open up between the general rule and the individual act. Rule-utilitarianism becomes a genuinely distinct theory, different from act-utilitarianism. But it achieves the distinctness only by leaving it unclear why anyone should accept it. To the question 'What would happen if everyone did that?' there is an obvious answer—'But *not* everyone is doing it.' It is plausible enough that the *actual* consequences of an action should be relevant to whether one ought to perform it. It is quite unclear why the entirely *hypothetical* consequences of innumerable *other* actions should be relevant. It may be true that if people in general disregarded the rule against stealing, security of property would disappear, and social life would break down. But since social life has not broken down, and the property system continues to be perfectly viable, why should I not make use of the fact to do some good by stealing from those who have more than they need?

In short, any rule-utilitarian is caught in the following dilemma. Either the reasons for following a (perhaps complex) rule are simply reasons for performing a certain kind of act, in which case the gap between rule and act disappears, and rule-utilitarianism ceases to be a distinctive theory; or there is a real gap between rule and act, in which case it is quite unclear why one should stick to the system of rules when breaking them can do more good. What Hume needs to explain is how one may come to be *committed* to certain social rules, despite the advantages of breaking the rules on particular occasions. This in turn requires an explanation of how one comes to be committed to the social institution or community whose rules they are. Some more satisfactory account is needed of the relation between the individual and society, and we shall look at a possible source for this in Chapter 8.

General Standards

Let us now revert to Stage two of Hume's scheme, the correction of sympathy by general standards. Hume, we saw, presents this as a matter of practical convenience: human beings could not converse effectively on moral matters if their judgements reflected the varying strength of their feelings of sympathy. As a factual claim this is unconvincing. Hume is presumably impressed by the fact that our moral language includes not only the direct expression of personal sentiments ('I admire Brutus') but also the impersonal ascription of objective qualities ('Brutus was a good and noble citizen'). But why should we not manage perfectly well with a moral vocabulary confined entirely to the former? There may be good reasons why we need also the language of objective qualities, but Hume does not tell us what these reasons might be. Moreover, even if we do need it, could we not employ such language in a way which mirrored the variability of our feelings? Other areas of discourse operate perfectly well in that way—the language of tastes, for example. One person may say, 'I find cream cakes rather sickly', and another may say, 'I don't find them sickly at all'. The question, 'Are cream cakes *really* sickly?' has no clear sense, in the absence of any 'general unalterable standard' by which it can be answered, but it does not follow that communication has broken down. The person who finds cream cakes sickly will act on that basis, his less sensitive interlocutor will do likewise, and no further problem need arise. If ease of communication is the only consideration, I do not see why moral language should not operate in the same way. I shall suggest in a later chapter that ease of communication is *not* the only consideration, and that Hume's point can be restated more convincingly. Hume himself, however, fails to do so.

Sympathy

I turn finally to Stage one, the claim that our judgements of moral approval or disapproval are generated by our feelings of sympathy. This claim is vital to Hume's ethical theory. It is what sets him apart from the egoistic perspective of Plato and Aristotle. What are we to make of it?

The difficulties emerge when we ask, 'What if someone fails to feel sympathy?' Hume does not raise this question. He simply assumes that sympathy is universal. If we bear in mind what he means by 'sympathy', this assumption is less implausible than it might appear. He is not assuming that everyone is always motivated by feelings of kindness and concern for others. His claim is merely that everyone is to some degree affected by other people's happiness or suffering. However little they might be moved to act on it, Hume would claim, no one can be totally indifferent to the contemplation of others' pleasures and pains. Though even this limited claim is not strictly true, we may, I think, concede this much to Hume, that someone who is incapable of sympathy in this rudimentary sense would normally be regarded as an instance of a psychopathic condition. We are envisaging not just someone who acts inconsiderately or cruelly towards others, but someone who is literally incapable of responding to other people as human beings. An actual example of such a condition would be the autistic child who 'treats people as if they were inanimate objects, exploring their shape as he would a toy or a piece of furniture. He appears to feel and behave as if alone in a world uninhabited by other persons.'[4]

Sympathy, we may allow, is, if not universal, at any rate a feature of any normal human being. This, however, will not take Hume very far in answering our question. If sympathy is something possessed by even the most cruel and ruthless of characters, it must be compatible with a wide range of behaviour. How much weight, then, ought it to carry in determining our actions? One might suppose Hume's view to be that it should be a decisive influence on our judgements about how to act. But why *should* it have this dominant role? Again Hume evades the question. Indeed, he would see it as a question which is simply not his concern. His task, he would say, is to describe and explain how we do in fact make our moral judgements, not to tell us how we *ought* to make them. He is not in the business of recommending, but merely of recording.

There is a further reason why he can avoid addressing the question. Recall that the kinds of moral judgements he is concerned with are judgements about personal qualities rather than judgements about actions. He thereby avoids offering any account of how we make difficult decisions about how to act. Take the case of a woman who is confronted with the choice of whether to walk out of a marriage which has stunted and oppressed her. If she does so, she may be exhibiting the qualities of courage and self-respect. If she decides to stay, perhaps out of an enduring loyalty to her husband, or a concern for her children, she may be exhibiting the qualities of fidelity or benevolence. But it is no comfort to her to know that whatever she does, she will be exhibiting morally admirable qualities. She still has to decide what to do. Should sympathy be the decisive consideration? If so, does that mean she should be influenced by other people's needs and interests at the expense of her own? Why should she? Why indeed should sympathy play any effective role at all in her decision? Why should she not simply act out of self-love on this occasion? Hume offers no way of answering these questions.

We can imagine possible answers. Hume could say that if her judgement about what to do is to be a moral judgement, it will be guided by sympathy, since the defining feature of moral judgements is precisely that fact that they stem from sympathy. Such an answer, however, would merely beg the question. Even supposing that moral judgements are by definition those which are guided by sympathy, why should one's judgement about what to do be a *moral* judgement rather than some other kind of practical judgement? Why should one decide on the basis of sympathy rather than on some other basis such as self-love?

A further answer which Hume might supply is that only by judging on the basis of sympathy, can one produce a judgement with which other people can agree. He says:

When a man denominates another his *enemy*, his *rival*, his *antagonist*, his *adversary*, he is understood to speak the language of self-love, and to express sentiments peculiar to himself and arising from his particular circumstances and situation. But when he bestows on any man the epithets of *vicious* or *odious* or *depraved*, he then speaks another language, and expresses sentiments in which he expects all his audience are to concur with him. He must here, therefore, depart from his private and particular situation and must choose a point of view common to him with others; he must move some universal principle of the human frame . . . (IX.6).

This universal principle is the sentiment of humanity or sympathy.

And though this affection of humanity may not generally be esteemed so strong as vanity or ambition, yet, being common to all men, it can alone be the foundation of morals or of any general system of blame or praise. (ibid.)

Hume is still talking here about judgements of personal qualities, rather than judgements of actions. One could, however, suggest in the same vein that judgements about what to do should take the form of moral judgements, based on sympathy, because those are the kinds of judgements on which people can agree.

Again the answer would beg the question. Why give priority to judgements on which people can agree? Hume has allowed in this passage that people can speak the language of self-love and be perfectly intelligible to one another. Why, then, should we not act on self-love, and forgo the luxury of other people's concurrence with our judgement about what to do?

The problem, then, is this. It may be that the distinctive feature of moral judgements is their connection with sympathy, and it may be that sympathy is an almost universally shared sentiment. This, however, constitutes no reason why we should form judgements from a moral point of view rather than some other, or why we should act on such judgements. And when Hume himself eventually tackles the problem directly, he abandons his reliance on sympathy and reverts to an appeal to self-love. Part II of the *Enquiry*'s Conclusion begins: 'Having explained the moral *approbation* attending merit or virtue, there remains nothing but briefly to consider our interested *obligation* to it, and to enquire whether every man who has any regard to his own happiness and welfare will not best find his account in the practice of every moral duty.' The implication is that the way to demonstrate the obligation is to show that the path of moral duty is the path most conducive to one's own happiness and welfare. Accordingly, Hume proceeds to remind us that possession of the social virtues put one on good terms with one's fellows, and that 'no society can be agreeable or even tolerable where a man feels his presence unwelcome and discovers all around him symptoms of disgust and aversion' (IX.18). Even in the case of justice, 'where a man, taking things in a certain light, may often seem to be a loser by his integrity', the fact remains that 'inward peace of mind, consciousness of integrity, a satisfactory review of our own conduct . . . are circumstances very requisite to happiness.' (IX.22–3.)

As with Plato and Aristotle, the appeal to self-interest is not a crude one. The argument is not that possession of the virtues is *instrumentally* advantageous, bringing compensatory benefits in its wake, but rather that possession of them is *itself* a state of happiness and well-being. Such an argument nevertheless remains unsatisfactory, for reasons which we considered in the previous chapter. And by reverting to the appeal to self-love, Hume shows that his use of the concept of sympathy does not after all enable him to succeed where Plato and Aristotle failed. We remain confronted by the same dilemma. Either the moral desirability of altruistic actions remains unjustified, as when Hume asserts that we just do as a matter of fact adopt the standpoint of sympathy, and form our judgements accordingly; or some further justification is offered, which then reduces altruism to a form of self-love. Hume oscillates between these alternatives, but never transcends the opposition between them.

Reason and Sentiment

So far I have been contrasting Hume with Plato and Aristotle on the problem of egoism and altruism. In the remainder of this chapter I shall examine a second contrast with the

Greeks—on the problem of moral knowledge. Plato and Aristotle, it will be recalled, disagreed on the nature of such knowledge. Plato's explicit doctrine viewed moral knowledge as a purely intellectual acquaintance with abstract universal forms. Implicit in Plato's own practice, however, we found a rather different view, much more in line with Aristotle's position: that moral knowledge is to be derived from an empirical study of the facts of human existence. This position I referred to as *ethical naturalism*.

Hume's disagreement with Plato and Aristotle is as radical as it could be. Quite simply, he denies that there can be such a thing as moral knowledge. Moral approval and disapproval derive from sentiment rather than from reason.

As a first step to a fuller understanding of this stark claim, we need to look at what Hume means by 'reason' and 'sentiment'. In other philosophical contexts 'reason' is sometimes opposed to 'experience' and equated with pure thought, the operation of the intellect without any reliance on the senses. In the present context, however, Hume uses 'reason' (for which he sometimes substitutes the term 'understanding') in a more comprehensive sense, to mean our capacity to judge of truth and falsity, that is, to obtain any kind of knowledge, whether from pure thought or from experience. Whereas the sphere of reason, then, is that of knowledge, the sphere of sentiment is that of feelings and emotions, and Hume insists on the sharp division between the two.

> The distinct boundaries and offices of *reason* and of *taste* are easily ascertained. The former conveys the knowledge of truth and falsehood; the latter gives the sentiment of beauty and deformity, vice and virtue. (Appendix I.21.)

Reason, he allows, has a role to play in our moral thinking. Through the use of reason we discover the consequences of various human qualities and actions. Take the case of justice. Hume claims that the upholding of justice, that is, of clear and simple property rules, will make for good order and prosperity in any society. Conversely, the violation of such rules will make for chaos and destruction. These are straightforward factual claims, and the establishing of their truth or falsity is the province of reason. Even if they can be shown to be true, however, this is not sufficient to establish that justice is a virtue. That conclusion follows only if it is also accepted that order and prosperity are desirable, and that chaos and destruction are undesirable. These further assertions are not factual claims, and they cannot be established by reason. To accept them is to feel a certain kind of sentiment. As we have seen, Hume thinks that the sentiment in question is the feeling of sympathy or humanity, which leads us to approve of the virtues because of their useful and agreeable features. He also thinks that everyone shares this feeling. Nevertheless, he would have to agree that if someone did not feel the requisite sympathy, if someone revelled in chaos and destruction, and therefore regarded justice as a vice and injustice as a virtue, we could not show him to be mistaken. We could not do so, not because it would be beyond our powers, but because *nothing could count as* his being mistaken. Moral utterances are simply not the kind of thing that could be either true or false.

A passage in Hume's *Treatise*, much quoted by recent philosophers, has commonly been interpreted as making the same point. The passage runs as follows:

In every system of morality which I have hitherto met with, I have always remarked that the author proceeds for some time in the ordinary way of reasoning, and establishes the being of a god, or makes observations concerning human affairs; when of a sudden I am surprised to find that instead of the usual copulations of propositions *is* and *is not*, I meet with no proposition that is not connected with an *ought* or an *ought not*. This change is imperceptible, but is, however, of the last consequence. For as this *ought* or *ought not* expresses some new relation or affirmation, it is necessary that it should be observed and explained; and at the same time that a reason should be given for what seems altogether inconceivable, how this new relation can be a deduction from others which are entirely different from it. (*Treatise* Book III Part 1, Section 1.)

Here Hume seems again to be saying that moral assertions are not statements of fact, and therefore cannot be derived by reason from other statements of fact. Given any set of 'is'-propositions, one will proceed from them to the acceptance of an 'ought' only if one has the appropriate sentiment.

That is the traditional interpretation. It has however been questioned, and with the questioning goes a reinterpretation of Hume's general account of reason and sentiment. It has been pointed out that Hume does not, in this passage, say that the derivation of an 'ought' from an 'is' is impossible, only that it 'seems altogether inconceivable'. Perhaps, therefore, he is to be taken literally: the derivation *seems* inconceivable, but with care it can be done. 'Ought'-propositions do follow from 'is'-propositions, but only from certain kinds of 'is'-propositions. And Hume's 'reason'/'sentiment' doctrine is then reinterpreted as the claim that the 'is'-propositions from which 'oughts' do follow are statements of fact about human sentiments. Such a claim is perhaps to be found in these sentences of the *Enquiry*:

The hypothesis which we embrace is plain. It maintains that morality is determined by sentiment. It defines virtue to be *whatever mental action or quality gives to a spectator the pleasing sentiment of approbation*; and vice the contrary. We then proceed to examine *a plain matter of fact*, to wit what actions have this influence. (Appendix I.10—my italics in final sentence.)

Here Hume does seem to be saying that, by establishing the relevant facts as to which actions and qualities produce a certain kind of sentiment, we can arrive at moral conclusions about which qualities and actions are good or bad, virtuous or vicious. If this is what he means, then he turns out to be an ethical naturalist after all.

Now we can agree that Hume is indeed, in one sense, a proponent of ethical naturalism. He sees ethics as a part of the study of human nature and insists that the proper method in ethics is the experimental method. What we need to do is to investigate the facts about what people's moral sentiments are actually like. But the question is: in what sense can these facts be called 'moral facts'? I want to suggest that they are moral facts only in a limited sense. When we establish that people feel a sentiment of approbation towards, say, acts of kindness, we do not thereby establish that kindness *is* a virtue, but only that people *regard* it as a virtue. The 'moral fact' which has been established is a second-order moral fact, not a first-order moral fact. It is true that, in the passage just quoted, Hume says that he *defines* virtue, as 'whatever mental action or quality gives to a spectator the pleasing sentiment of approbation'. This would imply that

'Kindness is a virtue' simply *means*, 'Kindness elicits from people a sentiment of approbation', and that therefore in establishing the latter, one is also establishing the former. I think, however, that Hume must be taken to be speaking loosely when he offers this as a 'definition'. The two cannot strictly mean the same, for it is essential to his theory that whereas 'Kindness elicits approbation' is a fact discoverable by reason, 'Kindness is a virtue' is not a deliverance of reason but an expression of sentiment. That, surely, is what the distinction between reason and sentiment is all about.

Hume's Arguments

Assuming that the traditional interpretation is correct, let us look at the arguments which Hume offers in defence of his position. There are five of these.

1. 'Reason', says Hume in the first argument, 'judges either of *matter of fact* or of *relations*' (Appendix I.6). But whatever fact or whatever relation we consider, it can be sometimes virtuous and sometimes vicious. Therefore virtue and vice cannot be identified with any particular facts or relations.

Reversing Hume's order, let us take first the case of 'relations'. Consider, he says, the example of ingratitude. This may be defined as occurring when A shows ill-will to B after B has shown good-will to A. The relation exhibited here is, according to Hume, the relation of *contrariety*; A's ill-will is contrary to B's good-will. The wrongness of ingratitude cannot, however, consist in this relation of contrariety, for the same contrariety would exist if A displayed good-will towards B in response to B's ill-will towards A, but in such a case the action, far from being wrong, might even be regarded as praiseworthy.

It is clear that Hume is using the term 'relation' in a special and limited sense. A natural response to the example would be to insist that 'returning ill-will for good-will' is a *different* relation from 'returning good-will for ill-will'. Hume takes them to be instances of the same relation, contrariety, because he assumes that the relations we should be looking for are purely *formal* or *logical* relations. Why should he make this assumption? Because the opponents he has in mind are philosophers who have expressly declared that moral right and wrong do consist in certain formal relations. Samuel Clarke, for instance, writes in his *Discourse on Natural Religion* of 1705 that:

In respect of our Fellow-Creatures, the Rule of Righteousness is, that in particular we so deal with every Man, as in like Circumstances we could reasonably expect he should deal with Us . . .[5]

Clarke explains that:

The Reason which obliges every Man in Practice, so to deal always with another, as he would reasonably expect that Others should in like Circumstances deal with Him, is the very same, as That which forces him in speculation to affirm, that if one Line or Number be equal to another, That other is reciprocally equal to It. Iniquity is the very same in Action, as Falsity or Contradiction in Theory, and the same cause which makes the one absurd, makes the other unreasonable.

He thus asserts precisely the view which Hume attacks, that wrongness in such cases is identical with the formal relation of contrariety. Against such a view, Hume's counter-example may be a sufficient refutation. It remains possible, however, that other more concrete, non-formal relations are constitutive of moral wrongness. Why should not ingratitude itself, for example, be such a relation? In Hume's categorization, 'ingratitude' would count as a 'fact' rather than a 'relation'. What does he say about it under that head?

His use of the term 'fact' seems also to be unnecessarily restricted. When we examine the crime of ingratitude, he says, and look for the facts,

nothing is there, except the passion of ill-will or absolute indifference. You cannot say that these, of themselves, always and in all circumstances are crimes. No, they are only crimes when directed towards persons who have before expressed and displayed good-will towards us. Consequently, we may infer that the crime of ingratitude is not any particular individual *fact* . . . (Appendix I.6).

But why should not someone's having displayed ill-will *in return for good-will* be itself a fact? In asserting that the only fact here is the display of ill-will, Hume seems to be assuming that a fact must be something which can be taken in at a glance, without any reference to a wider context. In particular, the context of relationships within which an action is performed has been excluded from Hume's category of 'facts', just as it was excluded from his category of 'relations'. It is, then, not surprising that neither any 'fact' (in this restricted sense) nor any 'relation' (in this restricted sense), can be equated with moral right or wrong. It remains perfectly possible that facts or relations in some wider sense might be identifiable as moral facts or relations.

2. Hume's second argument is virtually a restatement of the first. In moral deliberations, he says, 'we must be acquainted beforehand with all the objects and all their relations to each other.' This is the province of reason, to determine the relevant facts and relations.

> But after every circumstance, every relation is known, the understanding has no further room to operate, nor any object on which it could employ itself. The approbation or blame which then ensues cannot be the work of the judgment, but of the heart, and is not a speculative proposition or affirmation, but an active feeling or sentiment. (Appendix I.11.)

Hume here assumes that when all the facts and relations are known, and when therefore, by definition, reason can do no more, some further step is still necessary. In other words, he assumes what he assumed in the first argument, that facts and relations cannot themselves have a moral significance. This is simply to beg the question. To take the previous example, in establishing all the facts and relations, may we not establish that a particular act is one of ingratitude, and is this not to say that, whatever sentiments people may feel about it, the act is wrong? What need is there for any further step?

3. Hume's next ploy is to compare moral approval with the perception of beauty, and to suggest that since the latter is a matter of sentiment and taste, the former must be likewise.

> Euclid has fully explained all the qualities of the circle, but has not in any proposition said a word of its beauty. The reason is evident. The beauty is not a quality of the circle. It lies not in any part of the line,

whose parts are equally distant from a common centre. It is only the effect which that figure produces upon the mind . . . (Appendix I.14).

Hume again begs the question—or rather, two questions. The reason why Euclid says nothing about the beauty of the circle is not as evident as Hume supposes. It may be not that 'the beauty is not a quality of the circle', but simply that it is a different *kind* of quality from the geometrical qualities with which Euclid is concerned. For all that Hume has said, it remains perfectly plausible to suppose that the beauty is something objectively present in the circle, and that someone who fails to appreciate its beauty has failed to see something which is there to be seen.

Even if Hume is right about beauty, he begs a further question in supposing that moral qualities must be like aesthetic ones. We might allow that judgements of beauty are ultimately matters of personal taste, but still insist that moral judgements are different. The distinction is a plausible one. If someone insists on painting all the walls of his house a uniform black, we might simply say, 'Well, if that's how you like it, it's up to you'; but if someone goes in for sadistic child-murder we are hardly likely to produce the same response. The example suggests a difference between aesthetic judgements and moral judgements, and Hume has given us no reason for denying the difference.

4. The brief fourth argument is merely a particular application of the first. Rightness or wrongness cannot consist in any particular relations, he argues, since the same relation may exist between inanimate objects as between moral agents, and be virtuous or vicious in the latter case but not in the former.

A young tree, which over-tops and destroys its parent, stands in all the same relations with Nero when he murdered Agrippina and, if morality consisted merely in relations, would no doubt be equally criminal. (Appendix I.17.)

Like the first argument, this depends entirely on Hume's specialized use of the term 'relations' to mean 'formal relations'. Without that restriction we could perfectly well insist that the relation of Nero to Agrippina is *not* the same as that of the tree to its parent. Nero wills the death of his mother, the tree does not, and that is why the one act is wrong and the other is not.

5. Only in Hume's last argument (and then only towards the end of his formulation of it) does a substantial point emerge. Moral responses must be the product of sentiment rather than reason, he says, because sentiment, unlike reason, has a necessary connection with *action*. In pronouncing something to be virtuous or vicious, we are not engaging in mere theoretical speculation, we are inclining ourselves and others to act in a certain way. This is something which reason by itself cannot do.

> Reason, being cool and disengaged, is no motive to action, and directs only the impulse received from appetite or inclination, by showing us the means of attaining happiness or avoiding misery. Taste, as it gives pleasure or pain, and thereby constitutes happiness or misery, becomes a motive to action, and is the first spring or impulse to desire and volition. (Appendix I.21.)

Hume here supplies the missing ingredient which is needed in order to give force to the previous arguments. Facts cannot by themselves have a moral significance, because a moral response is a commitment to action, whereas reason by itself is wholly inactive. This is why, when reason has done all its work, some further step is still necessary, and this step has to take the form of a sentiment, because sentiments are the mental processes which motivate us to action.

Hume's whole thesis concerning reason and sentiment, then—his denial of the idea of moral truth and falsity, and his denial that reason can establish moral conclusions—depends upon his claims about the connection between morality and action, and about the inactive character of reason. I shall assess these claims when, in my final chapter, I have looked at some latter-day versions of them.

Notes

1 In the *Treatise* Hume shows some inclination to analyse 'sympathy' into its component psychological mechanisms (see *Treatise* Book III, Part III, Section I). In the *Enquiry*, however, he is content to state that 'It is needless to push our researches so far as to ask why we have humanity or a fellow-feeling with

others. It is sufficient that this is experienced to be a principle in human nature. We must stop somewhere in our examination of causes . . .' (footnote to V.17).

2   The classic example is to be found in Thomas Hobbes's *Leviathan*, published in 1651.

3   For a defence of equality against Hume and his modern followers, see my article 'Does Equality Destroy Liberty?' in Keith Graham (ed.): *Contemporary Political Philosophy* (Cambridge, 1982).

4   Philip Barker: *Basic Child Psychiatry* (London, 1971), p. 69.

5   L. A. Selby-Bigge (ed.): *British Moralists* (Oxford, 1897), Vol. II, p. 23.

6 Kant
Respect for Persons

Reading: Immanuel Kant: *Fundamental Principles of the Metaphysic of Morals* (first published 1785). I shall concentrate entirely on Sections I and II. Quotations are from the translation by Thomas K. Abbott, available in the Library of Liberal Arts. References are to paragraph numbers. The paragraphs of Section I should be numbered from 1 to 22, and the paragraphs of Section II from 1 to 90. Abbott occasionally deviates from the paragraph divisions in the original text. In the First Section he runs together paragraphs 17 and 18; paragraph 18 should begin at the words 'Let the question be . . .'. And in the Second Section he runs together paragraphs 88 and 89; paragraph 89 should begin at 'An absolutely good will . . .'.

The Protestant Ethic

With the ethics of Immanuel Kant we are firmly in a Christian context, that of eighteenth-century German Protestantism. Kant's parents were adherents of Pietism, a tendency (not an independent sect) within the Lutheran church. This background was an important influence on Kant, and his moral philosophy has its starting-point in certain general features of Protestant Christianity. The sociologist Max Weber, in his classic study of the Protestant ethic, says of its Lutheran origins:

at least one thing was unquestionably new: the valuation of the fulfilment of duty in worldly affairs as the highest form which the moral activity of the individual could assume. . . . The only way of living acceptably to God was not to surpass worldly morality in monastic asceticism, but solely through the fulfilment of the obligations imposed upon the individual by his position in the world. That was his calling.[1]

As Weber here indicates, the attitude of 'worldly asceticism' stands in contrast to the monastic tradition of 'other-worldly asceticism'. Unlike the latter, it does not conclude from the devaluation of the things of this world that the individual should withdraw from worldly affairs in order to seek spiritual perfection. The world of social and economic obligations is the world in which one has been placed by God to live a good life. On the other hand there is no suggestion, as there would be for Aristotle, that in engaging in these activities one is directly achieving one's own fulfilment as a human being, and giving expression to the highest potentialities of human nature. Worldly activities provide the setting in which one is required to exhibit moral goodness, but the actual content of these activities has no intrinsic value.

In these features of the Protestant ethic we can locate the source of Kant's stress on 'duty for duty's sake'. Kant is the first philosopher to put the concept of 'duty' at the very centre of ethics. Traditionally the concept refers to the requirements that are imposed on one by one's occupancy of particular social, economic, and political positions— one's duties as a parent, as an employer or employee, as a citizen, as a holder of political office, and so on. Kant extends the concept from these specific 'duties' to a generalized 'duty', and proposes that moral goodness consists in the performance of this generalized 'duty' for its own sake. But in detaching the concept from specific roles and offices, Kant also seeks to detach it from any idea of utility. The fulfilment of 'duty' becomes simply an abstract moral requirement, not something required for the effective functioning of human social institutions. Duty is to be performed entirely for its own sake, not in order to promote human happiness or fulfilment. The background of the Protestant ethic can help us to understand the emergence of this idea.

Two other features of Protestant thought may be mentioned. The first of these is the priority of 'faith' over 'works'. A vital element of Protestantism was the idea that good works are not a means by which one can win salvation, and have no importance in themselves, but only as the outward expression of an inner state of faith, through which alone we are saved. We can see this idea at work in Kant's ascribing supreme value to the 'good will' which is 'good not because of what it performs or effects, not by its aptness for the attainment of some proposed end, but simply by virtue of the volition' (I.3). The other feature to bear in mind is Protestantism's stress on the radical corruption of human nature. This is, of course, a permanent strand in Christian belief, but it was given new emphasis by the Protestant reformers. Man can achieve nothing good through his own qualities, but only through the grace of God within him, and this will be in direct conflict with worldly desires, which are by their very nature corrupt. We can see this conflict translated into more purely philosophical terms in Kant's opposition between duty and inclination. For Kant, natural human inclinations can have no moral value, and the nature of morality is most readily apparent in situations where duty and inclination conflict.

My reason for referring to the Protestant background to Kant's thought is not just as an exercise in the history of ideas. The First Section of Kant's *Fundamental Principles* establishes the main outlines of his ethics by appealing to the evidence of 'common understanding', 'the moral knowledge of common human reason'. What is this common moral understanding? I would suggest that it is, in effect, the ethics of Protestant Christianity. That is to say, it does not possess the universal quality which Kant might want to claim for it. It is the ethical common sense of a particular society and a particular historical epoch. We therefore need to identify the historical and social limits of this conception of morality, in order properly to assess Kant's argument. The whole of his moral philosophy in fact seems to me to depend very heavily on this appeal to what he regards as the ordinary moral consciousness. Not only does the First Section explicitly set out from this point. The argument of the Second Section appears to presuppose the conception of morality set out in the First Section. I am not sure whether Kant thinks that he is, in the Second Section, providing independent arguments for the validity of that conception of morality. Whatever his intentions, however, I would claim that he fails to do so. At most he supplies hints as to how we might work out an independent justification; in the

main, what I find in the Second Section is a further clarifica-
tion and elaboration of the ethical theory which has previously been derived from the ordinary moral consciousness.
Nor does the Third Section supply the required independent
justification. In it, Kant sketches the metaphysics which is
needed to explain the possibility of morality. In a world
where everything that happens is causally necessitated,
human beings can nevertheless possess the free will which
morality presupposes because, as selves, they belong to the
realm of *noumena* (or 'things in themselves'), as well as to
the world of *phenomena* (or 'appearances'). In this way
Kant attempts to demonstrate that morality is *possible*,
but not that it is *necessary*—that is, he has still not told us
why we ought to understand morality in this way, and why
we ought to act in accordance with such morality. Ultimately
he sets out no answer to this question, other than the claim
that his account of morality is that of the ordinary moral
consciousness. And if this consciousness is effectively the
consciousness of Protestant Christianity, we may find it
more questionable than Kant does.

First Section

Let us now look more closely at how, in the First Section,
Kant derives his ethical theory from the ordinary moral
consciousness. He begins with the assertion that nothing is
unconditionally good except a good will, whose worth is
entirely separable from the value of the results it brings
about. This initial claim derives its plausibility from the
widely held idea that moral evaluations focus primarily on
people's *intentions*. People are not morally blamed if,
through no fault of their own, their good intentions lead
to unfortunate results. If A dives into the sea to rescue B,
who is being carried away by the current, but because the
current is stronger than she thought, fails to effect the
rescue and is herself drowned, she will have done no good
and have produced only additional loss of life and the additional grief of her family and friends; nevertheless, in virtue
of her intentions and her efforts to realize them, she is
liable to be morally praised rather than criticized. Note

however that in the obvious examples of this kind the intention must itself be described as an intention to perform or effect something. Results are thus not irrelevant; the contrast is between the *intended results* and the *actual results*, and the former are the objects of praise or blame.

At paragraph 8 Kant introduces the central concept of 'duty', the term by which we are to refer to the good will when it is seen as being in opposition to inclinations. Actions have moral worth only if they are done from duty, not from inclination, and since 'inclination' contrasts also with 'reason', actions done from duty must coincide with actions governed by reason. It is not clear whether Kant wants to say that an action can have *no* moral worth if it is *at all* in accordance with one's inclinations. A charitable interpretation would, I think, have to take him to be saying something weaker: that an action motivated by inclination has no moral worth unless it is *also* motivated by a concern for duty. And presumably to say that it is also motivated by duty would be to say something like this: that as well as having an inclination to perform the action one also recognizes it to be one's duty, and on the strength of this recognition one *would have* performed the action *even if* one had had *no* such inclination. The philanthropist who enjoys helping others would not then be barred from exhibiting moral worth, provided he also had a sense of duty. On this interpretation Kant would be saying only that if someone has a direct inclination to perform the action, it is *more difficult to determine* whether he is also motivated by duty, whereas when inclination and duty conflict, the force of the sense of duty is obvious. Such an interpretation is marginally favoured by paragraph 9, and more strongly supported later when, at II.42, Kant says: '. . . the sublimity and intrinsic dignity of the command in duty are so much the more evident, the less the subjective impulses favour it and the more they oppose it'.

If Kant is interpreted in this way, his position will indeed get a certain amount of support from commonly accepted moral ideas. There does seem to be a certain plausibility in the idea that if an action is done solely because one enjoys it, it has no moral worth, because it does not involve any effort of will.

It is in paragraph 14 that Kant really begins to go beyond the ordinary moral consciousness, and radically to extend his own previous claims. He has previously maintained that the goodness of the good will is independent of the *results which are achieved*. He now claims that it is independent of the results which are *aimed at*, and that, as I mentioned previously, is very different. Again, he has previously maintained that duty is contrasted with *inclination*. What he now introduces is the much stronger claim that duty is to be contrasted with all specific *purposes*. Take our previous example of the unsuccessful rescuer. I agreed that she might be morally admired even though she failed to achieve anything. Nevertheless, as I also mentioned, this admiration is inseparable from our recognition of what it was that she tried to do. The natural assumption would be that she acted with the purpose of saving the life of another person, and it is this that makes her morally admirable. Again, to say that she acted with that purpose would not be to say that, in any normal sense, she did it out of inclination. Presumably she does not enjoy pitting her strength against a raging sea. The purpose which we attribute to her, so far from constituting an inclination, may be precisely what she sees it as her duty to do.

I suspect that in paragraph 14 Kant sees himself as simply developing further the themes of the previous paragraphs. I am suggesting, however, that in reality the case is quite otherwise. The paragraph marks a radically new departure, and cannot be supported by what has gone before. What can support it, then? Not an appeal to the common moral understanding, either, if that is supposed to be something widely shared across different societies and cultures. It can be given plausibility only by the previously mentioned features of the Protestant ethic.

If the idea of 'duty' is abstracted in this way from all specific purposes, a further problem arises, for there now seems no way of determining what this 'duty' consists in. It would appear to be completely empty. Kant's answer, in paragraphs 15 and 16, is that since all consideration of inclinations and effects is excluded, duty must be defined not in terms of its content, but as a purely formal requirement.

It is the requirement of acting from respect for the moral *law*. Why 'law' specifically? Because the idea of duty involves that of acting on *principle*, following a *universal* principle, and not simply reacting to the immediate and particular situation. The vocabulary of 'moral law' carries with it religious connotations, it suggests the conception of morality as something laid down by a divine lawgiver, and thereby gives this talk of 'law' an initial intuitive plausibility. Kant, however, would certainly repudiate this conception (and does so at II.85). The moral law is not, in his view, something imposed on us from without by any arbitrary will, divine or otherwise. It is the expression of pure reason, and in so far as this law involves a lawgiver, it is legislated by any rational being. Thus, in the only sense in which the moral law is laid down by God, it is also laid down by all of us as human beings possessing reason. This idea of the moral law as something laid down by every rational agent for himself is elaborated by Kant at II.55–60.

If, in obeying the moral law, one is only obeying oneself and following one's own will, why speak of 'obedience' and 'law' at all? Because we are divided beings, split between reason and inclination. In so far as we are rational, morality is simply the expression of our own free will. In so far as we are also creatures of inclination, however, morality is something which we have to obey. The popular conception to which Kant comes closest is not that of morality as obedience to God, but that of morality as obedience to one's conscience, the obedience of the lower self to the higher self.

But now, if duty is defined as respect for the moral law, this seems merely to shift the problem. How are we to determine what the moral law commands? Kant maintains that the moral law, like the idea of 'duty', cannot be defined by its content. Consequently, he accepts, there is nothing left for it to command, other than simply that one's actions should be law-abiding. This, at first, looks like an entirely empty requirement, a law which says only, 'Obey this law'. Kant claims however that, though entirely formal, it is not entirely empty, for when we abstract from all particular content, what remains to the idea of law is the requirement of universality. A law which commands simple law-abidingness thus has the form: so act that you can will that your maxim should become a universal law.

Kant claims that everyone actually recognizes this moral law. There is a certain truth in this. We might think here of the way in which people regularly question the rightness of an action by asking: what if everyone did that? Kant's moral law also has a certain affinity with the Golden Rule: 'Act towards others in the way in which you would like them to act towards you' (although Kant points out the limitations of this principle, especially in its negative formulation, in his footnote to II.52). Whether 'common human reason' understands by these principles what Kant understands by them, and in particular whether it understands them as purely formal principles, is another question. We shall be in a better position to answer it when we have looked at his attempt to show, in the Second Section, how this moral law can guide our actions.

Second Section

Kant's most important innovation in the Second Section is to introduce the concepts of 'hypothetical imperatives' and 'categorical imperatives'. An *imperative* is the linguistic form in which a *command* is expressed. *Commands* are related to *laws* as *duty* is to the *good will*: in each case the former adds to the latter the idea of an opposition to inclination. Thus all rational beings act according to the conception of laws. A being whose will was wholly determined by reason and who had no inclinations (a non-physical being not affected by sensory stimuli) would not experience these laws as commands, and would be what Kant calls a 'holy will'. Beings such as ourselves who have both reason and inclinations, and in whom the two can conflict, do experience the laws of reason as commands, in so far as our inclinations may prompt us to deviate from them.

Hypothetical imperatives are the expression of commands which are conditional on inclinations or purposes. They have the form, 'Do this in order to achieve that'. Examples would be, 'Tear back to open', or 'Make friends if you want to be happy'. The first of these is an example of what Kant calls 'imperatives of skill', expressing commands which are conditional on purposes which one may or may not share—one may or may not be interested in opening a packet of cornflakes. The second is an 'imperative of prudence', since the command derives from the one purpose which is necessary for all human beings, the pursuit of happiness. Categorical imperatives, on the other hand, express commands which are not conditional on any purpose at all. They are not of the form, 'Do this in order to achieve that', but simply 'Do this'. It therefore follows from the account of morality in the First Section that categorical imperatives are the form in which the commands of the moral law are expressed.

Kant provides four different formulations of the categorical imperative, and has left his readers in some confusion as to how the various formulations are related to one another. A clear explanation is, however, eventually given at II.72–5. Strictly speaking, there is only one categorical imperative. It can be given an entirely general formulation (which I shall refer to as G), and it can be given three other, more specified formulations (which I shall refer to as S1, S2, and S3). The more specified formulations rephrase G in such a way as to indicate more clearly how it can be applied in practice. The four formulations are:

G.   Act only on that maxim whereby you can at the same time will that it should become a universal law.

S1. Act as if the maxim of your action were to become by your will a universal law of nature.

S2. So act as to treat humanity, whether in your own person or in that of any other, never solely as a means but always also as an end.

S3. So act as if you were by your maxims in every case a legislating member in the universal kingdom of ends.

S1 is clearly only a slight variation on G. The only significant change is the extension of the phrase 'universal law' to 'universal law of nature'. The minimal interpretation of S1 would be that it simply requires us to apply G in the world as we know it. We are to consider whether the maxims of our actions, when universalized, could be consistent with the empirical facts of the natural world in which we have to act.

Some of Kant's interpreters have, however, wanted to read rather more into the phrase 'law of nature', and I shall consider their suggestions in due course.

What of S2 and S3? They appear to differ more radically from G. How then can they be called reformulations of it? To make sense of this, it is helpful to see all the formulations as permutations on the concepts of *rationality* and *universality*. G and S1 require that as rational beings we should be able to universalize the maxims of our actions, that is, we should be able to will them as universal laws. S2 then requires us to universalize our conception of ourselves as rational beings, and to treat all other human beings likewise as rational beings. Finally S3 synthesizes S1 and S2, bringing together the two ideas of 'universal laws' and 'rational beings'. In so far as we are rational beings, we would all will the same things as universal laws. Therefore these universal laws are ones which would be agreed on in a hypothetical community of rational beings, and they are laws which would enjoin respect for all the members of that hypothetical community as rational beings. This hypothetical community is what Kant calls a 'kingdom of ends', and a further requirement of right action is, therefore, that it should be compatible with the laws of a kingdom of ends.

Kant says very little about how S3 would be applied in practice. He has a good deal more to say about S1 and S2, and examines their application to four examples. I shall devote the remaining two sections of this chapter to questions concerning the practical application of S1 and S2, and Kant's discussion of it in connection with his examples. First, however, a word about the overall structure of the examples.

The four examples are systematically chosen. They are: (i) the duty to refrain from suicide; (ii) the duty to refrain from making false promises; (iii) the duty to develop our talents; (iv) the duty to help others. Examples (i) and (iii) are duties to ourselves, and (ii) and (iv) are duties to others. Examples (i) and (ii) are called by Kant 'perfect duties', and (iii) and (iv) are 'imperfect duties'. Kant's explanation of the terms 'perfect' and 'imperfect' is rather perplexing. He says (in the footnote to paragraph 34): 'I understand by a perfect duty one that admits no exception in favour of inclination'. Since, however, Kant normally seems to suppose that *no* duty admits of any exception in favour of inclination, it is difficult to see how he can use this feature to distinguish between perfect and imperfect duties. It would be tempting to interpret him as meaning that perfect duties are those which admit of no exceptions *at all*, whereas imperfect duties are those which can be overridden by perfect duties or by other imperfect duties (but not by inclinations). This is tempting because Kant certainly wants to say that some duties admit of no exceptions, and since it would be highly implausible for him to maintain this of all the things which he regards as duties, he does need some distinction between duties which do and duties which do not admit of any exceptions. Such an interpretation would be in keeping with the nature of Kant's examples. Duties not to commit suicide, or to make false promises, do seem to be of a kind which he might regard as having no exceptions, whereas this could hardly even be said intelligibly of duties to develop one's talents or to help others. If an opportunity were to present itself for me to develop my talents or help someone else by making a false promise (perhaps in order to obtain money on false pretences so that I can put myself through college or give it to a friend in need), one would expect Kant to say that the duty not to make false promises should be the overriding one. This would also make sense of what he says when he comes to apply S2 to the examples, for he then classifies examples (i) and (ii) as 'necessary duties, or those of strict obligation', and (iii) and (iv) as 'contingent or meritorious duties'. Finally, it would fit in with what Kant says in other writings. All in all, the interpretation would be irresistible, were it not for the fact that it is not what Kant actually says. Perhaps, then, we should simply convict him of carelessness.

There is one other general point to be made about how Kant applies the categorical imperative to his examples. The application of it is primarily a *negative* test. Actions whose maxim does *not* accord with the categorical imperative are ones which we ought *not* to perform. If they cannot be universalized, or if they involve treating human beings simply as means, then they are morally impermissible. Kant is not saying, however, that all actions which *do* accord with the categorical imperative are ones which we *ought* to perform. That would be nonsense. There are innumerable actions which can perfectly well be universalized, and do not involve treating people solely as means, but which are certainly not obligatory. I can certainly will it to be a universal law that everyone should take up jogging. This does not mean that I have a moral duty to do so myself. All that Kant wants to say of any such actions which accord with the categorical imperative, is that they are morally permissible, not that they are obligatory. And this is in keeping with the popular conception of morality, which is commonly thought of as setting limits to what we can do, forbidding rather than requiring.

Primarily, then, the categorical imperative serves to distinguish between permissible and impermissible actions. Now Kant does want to say that there are positive as well as negative duties. How, then, can these be identified by the categorical imperative? They can be identified because positive duties of the form, 'You ought to do X', can be restated in the negative form, 'Failure to do X is impermissible'. Kant would claim that a refusal to help others in need cannot be universalized. Therefore, he would conclude, the refusal to help others is impermissible, and hence it follows that helping others is obligatory. The test remains a negative one, but it can in this way generate positive duties. Notice that of the four examples it is (i) and (ii), the 'perfect' duties, which are negative, and (iii) and (iv), the 'imperfect' duties, which are positive. This provides further support for the suggested interpretation of 'perfect' and 'imperfect'. It makes sense to say of negative duties that one should *never* commit suicide out of self-love, *never* make false promises, etc., whereas it is quite unclear what it could mean to say that one should *always*, without exception, develop one's talents or help others. Thus negative rather than positive duties can plausibly be said to admit of no exceptions.

Universalizability

I turn now to a closer examination of G and S1, the two formulations which require that the maxim of any action should be universalizable. I assume that Kant does not envisage G being applied to particular actions independently, but only via S1 (or via S2 or S3). I shall therefore concentrate on S1 and consider how effectively this can serve as a basic moral principle.

I have said that Kant does not offer any fully worked out justification for any of the formulations of the categorical imperative, other than the derivation from the ordinary moral consciousness in the First Section. There are, however, hints as to how such a justification might be devised. 'Rationality' and 'universality' are, we have seen, the two key concepts, permutation of which produces the different formulations of the categorical imperative. Now, I think there is a case for saying that of the two, 'rationality' is the more fundamental, and that the requirement of universality can be derived from that of rationality. In other words, the claim would be that it is a necessary condition of my acting rationally that my actions should be universalizable. The question, 'Why act rationally?' cannot be answered. No further reason can be given, but someone who asks, 'Why?', is already committed to the search for reasons, and has therefore already accepted the requirement of rationality. If we can show, then, that in order to be rational my actions must also be universalizable, we can provide a defence of Kant which does not have to rely upon the assumptions of the ordinary moral consciousness.

Now there is certainly a weak sense in which rationality involves universality. To be rational, my behaviour must be universalizable in the sense of being consistent. Let us take Kant's example of false promises. Kant imagines some-one who 'finds himself forced by necessity to borrow money. He knows that he will not be able to repay it, but sees also that nothing will be lent to him unless he promises stoutly to repay it in a definite time' (II.36). Suppose that he decides to make such a promise, knowing that he cannot keep it. If he believes his actions to be rationally justified, then he is, as Kant says, committed to the universal principle or maxim, 'Whenever I believe that I am in need of money, I will borrow money and promise to repay it, although I know that I can never do so'. And if he cannot accept this as a universal principle, then he cannot rationally regard himself as justified in the present case, unless he can point to some additional relevant feature of the present situation which justifies his action.

This, then, is the weak sense of universalizability, as consistency. An action cannot be rational unless it falls under a universal principle which commits me to acting in the same way in all relevantly similar circumstances. Kant, however, wants a stronger sense of universalizability. He wants not just a principle of consistency, but what we might call a principle of the *impersonality of reasons*. The idea here is that reasons cannot be specific to particular individuals. If R is a valid reason for *me* to do action A, then it must also be a valid reason for *anyone* to do A in the same circumstances. Reasons are, by their very nature, reasons for anyone. Thus in the promising example, if our false promiser thinks that he is rationally justified, then he must also accept that everyone else would be equally justified in making such a promise whenever they needed money and could not repay it. And if he cannot accept this, then he cannot rationally regard himself as justified in the present case.

This is a more controversial sense of universalizability, but it does seem fairly convincing. It does seem correct that reasons, to be reasons at all, must be impersonal in this sense. Suppose, then, that we allow Kant this assumption, and accept that the categorical imperative in form G or S1 can be defended along these lines. The question now is: can such a principle, when applied to particular cases, effectively serve to distinguish permissible from impermissible actions? Can it, in other words, give concrete results?

There are two difficulties which have standardly been thought to arise for Kant at this point, and many critics would claim that they are insuperable. The first of these is the problem: *under what description* is an action to be universalizable? Any action can be described in a number of different ways. In our promising example we could imagine various possible descriptions, such as:

(a) making a promise when one cannot keep it;
(b) making a promise when one needs money and cannot keep the promise;
(c) making a promise when one needs money to pay one's way through college but cannot keep the promise;
(d) making a promise when one needs money which will eventually enable one to be of great benefit to humanity, even though one cannot keep the promise.

Whether or not the action is universalizable may depend very much on which description is taken. Kant assumes that something like description (b) would be the appropriate one, and claims that on such a description it could not be universalizable. If it were universalized, 'the promise itself would become impossible . . . since no one would consider that anything was promised to him, but would ridicule all such statements as vain pretences'. In any such case, however, a more precise description along the lines of something like (c) or (d) would be possible, and when so described, the action might well be universalizable. It is arguable that if everyone made false promises in the circumstances of (c), the general level of trust might be lowered, but not to an extent which would make promises impossible. This could be argued even more plausibly of (d). Moreover, one can imagine building more and more precise details, of an absurd kind, into the description of the action, just in order to make it universalizable, for example:

(e) making a promise when one needs money and cannot keep the promise, when it is a Thursday, and there is an 'r' in the month, and there are eighteen letters in one's name.

Given that this combination of circumstances would be fairly rare, the general level of trust would not be greatly impaired if everyone were prepared to act on this principle, and therefore one could claim that it would in fact be universalizable.

Kant's answer would be that the universalizability test is not to be applied to an action under just any description. What must be universalizable is the *maxim* of the action.

I have made frequent use of Kant's term 'maxim' in stating his position, and it now needs to be explained. Roughly speaking, the maxim of an action is a statement of the agent's intention formulated as a universal principle. Such a principle is universal in the weak sense referred to above. Thus it encapsulates the agent's initial reason for wanting to perform the action—the description under which he regards it as justified, prior to the application of the categorical imperative. A description such as (e) may be a correct description of a proposed action, but it is hardly likely to be the description which features in the agent's maxim, for presumably he does not contemplate making the promise *because* it is a Thursday, and there is an 'r' in the month, and there are eighteen letters in his name. Therefore the fact that the action may be universalizable under that description is not enough to legitimate it.

Kant's insistence that the agent's own maxim must be universalizable may, then, suffice to rule out absurd and far-fetched descriptions. It is not clear, however, that it can serve as the appropriate guide for determining the one description to be chosen, and for ruling out all other possibilities. In the first place, people's maxims may not be all that determinate. If we were to ask of our false promiser, 'Is it under description (b), or (c), or (d) that he is considering performing the action?', there may be no clear answer, not because we cannot find out but because he may simply not have formulated it for himself with such precision. He may have a vague conviction that the circumstances are pressing ones and make a false promise necessary, but not have thought out exactly what it is about the situation that necessitates the false promise. Even if he has done so, however, why should that provide the appropriate way of pinning down the correct description? This seems to make the rightness or wrongness of an action depend too much on the vagaries of individual psychology. If the action is universalizable under one description and not under another, whether or not it is morally permissible will then depend on how the agent himself happens to think about it. If he formulates his reasons very carefully and contemplates the action under description (d), and if it is universalizable under that description, then we shall have to say that it is morally permissible. If he formulates his reasons only vaguely and thinks of the action only in the more general terms of (b), and if the action is not universalizable under that description, then we shall have to say that the action is morally impermissible, even though (d) might still be a correct description of it.

Kant might accept these implications. He might remind us that, in his view, the proper objects of moral evaluation are not actions but motives. Therefore, he might say, if one and the same action can be right or wrong depending on the terms in which the agent thinks of it, that is as it should be; the moral assessment varies because the motives vary. We might perhaps retort that what the universalizability test seems likely to assess is the agent's sophistication in formulating his motives, rather than their moral qualities. But let us leave this objection now, for there is another which is even more formidable. This is the problem of Kant's *formalism*.

Kant explicitly asserts that the principle of universalizability is a purely formal principle. That, for Kant, is a condition of its being an authentically moral principle, which it could not be if it were tied to a particular content. Therefore when his critics accuse him of formalism, there is as yet no disagreement. What the critics will add, however, is that because the principle is a purely formal principle, it is useless. Absolutely any action can be universalized without contradiction. The principle rules out nothing, and therefore cannot be used to distinguish between right and wrong actions. Hegel put the point succinctly:

by this means any wrong or immoral line of conduct may be justified . . . The absence of property contains in itself just as little contradiction as the non-existence of this or that nation, family, etc., or the death of the whole human race. But if it is already established on other grounds and presupposed that property and human life are to exist and be respected, then indeed it is a contradiction to commit theft or murder; a contradiction must be a contradiction of something, i.e. of some content presupposed from the start as a fixed principle.[2]

The phrase 'the absence of property' refers to an example used elsewhere by Kant, but the example of promising will illustrate the point equally well. Kant claims that the maxim of making a false promise cannot without contradiction be universalized, since if it were universalized promising itself would become impossible. Hegel's retort would be: the non-existence of promising is not self-contradictory, it is simply in contradiction with the presupposition that promising ought to exist. Thus the formal principle can generate a moral conclusion only if an additional content is smuggled in. And Hegel's criticism has subsequently been repeated by innumerable other critics of Kant.

Now Kant himself is happy to admit that the principle of universalizability cannot entail moral conclusions just by itself. It has to be applied, and in applying it we have to take into account facts about the world in which it is applied. I have already indicated that this, at the very least, is what must be meant by Kant's phrase 'universal law of nature'. In the promising example, Kant employs the assertion that if it were a universal law for people to make false promises when in difficulties, promising would become impossible because promises would never be taken seriously; and this is a factual claim which has to be combined with the principle of universalizability in order to produce the moral conclusion. This Kant would certainly accept. The real criticism, however, is not that Kant needs these factual additions, but that he also needs *additional moral or other evaluative presuppositions*—in the promising example, the presupposition that the practice of promising ought to exist. If this is the case, it must surely be a defect in Kant's ethics, and I think we shall find that it *is* the case, if we look at the various attempts to defend or supplement Kant.

a. *Maxims* One suggestion is that Kant does not need to bring in any external ethical content to combine with the formal principle, because the content is supplied by the maxim itself.[3] The maxim, 'When in difficulties, make false promises', already presupposes the institution of promising, and thus the non-existence of promising which would follow from its being universalized would be in contradiction, not indeed with itself, but with the original maxim. If promising became impossible, then the maxim, 'When in difficulties, make false promises', would itself become impossible.

Similarly stealing could not be universalized, for if it were, property would cease to exist, and stealing would then be impossible.

This defence can give Kant only temporary respite. He cannot, perhaps, be accused of importing the presupposition of promising, since this is already presupposed in the original maxim. Still, the fact remains that it is presupposed, and that some account has to be given of it. That is to say, an adequate ethical theory needs not just the principle of universalizability, but a full account of these institutions such as promising, property, punishment, marriage, etc., which have ethical implications built into them. This is the direction in which Hegel takes his criticism of Kant, substituting for Kant's concept of 'duty for duty's sake' a theory of the duties which attach to social institutions.

b. *Natural purposes* A second suggestion offered in defence of Kant involves reading more into the phrase 'universal law of nature' than I have so far done. Nature, it has been suggested, should here be understood as something *purposive*, and S1 requires that a maxim when universalized should be consistent with *purposes in nature*.[4] There are various indications that Kant was prepared to employ this concept in his ethical theory. In a passage in the First Section he argues that reason must exist for a higher purpose than the promotion of our happiness, and he there subscribes explicitly to the idea of natural purposes: 'In the physical constitution of an organized being, that is, a being adapted suitably to the purposes of life, we assume it as a fundamental principle that no organ for any purpose will be found but what is also the fittest and best adapted for that purpose' (I.5). He wants to apply the same principle not only to physical organs, but also to psychological faculties. In the first of the four examples, it is important that the contemplated action is suicide *motivated by self-love*, and Kant says that it cannot be universalized because 'a system of nature of which it should be a law to destroy life by means of the very feeling whose special nature it is to impel to the improvement of life would contradict itself' (II.35). In other words, a universal law of suicide motivated by self-love would contradict the

natural purpose of self-love. Similarly, in the third example
Kant argues that a rational being cannot will a universal law
not to cultivate one's talents, because 'he necessarily wills
that his faculties be developed, since they serve him, and have
been given him, for all sorts of possible purposes' (II.37).
Given him by whom? Again the answer is 'by nature', as
Kant indicates when he returns to the example at II.53
and speaks of 'the end that nature has in view in regard to
humanity'.

It is clear that Kant does employ the concept of natural
purposes, and that in conjunction with the principle of
universalizability it can generate concrete moral conclusions.
It is much less clear that this vindicates Kant's ethical theory.
The concept of natural purposes is not just a minor supplement to the categorical imperative. It embodies a substantial
ethical position, and a highly controversial one at that.
This does not mean that we should dismiss it; we have seen
that it gains support from Aristotle and the Christian 'natural
law' tradition. But it does mean that if Kant is going to use
it he should elaborate a defence of it, and this would give
his ethical theory a very different character indeed. It would
be the idea of natural purposes, rather than the principle of
universalizability, that would do all the work, and indeed the
latter would become redundant. If suicide out of self-love,
when universalized, is contrary to the natural purpose of
self-love, then it is equally true that a single act of suicide
out of self-love is contrary to that natural purpose, and in
that case we do not need to invoke the principle of universalizability at all.

c. *Intuitions* The two suggestions so far considered have
been attempts to defend Kant. I turn now to three attempts
to improve upon Kant, rather than defend him. I shall argue
that these attempts either fail to produce a workable ethical
principle, or do so only by demoting the categorical imperative to a minor role. The first of these suggestions is that,
though the categorical imperative cannot itself tell us what
we ought or ought not to do, 'its value—a great value—lies
in putting us in the right attitude, by requiring us to ignore
our own particular wishes and to adopt an impersonal point

of view'.[5] Once we have been 'put in the right attitude', however, something further is needed, some kind of moral perception or intuition which will enable us to see where our duty lies.

The trouble with this is, as before, that the proposed addition is in fact a whole new ethical theory. Like the concept of 'natural purposes', that of 'moral perceptions' is extremely controversial, and if an ethical theory could be built up to justify it, it could function as a complete theory in itself, and Kant's own ethics could simply be left to take a back seat.

d. *Utility* Much the same goes for the next proposal. Some writers have suggested that the principle of universalizability needs to be supplemented with utilitarian considerations. In envisaging our maxim as a universal law we should then have to ask not, 'Does it become self-contradictory?' but, 'Would its universalization lead to undesirable consequences? Would it tend to produce more suffering or less happiness that some alternative action?' Such a proposal looks attractive when applied to examples like that of false promising. Having established that the maxim to make a false promise would, if it became a universal law, make promising impossible, we have not thereby revealed any contradiction. What we can say is that such an eventuality would be highly undesirable. Human beings without the institution of promising would be at a great disadvantage, deprived of all the conveniences which that institution carries with it.

In the previous chapter we saw that Hume, in his discussion of justice, makes one such attempt to combine the concepts of utility and universalizability. I pointed out some of the difficulties. In the present chapter what needs to be added is that in any marriage of utilitarian and Kantian ethics, the utilitarian component is bound to be the dominant partner. Such a marriage would be very much at variance with the whole spirit of Kant's ethics, with its constant stress on the irrelevance of consequences and happiness. Strictly speaking, it is not incompatible with what Kant actually says in this vein. What he says is that an action has no moral worth if it is done *for the sake of* consequences such as the promotion of happiness, or the prevention of suffering. If, however, we say of an action that *when universalized* it would produce happiness or suffering, and if we perform or refrain from the action on those grounds, we are not acting *for the sake of* such consequences, since the individual action itself *would not have* those consequences. An individual act of false promising, for example, need not itself have any of those undesirable consequences which universal false promising would have. Thus Kant could consistently maintain that morally good actions do not aim at utilitarian consequences, while agreeing that utilitarian considerations should be taken into account, in determining whether the maxim of an action could be universalized. It would be logically consistent, but it would nevertheless be incongruous.

e. *Inclinations* A further suggestion would be that the principle of universalizability needs to be supplemented with the agent's own inclinations. One would then have to ask not, 'Can my maxim be universalized without contradiction?', but, 'Would the universalized maxim be consistent with my own inclinations? Would I *want* my maxim to be a universal law?' It is in this version that the idea of universalizability has enjoyed a considerable vogue among ethical philosophers recently.[6] As an interpretation of Kant, it would seem to have the same incongruity as the previous proposal. The idea that inclinations could play such a role in helping to determine our duty seems entirely foreign to Kant's insistence on the opposition between duty and inclination. And yet, surprisingly enough, Kant himself eventually works round to such a position. Of examples (iii) and (iv) he says that the maxim of the action could in fact be universalized without contradiction; what makes the maxim wrong is that 'it is impossible to *will* that such a principle should have the universal validity of a law of nature'. It is not clear what 'willing' means here, but in the case of (iv) it seems to amount to something very much like inclination. Kant says that the maxim not to help others in distress could without contradiction be a universal law; nevertheless one cannot will that it should be universal, because 'many cases might occur in which one would have need of the love and sympathy of others, and in which, by such a law of nature, sprung from his own will, he would deprive himself of all hope of the aid he desires' (II.38). What can this mean, if not that such a universal law would be contrary to one's inclinations?

The attraction of this option is that, although it involves supplementing the principle of universalizability with an additional source of evaluation, the latter is not an additional *moral principle*. Thus it does not require a whole new ethical theory to justify it. We do not, in fact, have to go outside the limits of Kant's own conceptual structure. We can work within Kant's moral psychology, employing his antithesis of reason and inclination, and modifying it to state not that the requirements of reason *exclude* the inclinations, but rather that the requirements of reason (in the form of universalizability) are to be *imposed upon* the inclinations.

It is an attractive proposal, but I do not think that it will work, and my objection to it is not, as with its predecessors, that the proposed addition to Kant is too strong, but that it is too weak. I do not think that the combination of universalizability and inclinations will generate the concrete moral conclusions which it is supposed to produce. To do so would require a stronger notion of universalizability than is legitimate. I have said that the principle of universalizability is defensible in this sense: that if I believe I have good reason to act in a certain way, I am thereby committed to *recognizing that others have good reason* to act in the same way in relevantly similar circumstances. I am not, however, thereby committed to *willing* that they should act in the same way. Therefore there need be no inconsistency between my universalized maxims and my own inclinations. I can perfectly well recognize that others have good reason to act in a certain way, while wanting them not to.

To make the point clearer, consider Kant's fourth example. We are to imagine someone whose maxim is not to help others in distress. Kant claims that he cannot universalize this maxim, because if he were in distress he would want others to help him. I am suggesting that despite that fact, he *can* universalize his maxim. He can quite consistently say something like this: 'I see no reason why I should help others in distress. I accept that this logically commits me to the view that if I were in distress, there is no good reason why others should help me. Now certainly I would want them to help. If I were in a position to do so, I would try to induce them to help me. But at the same time I entirely accept that they would be rationally justified in refusing to help me.' This is perfectly consistent. And it is as far as the combination of universalizability and inclinations can take us. I have allowed that, if we are to be rational, our practical maxims must be universalizable in two senses. These are:

(i) universalizability as *consistency*—the requirement that one's reason for performing a certain action in certain circumstances must be a reason for one to perform *the same* action again in relevantly similar circumstances;

(ii) universalizability as *impersonality*—the requirement that one's reason for performing a certain action in certain circumstances must be a reason for *anyone* to perform the same action in relevantly similar circumstances.

It does not follow however, that one's practical maxims must be universalizable in a third sense, that of:

(iii) universalizability as *impartiality*—the requirement that one's reasons must give equal weight to everyone else's desires and interests, along with one's own.

The requirement of impartiality is quite distinct from the previous two, and unlike them it cannot legitimately be presented simply as a requirement of formal rationality. It is not, therefore, a defensible interpretation of the notion of universalizability.

f. *Further formulations* There remains one other possibility: that G and S1 can be applied to concrete cases, and produce concrete conclusions, only when supplemented with the other formulations, S2 and S3. This is not, on the whole, Kant's position. He certainly claims to be applying S1 in its own right to the four examples. Later, however, he does suggest that the relation between S1 and S2 is that they specify respectively the *form* and the *matter* of morality (II.73-4). Certainly S2 appears to be less of a purely formal principle than S1. We might therefore incline to the view that, though S1 is not a workable principle in itself, its real value is to pave the way for S2, and that with the formulation of S2 we do indeed have a viable moral principle. Let us, then, consider S2.

Respect for Persons

S2 requires us to treat human beings (including ourselves) as ends, and never only as means. The world 'only' is important. Kant is not saying that we should never use human beings as means at all. Human society would be impossible if people could never make use of one another. Every time I eat a meal, I make use of the people who produced and marketed the food, every time I ride on a bus I make use of the driver, every time I read a book I make use of the author. Examples could be multiplied. Kant's point is that we should not regard people *simply* as means to our own ends. All human beings are ends in themselves, and when the circumstances arise (which they may not), we should treat them as such. The question is, then: What is it to treat someone as an end?

Kant's choice of the term 'end' is thoroughly confusing. The word normally indicates something to be brought about, something which we aim at in our actions. To regard people as ends in this sense would presumably be to aim at bringing into existence as many people as possible, and we should then have to take Kant as advocating a life of maximum sexual indulgence. This is not, I think, what he has in mind. The only continuity between Kant's talk of 'persons as ends' and the normal meaning of 'ends', is that in both senses 'ends' are contrasted with 'means'. This however seems to leave us where we started—with the negative injunction that treating people as ends is treating them not merely as means. Perhaps we can best interpret Kant, initially, as saying that to treat people as ends is to treat people as beings who *have* ends. I should not treat human beings as mere means to my own ends, because I should recognize that they themselves have ends of their own. They have ends, because they are free, rational and autonomous agents, they can act in accordance with purposes and principles, they are persons, not things (II.48).

This is still very vague, and I shall attempt shortly to make it more precise, but first I want to look at how Kant wishes to justify S2. In general terms, I have suggested that the justification depends on a further redeployment of the concepts of 'rationality' and 'universality'. A key passage is the following:

rational nature exists as an end in itself. Man necessarily conceives his own existence as being so; so far then this is a *subjective* principle of human actions. But every other rational being regards its existence similarly, just on the same rational principle that holds for me; so that it is at the same time an objective principle from which as a supreme practical law all laws of the will must be capable of being deduced. (II.49.)

What this amounts to is the application of the requirement of universalizability to one's conception of oneself as a rational being. We can rephrase it as the three-step argument: (i) one necessarily regards oneself as a rational being, as an end; (ii) one therefore has to accept that everyone else is justified in regarding himself/herself as a rational being and as an end; (iii) it is therefore an objectively valid principle that everyone should be treated as a rational being and as an end. The move from (i) to (ii) is justified by the notion of universality as the impersonality of reasons. The difficulty resides in the move from (ii) to (iii), for this requires an extension of the idea of universalizability, of the kind which I criticized in connection with proposal (e) above (pp. 115–17). It requires a shift from 'universality as impersonality of reasons' to 'universality as impartiality', and there are no good grounds for thinking that one can derive the latter from the former. If I treat myself as a person, I may be logically committed to accepting that others have good reason to treat themselves as persons, but I am not logically committed to the principle that *I* should treat *them* as persons. A world of self-respecting egoists is not an irrational world.

I conclude that, to the extent that it is contained in the brief passage I have quoted, Kant's defence of S2 fails. I do not think that he has provided any further arguments, other than the appeal to the ordinary moral consciousness. Nevertheless, the idea of respect for persons, though it lacks a sound justification in Kant, is an immensely fruitful idea, and I want to bring out some of its implications.

I have said that, initially, we could understand the idea of 'treating persons as ends' to mean 'treating persons as beings who have ends'. Part of what this will require, then, is that we should be motivated by other people's ends, as well as by our own. This is asserted by Kant when he applies S2 to example (iv); 'the ends of any subject who is an end in himself ought as far as possible to be *my* ends also' (II.54). This will involve a concern for the interests of others, helping to promote their happiness and to prevent their suffering. Such a conception of morality forms the substance of the utilitarian ethic, which we shall consider in the next chapter, and it is by no means distinctive of Kant. There is, however, in Kant's position something much more distinctive. In so far as treating human beings as ends involves helping to promote their ends, this stems from something more basic, an attitude not just towards their interests, but towards the persons themselves. It is the attitude which Kant tries to capture with the concepts of 'respect' and of 'dignity'. At II.68-9 Kant contrasts 'value' and 'dignity'. 'Whatever has a value', he says, 'can be replaced by something else which is equivalent'. 'Value' is thus the kind of worth possessed by all the various individual objects of desire, such as material goods, or personal qualities such as skill, or wit, or strength. Such things are essentially replaceable. If I buy a new copy of a book and immediately lose it, and if someone then gives me a replacement copy which is exactly the same as the previous one, it will be just as good as the previous one and I will have lost nothing. Moreover, different kinds of things which have value can to some extent compensate for one another. If I have a house with a large garden which I value, this may to some extent compensate for the smallness of the rooms, or the damp in the cellar, and I may be prepared to accept the one as the price I have to pay for the other. Likewise with personal qualities, if I have certain intellectual skills this may to some extent compensate me for my lack of skill as a games player. Now all such things have value, because of the role which they play in the lives of persons. Persons are what give value to things. Persons themselves, therefore, as the source of value, must have a quite different kind of worth; 'that which constitutes the condition under which alone anything can be an end in itself, this has not merely a relative worth, that is, value, but an intrinsic worth, that is, *dignity*' (II.69). In contrast to things which have value, persons, in so far as they have dignity, are irreplaceable. If I take the lives of ten people, I cannot compensate for this by bringing into existence ten more people. As possessors of dignity, persons are the proper objects of the attitude of respect. Respect for dignity is something quite distinct from the promotion of value. Respect for other persons may, as we have seen, require me to help promote their ends, but what it does, more basically, is to set limits on my own pursuit of my own ends. It is 'the supreme limiting condition of all our subjective ends, let them be what we will' (II.55). In pursuing our own ends, we are precluded from employing means which will violate the sanctity of other persons (II.70). Respect is not the same as either inclination or fear, but it has something analogous to both. It is like inclination in being something which we freely and voluntarily will, but it is like fear in being something to which we are subject, and which thwarts our pursuit of our own ends. It is one and the same respect which we feel for persons as rational beings, and for the moral law as the law of reason (footnote to I.16).

I do not have room to explore here the more concrete moral implications of this idea of respect for persons. I mention only the most basic of them: respect for persons involves respect for their *liberty and autonomy*. An ethic which was confined to the *promotion* of ends would incline to paternalism. It would require me to promote the happiness and prevent the suffering of others even at the cost of imposing on them, if necessary, the means to their happiness. For the Kantian ethic, on the other hand, the basic requirement is a respect for the other person's own pursuit of his or her own ends through his or her own free action, and I am to help in the promotion of those ends only in ways which are compatible with that basic respect. Accordingly, Kant lays great emphasis on the notion of human *rights*, in so far as these identify basic freedoms which have to be respected (II.52). In his *Lectures on Ethics* he declared:

There is nothing more sacred in the wide world than the rights of others. They are inviolable. Woe unto him who trespasses upon the right of another and tramples it underfoot! His right should be his security; it should be stronger than any shield or fortress. We have a holy ruler and the most sacred of his gifts to us is the rights of man.[7]

Whether human rights can be regarded as literally inviolable is a matter for argument. Certainly there are problems, for example, where rights conflict. If there is a 'right for life', for instance, what are we to say of cases where it may be necessary to kill one person in order to save the life of another? What a Kantian ethic will certainly insist on, however, is that rights cannot be violated simply for the sake of promoting desirable ends, whether for oneself or for others.

S2, I am suggesting, is a much more satisfactory formulation of the categorical imperative than S1, and a comparison between the two gives the true measure of the accusation of formalism directed against S1. What seems intuitively interesting, and even inspiring, about an ethic of universality is the idea of universal humanitarianism, the idea of refusing to discriminate between human beings, and of respecting the claims of all to have their humanity recognized. S2 makes this idea explicit, whereas S1 disguises it as a formal principle of pure reason.

On the other hand, I still want to insist that Kant has not provided an adequate justification of S2. The question *'Why should I respect all human beings as persons?'* remains unanswered. Kant's failure here is a failure to justify the strong version of universalizability, as impartiality rather than mere impersonality, and it is the same failure which vitiates also the most plausible interpretation of S1. Kant, then, unlike Plato and Aristotle, undoubtedly furnishes a morality of altruism. Like Hume, however, he presents the opposite problem. Can he, or anyone else, provide any good reason for adhering to an altruistic morality?

Notes

1 Max Weber: *The Protestant Ethic and the Spirit of Capitalism*, trans. Talcott Parsons (London, 1930), p. 80.
2 G. W. F. Hegel: *Philosophy of Right*, trans. T. M. Knox (Oxford, 1952), para. 135.
3 Marcus G. Singer: *Generalization in Ethics* (London, 1963), pp. 251-3.
4 The principal advocate of this interpretation is H. J. Paton in his book *The Categorical Imperative* (London, 1947).
5 W. D. Ross: *Kant's Ethical Theory* (Oxford, 1954), p. 94; cf. pp. 34-5.
6 The most influential formulation has been that by R. M. Hare in his book *Freedom and Reason* (London, 1963).
7 Immanuel Kant: *Lectures on Ethics*, trans. Louis Infield (New York, 1963), pp. 193-4.

7 Mill
The Greatest Happiness

Reading: John Stuart Mill: *Utilitarianism* (first published 1861). There are many editions. A useful one is the Fontana edition edited by Mary Warnock, which also contains Mill's essays on *Bentham* and *On Liberty* and parts of Bentham's *Introduction to the Principles of Morals and Legislation*, all of which are valuable additional reading for the present chapter. Warnock's introduction is also very helpful.

My references will again be to paragraphs, numbered within each chapter. There are 6 paragraphs in Chapter I, 25 in Chapter II, 11 in Chapter III, 12 in Chapter IV, and 38 in Chapter V. My occasional page references to other works by Mill and by Bentham will be to the page numbers in Warnock's edition.

Kant, Bentham, and Christianity

At the beginning of his *Utilitarianism* (paragraph 4) Mill takes his distance from Kantian ethics. He places at the centre of his own moral theory the very things which Kant wants to exclude—the assessment of actions in terms of their ends and consequences, their contribution to human happiness, and the prevention of human suffering. For all that, Mill was a great compromiser in philosophy, and he saw things of value in Kant's theory, which he wanted to retain. He draws on the alternative tradition represented by Kant in order to qualify what was, on balance, a much more positive influence on him—the philosophy of Jeremy Bentham.

Bentham's ethics can be compared in its crudity (or simplicity, according to how we view it) with the position presented by Glaucon in the *Republic*. All human action, he claimed, is motivated by the desire for pleasure and the avoidance of pain. The only rational moral theory, therefore, will be one which seeks to make such action as consistent and effective as possible. In practice each person's pursuit of his or her own pleasure will be modified, to take account of the pleasures and pains of others, by the influence of four 'sanctions'. These are the *physical* sanction (the pleasure and pain one experiences as a direct and natural consequence of one's actions); the *political* sanction (the influence of laws and political edicts on one's pleasures and pains); the *moral* sanction (the influence exerted by other people's responses to oneself and by popular opinion in general); and the *religious* sanction (the influence exerted by the prospect of divine rewards and punishments). The combined effect of all these sanctions is to induce people to pursue their own pleasure in such a way as to co-operate also in the production of pleasure and avoidance of pain for others. The task of the moralist and of the legislator is to manipulate the various sanctions, so as to maximize the happiness of all. Clearly, on this theory, I can attach to the happiness of others only an instrumental value, and my only reason for pursuing it will be for what it contributes to my own happiness. Bentham, however, thought that this reason would be an effective one. Individuals and legislators alike ought therefore to regulate their conduct by the *principle of utility*, by which 'is meant that principle which approves or disapproves of every action whatsoever according to the tendency which it appears to have to augment or diminish the happiness of the party whose interest is in question' (i.e. in the case of individual actions, the happiness of the individual, and in the case of social organization, the happiness of the community).

John Stuart Mill's father, James Mill, was Bentham's friend and collaborator, and with Bentham's help devised an ambitious scheme of education for his son. It is not surprising, therefore, that the younger Mill grew up a convinced utilitarian, but not surprising either (adolescence being what it is) that he then reacted against it. In what he later called 'a crisis in my mental history', he came to see Benthamite utilitarianism as too limited and uninspiring. Bentham's philosophy, as he subsequently wrote in his essay on *Bentham,* will do nothing (except sometimes as an instrument in the hands of a higher doctrine) for the spiritual interests of society . . . It can teach the means of organising and regulating the merely *business* part˅of the social arrangements. Whatever can be understood or whatever done without reference to moral influences, his philosophy is equal to: where those influences require to be taken into account, it is at fault. (Warnock: op. cit., pp. 105 f.)

The principle deficiency in Bentham's conception of moral influences is that

Man is never recognised by him as a being capable of pursing spiritual perfection as an end; of desiring, for its own sake, the conformity of his own character to his standard of excellence, without hope of good or fear of evil from other source than his own inward consciousness. (Ibid., p. 100.)

The concession to Kantian ethics is clear here.

The insights which Bentham lacks, Mill aspires to incorporate within what is still a utilitarian framework. He remains committed to the view that 'actions are right in proportion as they tend to promote happiness, wrong as they tend to promote the reverse of 'happiness', and that 'by happiness is intended pleasure, and the absence of pain; by unhappiness, pain, and the privation of pleasure' (II.2). Unlike Bentham, however, he puts a much more altruistic slant on the doctrine. In keeping with his emphasis on the nobility of disinterested devotion to moral duty, he interprets utilitarianism as requiring that one's actions should aim at the general happiness, regardless of whether this will increase one's own happiness. Interpreted in this light, utilitarianism is, he thinks, essentially concordant with the ethics of Christianity. 'In the golden rule of Jesus of Nazareth,' he says, 'we read the complete spirit of the ethics of utility' (II.18). Mill was certainly not a Christian. Like many of his contemporaries, however, he wished to extract from Christianity the essential spirit of its ethics, which should continue to inspire mankind under the guise of a 'religion of humanity'. This exalted ethical religion, detached from its Christian context, would have to rest upon the somewhat fragile foundations of Bentham's hedonistic psychology. We shall now have to consider whether the resulting structure is sufficiently stable to survive.

Higher and Lower Pleasures

Mill offers two kinds of defence of utilitarianism. In Chapter II, he mounts a negative defence, attempting to eliminate misunderstandings of the theory and to meet objections to it. The point of reference here is, as with Kant's defence, the ordinary moral consciousness, and Mill wants to show that utilitarianism is essentially consistent with that common-sense morality. He does not, indeed, claim that utilitarianism in its implications coincides exactly with the accepted moral beliefs of his day. He was critical of many of those beliefs, and the utilitarian theory provided the standpoint from which he would want to criticize them. What he would claim, however, is that the general body of widely-accepted moral beliefs, when properly reflected upon, made internally consistent, and modified in the light of empirical facts, will be found to be broadly in accordance with the principle of utility, which can therefore be adopted as its underlying principle. This is Mill's approach in Chapter II. Chapter IV is different. He there attempts a more positive defence, one which is independent of the ordinary moral consciousness and is in some sense a more basic proof. Just what form this proof is supposed to take, and in what sense it is a 'proof', I shall consider in due course, but I shall begin by examining the first kind of defence.

From the standpoint of commonly accepted beliefs and values, the point on which Mill feels his utilitarianism to be most vulnerable is its hedonism—its assertion that the sole ultimate value is happiness, and that this can be equated with pleasure and absence of pain. Mill envisages the response of his critics: 'To suppose that life has (as they express it) no higher end than pleasure—no better and nobler object of desire and pursuit—they designate as utterly mean and grovelling; as a doctrine worthy only of swine' (II.3). It is to deal with this kind of objection that Mill introduces, in Chapter II, his distinction between higher and lower pleasures. Pleasures differ from one another in quality as well as in quantity, and the superior pleasures are those which befit our nature as human beings, and utilize our capacities for intelligent activity.

To appreciate the force of the distinction between 'quantity' and 'quality', we must look to a comparison with Bentham. Bentham's theory is insistently quantitative. To estimate the value of an action we must measure the value of the pleasures and pains it produces, and Bentham asks us to do this by measuring their intensity, their duration, their certainty or uncertainty, their propinquity (how long we have to wait for them), their fecundity or purity (i.e. the further pleasures or pains they are likely to cause), and their extent (the number of people who experience them). Although Bentham can hardly have taken seriously the idea of assigning precise numbers to these measurements, it is fair to say that this is the ideal to which he would aspire.

In introducing considerations of quality as well as quantity, Mill is in part reverting to the position of Plato and Aristotle. Like them, he believes that to find out what constitutes full and genuine happiness, we have to look at what is specific to the nature of human beings and distinguishes them from other animal species. Unlike Aristotle, however, he does not attempt the transition from the view of human nature to the view of human happiness by means of the essentialist argument that because certain activities are essentially human, they constitute the natural and proper purpose of human life, and provide the content of human happiness. For Mill, the connection between human nature and human happiness is not this essentialist one but a psychological one. The description of utilitarianism as a doctrine worthy only of swine is, he says,

felt as degrading precisely because a beast's pleasures do not satisfy a human being's conception of happiness. Human beings have faculties more elevated than the animal appetites, and when once made conscious of them, do not regard anything as happiness which does not include their gratification. (II.4.)

The point, then, is not that because human beings have distinctive capacities, they *therefore ought to* (or are intended by nature to) find their happiness in the exercise of them; it is that because they have these distinctive capacities, they *are not fully satisfied by* a happiness which does not involve the exercise of them.

How can Mill say this? Is it not all too apparent that many people actively pursue trivial and mindless pleasures, and are entirely content with them? Mill's answer is that though, finally, the higher pleasures can be said to be superior only because human beings prefer them, the preferences which determine their superiority must be the preferences of those who have a real experience of the alternatives. Undoubtedly there are many people whose experience has been largely confined to trivial and mindless pleasures, and who continue to pursue them fairly exclusively. What Mill would claim is that if they could properly experience some of the more demanding enjoyments which human beings are capable of, they would themselves come to find those more rewarding. The phrase '*properly* experience' is important. The pleasures of literary and artistic enjoyment, of intellectual enquiry, of creative and imaginative work, or of energetic devotion to a cause, may not reveal themselves upon an immediate acquaintance. They require application and commitment over an extended period of time, a willingness to accept temporary set-backs, and in some cases a process of education. But anyone who has really experienced what such activities have to offer will not thereafter willingly forgo them.

This would also be Mill's answer to another common reaction, that his position is an 'élitist' one. When Mill says that the superiority of the higher pleasures is decided by the 'verdict of the only competent judges', his readers are often inclined to reply: Why should I accept that verdict? If I really am passionately and exclusively devoted to so-called 'animal' pleasures, what right does anyone else have to label those pleasures inferior? Mill's answer would have to be: No right at all—other than a right grounded upon what your own judgement would be if you could really experience the alternatives. Mill depends heavily on the assumption that if they could only experience them fully, everyone really would prefer the higher pleasures. He does qualify this slightly, but significantly. He admits that there are those who, having at one time been able to appreciate the higher pleasures, subsequently neglect them and relapse into habits of apathy. But such cases are, he thinks, susceptible of

explanations in social and psychological terms which will
show them to be cases of degeneration.

Two other qualifications ought to be added to Mill's
position, and these are ones which he does not himself add.
We should, I think, qualify Mill's rather severely intellectualist
account of the higher pleasures. He tends to assume that
the distinction between higher and lower pleasures corresponds to that between intellectual (or at any rate spiritual)
and physical activities. There is no need to assume this.
There are plenty of physical activities which offer more than
superficial pleasures—activities which require skill, energy,
care, and commitment, and which are appreciated and
enjoyed only when pursued in this way. Indeed, if we think
of examples, such as activities of skilled craftsmanship, the
intellectual/physical dichotomy seems positively misleading.
The second qualification is that the contrast between higher
and lower pleasures need not entail that the lower pleasures
have to be excluded from a worthwhile life. Mill was inclined
to exclude them. He tended to look on the pleasures of
physical sensation as simply degrading. This, however, is not
essential to his general position. The much maligned triad of
food, drink, and sex are surely pleasures without which any
human life is the poorer. While characterizing them as 'lower'
pleasures, Mill could quite consistently have allowed a place
for them, adding only that a life which was devoted over-
whelmingly to them, and which detached them from any
context of wider significance, however replete with pleasure
it might be, would be a trivial and empty life.

With these qualifications, Mill's position seems to me to
be a distinct advance on Bentham. Though tending in an
Aristotelian direction, it improves also upon Aristotle, in so
far as it does not rely on his essentialist argument. Many of
Mill's critics, however, though agreeing with this, would
add a new objection. They would say that Mill may be right
to recognize qualitative differences of pleasure, but that
he is inconsistent in so far as he also wants to hang on to
Bentham's quantitative version of utilitarianism. He continues to refer to it, for example, as the *Greatest* Happiness
Principle, and to say that an action is right if it produces
more happiness than any alternative.

Up to a point—but only up to a point—this objection can be answered. The categories of quantity and quality are not mutually exclusive. A difference may be a qualitative one, and at the same time be a quantitative one just because it is also qualitative. If, of two pleasures, one is richer and more rewarding because it employs more of one's faculties and energies, then it will for that very reason be *more* pleasurable, and a life encompassing it will be a life of *greater* happiness, even though the pleasure will be no more intense or long-lasting. The point is that, though ·one can speak of 'greater' pleasure or happiness in such cases, the quantitative difference is one which can be recognized *only on the basis of the qualitative difference*. Only if we can see that the pleasure is more demanding, less superficial, and therefore more rewarding, can we see that it is also a greater pleasure. If we look for a *purely* quantitative difference, we shall not find one.

Mill, then, is not necessarily inconsistent in using both quantitative and qualitative terminology. The real trouble is that he still, to some extent, wants to combine the qualitative conception with Bentham's arithmetical, additive conception of quantitative differences. He does, on occasion (though much less than is commonly supposed), continue to speak as though one could determine the rightness or wrongness of an action simply be *adding up* the quantities of pleasure and pain it will produce, by 'calculating and weighing the effects' (II.24), and thereby determining whether the action does or does not 'tend to increase the sum total of happiness' (II.17). To that extent he is indeed inconsistent. It is not enough, however, simply to charge him with inconsistency. The criticism is facile unless it also indicates in which direction the inconsistency should be resolved. I have already indicated my own view that its resolution should take Mill more firmly in the direction of Plato and Aristotle rather than of Bentham.

Duties

I turn now to the other most widespread objection to utilitarianism, and this is that it fails to give an adequate treatment of the concept of duty. A division is often made between *teleological* and *deontological* theories in ethics. A teleological theory is one which asserts that an action is right or wrong, in so far as it produces good or bad consequences. Utilitarianism is one form of teleological theory, distinguished from other teleological theories by its assertion that the 'good' of good consequences is identifiable with happiness. A deontological theory is one which asserts that at least some actions are right or wrong, and we have a duty or obligation to perform them or refrain from them, quite apart from considerations of consequences. Teleological theories thus treat 'good' and 'bad' as the basic ethical concepts, and define others such as 'right' and 'wrong' in terms of these, whereas deontological theories would treat 'right', 'wrong', 'duty', and 'obligation' as basic, or at least give them equal status with 'good' and 'bad'.

Kant's ethical theory would be one instance of a deontological theory. Many other philosophers, however, without being committed to Kant's account of duty and its derivation from the categorical imperative, have wanted to assert that there are duties which a utilitarian or other teleological theory cannot explain. A classic statement of this position can be found in W. D. Ross's book *The Right and The Good*, published in 1930. Ross offers the following classification of moral duties:

duties of fidelity (keeping promises, telling the truth, paying debts etc.);
duties of reparation (compensating for a harm one has done);
duties of gratitude (repaying a kindness);
duties of justice (distributing goods rightly);
duties of beneficence (improving the condition of others);
duties of self-improvement (improving our own condition in respect of virtue or intelligence);
duties of non-maleficence (not injuring others).

The last three could be regarded as very broadly utilitarian or at least teleological in character, but the others are not, and carrying them out may sometimes require us to produce less overall good than we could otherwise have done. Therefore, if there really are such duties, they pose an obvious problem for utilitarianism.

Ross argues the point effectively with respect to the example of promising, and the example is a good one. Now we can agree that keeping a promise will normally have at least some good consequences, and breaking it will have bad consequences, for if I keep it, the person to whom I made it will be pleased, and if I break it, he or she will be annoyed. We can also agree that in some cases the results of keeping a promise would be so bad, or of breaking it would be so good, that I ought to break it. If, for example, I have promised to meet you for a drink and, when I am about to set out, my child is taken ill and I have to rush her to hospital, it would generally be agreed that I am right to break my promise. Certainly, then, consequences are relevant to the keeping or breaking of promises. There is, however, another factor which is equally relevant to what I ought to do in such cases, namely *the fact that I have promised*; and this, according to Ross and others, is what utilitarians lose sight of when they assume that the rightness or wrongness of promise-keeping is simply a matter of consequences. According to Ross, I have a duty to keep a promise, just as such, simply because I have promised. This duty may be reinforced by potential consequences. It may be outweighed by consequences. It is, however, a duty in its own right, and utilitarianism cannot explain this.

Ross asks us to imagine an example. He presents it in highly abstract terms, and I will therefore concretize it. Suppose that I have arranged to visit a friend on my bicycle, and have promised my daughter that I will take her with me on the child-seat of the bicycle. As I am about to leave, my son says that he wants to go with me. I cannot take them both. Now suppose that my son and my daughter would equally enjoy going with me, and would be equally disappointed if they cannot go (and suppose that this is the case, even when we take into account the added disappointment which my daughter will feel as a result of having had her expectations roused). Or suppose that my son will even enjoy it very slightly more than my daughter would. The utilitarian will have to say that if my son would enjoy it even more, I ought to take him; and that if they would both enjoy it equally, it would be equally right for me to take either my son or my daughter. To say this, however, is to deny all significance to what is, in fact, the crucial difference between the two alternatives, the fact that I have made a promise to my daughter, but not to my son. In virtue of that fact it is clear that, even though the consequences might be just as good in either case, I ought to take my daughter. This shows that there is a duty to keep one's promises, quite apart from utilitarian considerations.[1]

Similar examples could be constructed to illustrate other duties. Take the case of justice. Ross understands justice as the duty of distributing rewards in proportion to merit. Others have understood it as requiring, at least to some degree, an *equal* distribution of goods. Suppose that we are comparing two modes of social and political organization, instantiated in society A and society B. Suppose that the overall level of general well-being (measured, perhaps, as the sum total of economic wealth) is slightly higher in A than in B. Suppose, however, that in A there are massive inequalities, such that a fortunate few enjoy unparalleled luxury, while a significant number of others live in abject poverty, whereas in B goods are distributed much more equally, and everyone enjoys a good life. It would surely have to be said that in comparison with B the organization of A is unjust and to that extent wrong, even though the sum of well-being in A is higher. Now there may be more to be said. Some might argue, for example, that the promotion of equality is possible only at the cost of coercion and the destruction of liberty, and that it would therefore be wrong to try to replace the mode of organization of A with that of B. Other arguments might be advanced for the same conclusion. What can hardly be denied, however, is that in assessing the rights and wrongs of the two societies, considerations of justice are relevant, and that they are distinct from, and may conflict with, considerations of maximizing utility.

What is common to the two examples, that of promise-keeping and that of justice? What they both bring out is that utilitarianism, focusing exclusively on the overall maximization of benefits, attaches no ethical significance to *who gets the benefits*, because it attaches no significance to the nature of the *relations* between the persons involved. Ross again puts this well. Any form of utilitarianism, he says,

> seems to simplify unduly our relations to our fellows. It says, in effect, that the only morally significant relation in which my neighbours stand to me is that of being possible beneficiaries by my action. They do stand in this relation to me, and this relation is morally significant. But they may also stand to me in the relation of promisee to promiser, of creditor to debtor, of wife to husband, of child to parent, of friend to friend, of fellow countryman to fellow countryman, and the like; and each of these relations is the foundation of a *prima facie* duty, which is more or less incumbent on me according to the circumstances of the case.[2]

Unfortunately Ross does not take this any further. What it calls for is a developed account of social relations and their ethical significance. Ross does not provide one, and without it we shall not be able to form a clear idea of what is valid in the deontological approach to ethics. In the next chapter we shall look at an attempt to provide such an account.[3]

The 'Proof'

So far we have been considering objections to utilitarianism from the point of view of generally accepted moral beliefs. Mill, like other utilitarians, thinks it incumbent on him to meet these objections, and to show that such beliefs are, in their main essentials, consistent with utilitarianism. There is, however, a shorter way which he could have taken with them. Mill thinks that he can also provide an independent defence of utilitarianism, an argument from first principles which does not require any appeal to accepted moral beliefs. Therefore, if those beliefs then turn out to be incompatible with utilitarianism in certain respects, it is open to Mill to respond: so much the worse for conventional morality—it must be mistaken on these points, since we have independently demonstrated that utilitarianism is correct.

The attempted demonstration has three stages (although they are not presented by Mill in this order):
(i) If everyone desires happiness for its own sake, then happiness is desirable as an end in itself.

(ii) Nothing else separate and distinct from happiness is desired as an end in itself.

(iii) If happiness is the only thing desirable as an end in itself, then the general happiness is the proper end of conduct.

The passage which gives us the essence of stage (i) is this:

> The only proof capable of being given that an object is visible, is that people actually see it. The only proof that a sound is audible, is that people hear it: and so of the other sources of our experience. In like manner, I apprehend, the sole evidence it is possible to produce that anything is desirable, is that people do actually desire it . . . No reason can be given why the general happiness is desirable, except that each person, so far as he believes it to be attainable, desires his own happiness. This, however, being a fact, we have not only all the proof which the case admits of, but all which it is possible to require, that happiness is a good . . . (IV.3).

Mill's argument in this passage has been attacked, most notably by G. E. Moore in his 1903 book *Principia Ethica*, on the grounds that something's being *desired* does not entail that it is *desirable*. From the mere statement of psychological fact that people *do actually desire* happiness for its own sake, one cannot, it is said, deduce the evaluative conclusion that happiness is desirable, i.e. that it *ought* to be desired. It is logically possible that people in fact desire something which they ought *not* to desire, something which is not really desirable. The argument is not, it is claimed, a valid proof.

Mill's defenders hasten to point out his quite explicit assertion that he is not offering a proof 'in the ordinary and popular meaning of the term'. 'Questions of ultimate ends', he says, 'are not amenable to direct proof' (I.5). He is not claiming that if people desire happiness, this *logically entails* that it is desirable. What then is he claiming? If he is not offering a proof in the normal sense, what is he offering? Here is his answer.

> questions of ultimate ends do not admit of proof, in the ordinary acceptation of the term. To be incapable of proof by reasoning is common to all first principles; to the first premises of our knowledge as well as those of our conduct. But the former, being matters of fact, may be the subject of a direct appeal to the faculties which judge of fact—namely, our senses, and our internal consciousness.

Can an appeal be made to the same faculties on questions of practical ends? Or by what other faculty is cognisance taken of them? (IV.1.)

It is clear from this passage that Mill's argument does not appeal to a general logical relation between words ending in '-ed', and words ending in '-ble'. That is not the point of the analogy with 'visible' and 'audible'. It would not suit his purposes, for example, to claim that the only proof that Manchester United are beatable is that they have been beaten. The appeal, rather, is to a specific view about the ultimate grounds of knowledge. This view is an *empiricist* one, the view that all valid claims to knowledge must ultimately be based on experience. Our knowledge of the external world is based on the experience of the senses—and this is the point of Mill's remark that we know that things are visible because we see them, and we know that things are audible because we hear them. Mill would also claim that our knowledge of our own mental states is based on the experience of introspection, our 'internal consciousness'. In these cases, then, the experience which is the grounds of our knowledge is provided by the faculties of sight, hearing, and the other senses, and by the faculty of internal consciousness. Mill then asks: what of our knowledge of values, of the ends of conduct? What kind of experience provides the grounds of this knowledge? What psychological faculty is the source of this experience? His answer is: the faculty of desire.

Now the experience of desire does not furnish any conclusive proof, any more than do the experiences of sight or hearing. If I want to convince you that the Post Office Tower is visible from Hampstead Heath, and I therefore take you to Hampstead Heath and let you see the Tower, this does not *prove* that it is visible. The senses are fallible, and the experience may be the result of some complex optical illusion. There are ways of checking on this, and these will involve further appeal to the evidence of the senses. If, after all possible checks have been made, you still insist that the Tower is not visible and that your experience must be some kind of illusion, I cannot prove you wrong. Nevertheless the fact remains that one normally convinces people that something is visible by appealing to their experience of seeing it, and if this experience consistently supports the claim, it provides the best evidence one could possible have. Similarly if one wants to convince people that something is desirable as an end in itself, the appropriate way of doing this is to point out to them that, as a matter of experience, they do in fact desire it. This will not, strictly speaking, prove that it is desirable, but it will provide 'all the proof which the case admits of, and all which it is possible to require'.

So far, so good. The first stage of Mill's argument is not fallacious in the way that it has sometimes been thought to be. Mill now has to show that people do in fact desire happiness for its own sake, and furthermore that nothing other than happiness is in fact desired for its own sake, for this is how he must make good the utilitarian claim that the production of happiness is the *sole* test of right and wrong. It is clear that people desire a host of different things. It is also clear that many of the things which people want are wanted, not for their own sake, but for the sake of something else. If I want some petrol, I want it not for its own sake, but so that I can drive my car; driving my car is something which I want not for its own sake, but so that I can get to work, and getting to work is in turn not something which I want for its own sake. Here we have a typical sequence of means and ends, each intermediate end being in turn a means to a further end. What Mill has to show is that every such sequence of means and ends eventually comes to a halt at happiness. He has to show that happiness is the one thing which is wanted purely for its own sake, and that everything else which people want is ultimately wanted for the sake of happiness. Can he show this?

It would seem not. He says:

Now it is palpable that they do desire things which, in common language, are decidedly distinguished from happiness. They desire, for example, virtue, and the absence of vice, no less really than pleasure and the absence of pain. The desire of virtue is not as universal, but it is as authentic a fact, as the desire of happiness. (II.4.)

The example takes us back to Mill's concession to Kantian ethics, and his revision of Bentham so as to allow that people can and should aim at disinterested devotion to moral duty for its own sake. The recognition of this possibility now poses problems for Mill's claim that happiness is the only thing desired for its own sake. He goes on to identify other apparent counter-examples. People like music for its own sake, they aim at health for its own sake, and, less admirably perhaps, they desire things such as money and power and fame for their own sake. We could construct other counter-examples of the same kind. How is Mill to deal with them? He does so as follows:

The ingredients of happiness are very various, and each of them is desirable in itself; . . . besides being means, they are a part of the end. Virtue, according to the utilitarian doctrine, is not naturally and originally part of the end, but it is capable of becoming so; and in those who love it disinterestedly it has become so, and is desired and cherished, not as a means to happiness, but as a part of their happiness. (IV.5.)

Here the crucial phrases are 'ingredient of happiness' and 'part of happiness'. Mill's way of dealing with the counter-examples is then to say that these other things such as virtue and health are indeed, or can come to be, desired for their own sake, but that this is quite consistent with the assertion that they are desired as parts or ingredients of happiness. Of any such thing we can say that

In being desired for its own sake it is, however, desired as *part* of happiness . . . The desire of it is not a different thing from the desire of happiness, any more than the love of music, or the desire of health. They are included in happiness. They are some of the elements of which the desire of happiness is made up. Happiness is not an abstract idea, but a concrete whole; and these are some of its parts. (IV.6.)

There is a positive merit in this formulation, but there is also a danger. As to the merit, we have encountered it previously in connection with Mill's discussion of higher pleasures. We saw there the need to move away from Bentham's purely additive and instrumental conception—the idea that happiness is simply a sum of homogeneous units of pleasurable experience, and that anything else of value is related to happiness simply as a means to the production of such units. To give an adequate account of happiness, we have to look at the character of a human life as a whole, and to consider what overall kind of life human beings experience as most deeply and fully satisfying. The vocabulary of 'parts' or 'ingredients' of happiness, as distinct from that of means and ends, is a move in this direction, though perhaps still conceding too much to the additive conception.

Such a vocabulary has its value, then, when used as part of an attempt to work out an adequate and substantial moral psychology. The danger arises when Mill uses it in the present context, as part of an attempt to prove that happiness is the only thing desired for its own sake. The danger is that any apparent counter-examples will *automatically* be redescribed by Mill in the language of 'ingredients of happiness'. Of anything which appears to be desired for its own sake Mill can simply say, 'That just shows that it is a part of happiness'. In other words, 'being desired for its own sake' would be regarded as *meaning* 'being desired as a part of happiness'. The claim that happiness is the sole end, and that everything else that people desire is desired as a means to, or as a part of happiness, would then have become an empty truism. 'Happiness' would simply have been redefined as 'satisfaction of desire', and the assertion, 'People desire happiness', would amount to no more than 'People desire the satisfaction of their desires'.

This might not matter if the third stage of Mill's argument could be accepted. That stage is supposed to provide the transition from the agent's own happiness to the general happiness. All that the previous two stages can have shown is that each person necessarily desires his or her own happiness, and desires nothing else, except as a means to or part of this, and that therefore each person's own happiness is desirable for that person, and is a rational end for that person to aim at. What now has to be shown is that it is equally rational and desirable for each person to aim at the happiness of everyone else. And even if the first two stages have established only that each person's satisfaction is a rational end for that person, still, if some argument could then be found to show that it is equally rational for each person to aim at the satisfaction of everyone, a substantial ethical theory would have been validated. This is, in fact, the form in which some contemporary utilitarians have re-stated the theory. They have replaced the concept of 'happiness' with something like 'preference-satisfaction'. They have adopted a version of utilitarianism which does not aspire to a theory of value, but simply a theory of distribution. It does not offer any substantial answer to the question, what kinds of things are valuable or desirable. It simply recognizes that people have preferences, whatever they may be, and argues that any human agent ought to aim at maximizing the satisfaction of preferences, whether they are one's own or other people's. If this is how Mill is to be reformulated, everything depends on the third stage of the argument.

Unfortunately that stage is the weakest of all. Indeed, it can hardly be said to exist. All that Mill gives us is half a sentence, the continuation of a passage I have previously quoted.

No reason can be given why the general happiness is desirable, except that each person, so far as he believes it to be attainable, desires his own happiness. This, however, being a fact, we have not only all the proof which the case admits of, but all which it is possible to require, that happiness is a good: that each person's happiness is a good to that person, and the general happiness, therefore, a good to the aggregate of all persons. (IV.3.)

If the last half-sentence contains any argument at all, that argument would presumably have to be:

(a) Each person desires his or her own happiness.
(b) Therefore each person ought to aim at his or her own happiness.
(c) Therefore everyone ought to aim at the happiness of everyone.

The move from (b) to (c) is, however, entirely fallacious. It is no more valid than would be the argument that, if each husband ought to love his own wife, every husband ought to love everyone else's wife.

In Chapter V, Mill makes one other perfunctory attempt to fill the gap. He says that the Principle of Utility is 'a mere form of words without rational significance, unless one person's happiness . . . is counted for exactly as much as another's (V.36). He adds, in a footnote, that 'equal amounts

of happiness are equally desirable, whether felt by the same
or by different persons . . . for what is the principle of
utility, if it be not that "happiness" and "desirable" are
synonymous terms?' In so far as there is any argument here,
it would have to be some kind of universalizability argument:
if I apply the word 'desirable' to my happiness, and you
apply the word 'desirable' to your happiness, then I must
apply the word 'desirable' to your happiness, for the word
'desirable' must be used consistently, with the same meaning
on each occasion of its use. This, however, is just another
attempt to squeeze too much out of the requirement of
consistency or universalizability. All that can be said is that,
if I regard it as rational (or linguistically appropriate) for me
to apply the word 'desirable' to my happiness, I must regard
it as equally rational (or linguistically appropriate) for you
to apply the word 'desirable' to your happiness. That is not
what Mill wants.

Ironically, the materials for a more satisfactory argument
are available to Mill in his own Chapter III. He there suggests
that utilitarian morality has 'a natural basis of sentiment',
and that this natural basis is 'the social feelings of mankind,
the desire to be in unity with our fellow-creatures'. The
social state is 'natural, necessary and habitual' for human
beings. All human beings grow to maturity within a social
environment, and in this way they 'grow up unable to conceive as possible to them a state of total disregard of other
people's interests'. Through innumerable experiences of
co-operating with others, people come to identify with the
interests and feelings of others, and to think in terms of
collective rather than individual interests (III.9–10). All of
this is offered by Mill not as a *justification* of the altruistic
aspect of utilitarianism, but simply as a psychological *explanation* of how it is possible. Nevertheless, properly employed,
this account of the social character of human experience
would have enabled Mill to show not just that such behaviour
is possible, but that it is rationally justifiable. That is a claim
which I shall try to substantiate in due course.

As an ethics of altruism, then, Mill's theory fails just as
Kant's did. He sets out to provide a completely universalistic
morality. Each of us is to treat every other person's happiness

and suffering as having just the same importance as our own; in Bentham's words, 'everybody to count for one, nobody for more than one'. It turns out, however, that Mill can provide no satisfactory account of why anyone ought to act in this way.

The Two Strands in Mill's Utilitarianism

We have found a pervasive tension between two strands in utilitarianism. On the one hand, there is what can be called the 'mathematical' strand, which derives from Bentham. Happiness is treated as an unproblematic concept, whether it be composed of Benthamite states of pleasurable sensation or the preference-satisfactions of latter-day utilitarianism. The individual's happiness is arrived at simply by adding together these units. And the general happiness which is supposed to be the aim of all conduct is treated as equally unproblematic; it is simply a matter of adding up the happiness of all the individuals. I have argued that this strand is inadequate on both counts. The concept of happiness can and should be given more than this superficial treatment; and the universalistic altruism of the theory lacks any satisfactory justification.

Mill is torn between this and what I will call the 'Platonic-Aristotelian' strand. The consistent development of this strand would involve treating happiness as an essentially qualitative notion. Happiness would then be a matter of the overall character of a person's life, such as would satisfy his or her most deeply felt needs. In order to identify the form such a life would take, we would have to look at what is distinctive about human beings, and what constitutes a fully human life. In the manner of Plato and Aristotle, this enriched conception of the agent's own happiness would then provide the overall framework within which relations to others would be located. An adequate account of these social relations, in all their complexity, would make it possible to do justice to the moral duties of deontological ethics. In the next chapter we shall look at a theory which tries to do all of this.

Notes

1 My formulation of Ross's example is indebted also to Russell Grice's version of it in his book *The Grounds of Moral Judgments* (Cambridge, 1967), pp. 57–63.
2 W. D. Ross: *The Right and the Good* (London, 1930), p. 19.
3 One other way in which many recent utilitarians have attempted to meet deontological objections, is by adopting some form of rule-utilitarianism. It may indeed, they say, be right to observe certain duties, even though in particular cases I could do more good by acting differently; but what makes it right is the fact that these duties are enjoined by general rules, the observance of which will do more good than the observance of any alternative set of rules. We encountered one version of rule-utilitarianism in the chapter on Hume, and I there indicated some difficulties and objections. There is no room to discuss the theory further here, but for some typical defences and criticisms see the articles by Urmson, Mabbott, Rawls, and Smart in Philippa Foot (ed.): *Theories of Ethics* (London, 1967).

8 Hegelian Ethics
Self-realization

Reading: F. H. Bradley: *Ethical Studies* (first published 1876).

This is available in paperback from Oxford University Press. There is a convenient abbreviated paperback edition in the 'Library of Liberal Arts' series, edited and with a useful introduction by R. G. Ross. It contains the following chapters, which are the only ones to which I shall refer:

Essay II : Why Should I Be Moral?;
Essay III : Pleasure for Pleasure's Sake;
Essay IV : Duty for Duty's Sake;
Essay V : My Station and its Duties;
Concluding Remarks.

Essays III and IV criticize aspects of utilitarian and Kantian ethics respectively, and are best read in conjunction with Mill and Kant. In this chapter I shall concentrate very heavily on Essay V, 'My Station and its Duties', with some reference also to Essay II, and briefly to the Concluding Remarks. References to paragraph numbers are needed only for Essays II and V. Essay II has 69 paragraphs, excluding the Note at the end, and Essay V has 74 paragraphs, again excluding the Note. In Essay V, paragraph 67 is the incomplete sentence beginning '(1) Within the sphere . . .', and paragraph 68 begins '(a) It is impossible . . .'.

Bradley and Hegel

Ideally, I should like this chapter to deal directly with the ethical philosophy of Hegel, the nineteenth-century German philosopher whose ideas on the history of philosophy I mentioned in Chapter 1. Hegel's ethics seems to me to be by far the most interesting theory to go beyond the deficiencies of Kantianism and utilitarianism in the direction of an ethics of social relations. (Hegel wrote before Mill, but was acquainted with Bentham's work.) Hegel's philosophy is, however, notoriously difficult—not, perhaps, as utterly forbidding as it is sometimes made out to be, but still a formidable task for the beginner.

There is, however, a solution readily available, for one of Hegel's foremost British interpreters, F. H. Bradley, is eminently readable (if sometimes over-rhetorical), and meets the needs of this chapter perfectly. Bradley was one of the group of philosophers known as the British Idealists, centred mainly at Oxford, who were responsible for introducing Hegel's philosophy into this country in the latter part of the nineteenth century. They drew on Hegel and his German idealist predecessors (including Kant), principally to counter the then-dominant tradition represented by Mill, not only in ethics but in all areas of philosophy.

It is a matter for argument whether Bradley's presentation of Hegelian ethics is a faithful reflection of the original. Bradley himself is not an orthodox Hegelian, and *Ethical Studies* is not an exegesis of Hegel, but an important work in its own right. The general methodology of the book is Hegelian, however, and the chapter entitled 'My Station and its Duties' is a sympathetic exposition of a broadly Hegelian position, buttressed with extended quotations from Hegel. Bradley's own judgement on it is that 'the theory which we have just exhibited (more or less in our own way) . . . seems to us a great advance on anything we have had before, and indeed in the main to be satisfactory' (V.64). He adds, however, that 'if put forth as that beyond which we do not need to go, as the end in itself, it is open to very serious objections', and he proceeds to state these. It is not clear whether in doing so he thinks that he is criticizing Hegel, that is, whether he thinks that Hegel would regard the ethics of 'my station and its duties' as 'that beyond which we do not need to go'. Certainly, the direction in which Bradley himself goes beyond it, into the religious faith of the Concluding Remarks, is not Hegel's. I shall, then, treat *Ethical Studies* as a work in its own right, not concerning myself too much with the question of its fidelity to Hegel, but recognizing that its underlying inspiration is Hegelian.

Some initial remarks are nevertheless needed about the

Hegelian influence on Bradley's method. I said something about this in Chapter 1, where I mentioned Hegel's idea of philosophical development taking place through the negation of limited and partial positions, and the retention of them in their negated forms as elements within a whole. This philosophical method is called by Hegel 'dialectical', and it is the method of Bradley's *Ethical Studies*. In Hegelian fashion that work exhibits a sequence of different conceptions of morality, each of which arises out of the negation of the previous conception. Each ethical position, when examined, is found to contain contradictions within it, and the resolution of these requires a progress to a new and higher position. The initial movement is from the hedonistic utilitarianism of 'pleasure for pleasure's sake' to the Kantian morality of 'duty for duty's sake', and from that to the social morality of 'my station and its duties'. This is subsequently incorporated within a rather hazily defined 'ideal morality', an examination of which reveals contradictions in the very idea of morality as such, and requires us to go beyond morality to religion. The most characteristically Hegelian part of this sequence is the first three stages, for it is a feature of Hegel's dialectic that particular positions come to be seen as defective in so far as they are *one-sided*. The typical movement is this: the first position is found to be one-sided, the second position corrects this only by being one-sided in the opposite direction, and a third position then incorporates the two opposites into a higher unity which retains what is valid in each. Since the second position is the negation of the first, the third can be described as 'the negation of the negation', and Hegel uses this phrase to indicate that, in negating the second position, we do not regress to our original starting-point, but rise to a higher position which is a unity of opposites.

That is the movement in *Ethical Studies* from 'pleasure for pleasure's sake' to 'duty for duty's sake' to 'my station and its duties'. I shall not go into the details of the critiques of utilitarianism and Kantian ethics, for this would be to repeat much of my previous two chapters (which themselves owe a good deal to Bradley). I can, however, indicate schematically how they exhibit the above pattern. Bradley's chapter 'Why

Should I be Moral?' identifies 'self-realization' as the central concept of ethics, and the fundamental aim of morality. The task for ethics is then to determine what self-realization consists in, and Mill and Kant each offer one-sided answers to this question, Mill identifying self-realization with the attainment of pleasure, and Kant identifying it with the achievement of a good will through the performance of duty. These answers are one-sided in the following respects: Mill emphasizes the aspect of the *particular* to the exclusion of the universal, whereas Kant emphasizes the aspect of the *universal* to the exclusion of the particular; and Mill emphasizes the aspect of *content* to the exclusion of form, whereas Kant emphasizes the aspect of *form* to the exclusion of content. Each of them fails to do justice to the unity of particular and universal, and to the unity of form and content.

Let me try to explain. Utilitarianism, in equating the good life with the maximization of pleasure, thereby identifies it with a mere series of isolated particulars, a mere succession of states of feeling, the only object being to achieve as many of these as possible. They are mere particulars, not standing in any significant relation to one another, and thus there is lacking any conception of a universal, which unites all these particular states of pleasurable feeling into a coherent whole. They are simply added up. They are therefore a mere content without form, for when added together they are not seen as falling into any significant overall shape or pattern. They are a mere accumulation. Kant, on the other hand, stresses the aspects of universality and form, but in such a way that they become a mere empty universality, and a mere empty form, divorced from any way of becoming particular and concrete. Kantian morality simply prescribes conformity to the idea of universal law, it proposes a purely formal test of right and wrong. But as we have seen, absolutely any action can be universalized, and therefore in order to derive from the universalizability test concrete results, Kant has to smuggle in a content from outside, and to bring in considerations of utility and of consequences which he had previously insisted on excluding.

Bradley, then, is looking for a conception of morality

which unites these two poles, and he claims to find it (at least partially) in the morality of 'my station and its duties'. This is the Hegelian morality which stresses the *social* character of the individual, and finds the content of moral life in the actions which derive from particular social relations and functions. Such a morality, according to Bradley, synthesizes particular and universal, content and form, in the concept of the *concrete universal*. This is a difficult idea, but it seems to mean something like the following. (a) The self to be realized is a concrete universal in the sense that it is a whole, an organized totality. It is not, like the Kantian self, an empty form and universality, but a self which expresses itself as a whole in each of its particular acts and experiences. Conversely, these individual acts and experiences are not isolated occurrences, but get their significance from their place in the context of an organized life. (b) The self to be realized is 'universal' in a second sense. It is a unity with other selves. The self which I am to realize is a social self—not the self which I am as an isolated particular, but the self which I am through my relations to other selves, the self which I share with others, as a social being. The relation of society to the individuals here mirrors that of the overall self to the particular actions. Just as the self is not simply the sum of individual actions, nor yet something divorced from them, but is their organized unity, so also society is not just the sum of individuals, but is actively and fully present in each of them; it is constitutive of the individuals, so that they cannot exist without society, but neither can it exist except through them. And this presence of the society in the individual is the concrete universal.

The Ethics of Social Relations

To support his Hegelian morality, then, Bradley has to vindicate the concept of the individual as essentially a social being. This he attempts in paragraphs 5 to 19 of 'My Station and its Duties', where he offers two main lines of defence. These we can refer to as the biological argument (13-15), and the cultural argument (16).

The biological argument is, in essence, that the individual is a social being because he or she is the product of genetic inheritance, and is therefore born as a member of a certain family and a certain race. This is a weak argument and will not, I think, take Bradley very far. Partly I have in mind the fact that the case for the inheritability of mental characteristics remains to this day extremely controversial (witness the disputes about IQ and inheritance, or about Chomskyan linguistics). More importantly, however, even if it could be demonstrated that genetic inheritance plays a very large determining role, this would still not show that human beings are *social* in any very strong sense. This relation between social influences and the individual would be a purely *causal* one. It would show only that the individual was a product of these social influences, and would be quite compatible with the assertion that, once one is born, one can exist essentially as an individual having no ties with and owing nothing to society. It need have no ethical implications.

Such implications properly emerge only when the biological argument itself shades into the cultural argument. It is initially a biological fact that the human child is born into and nurtured by some kind of family, which itself exists within some wider social group. What this also means, however, is that the mental growth and development of the individual is essentially a social process. One comes to understand who one is, as an individual, by coming to understand the relations in which one stands to other people, and the responsibilities which these carry with them, and by acquiring the habits and customs of one's community, through which these relations are understood. Bradley emphasizes especially, and rightly, the importance of language in this connection. Language is necessarily a social acquisition, and in acquiring it one is acquiring not just a set of words, but a set of ideas and conceptions, a way of thinking which is built into the language itself. This set of ideas is not something which one can take or leave at will. One can exist as a thinking, rational individual only by acquiring the language of a community, and then one necessarily apprehends the world through the concepts of that language.

Bradley claims, then, that the identity of the individual

is constituted by his or her relation to others. This claim undergoes a crucial transition in paragraph 19. Bradley says:

> To know what a man is (as we have seen) you must not take him in isolation. He is one of a people, he was born in a family, he lives in a certain society, in a certain state. What he has to do depends on what his place is, what his function is, and that all comes from his station in the organism. . . . There are such facts as the family, then in a middle position a man's own profession and society, and, over all, the larger community of the state.

Here the notion of 'relations of community' has already undergone a drastic curtailment. It has immediately been equated with the notion of one's social *function*, and that is something much more specific. According to Bradley the most important of these functions are the roles which one occupies in one's family, in one's profession, and as a citizen of the state. He is here echoing Hegel's division of ethical life into the family, civil society (Hegel's term for the sphere of work and economic life), and the state. Hegel's position is itself a limited one; my relations to others are certainly not exhausted by the facts of my being a father, a university lecturer, and an Englishman. Nevertheless Hegel does, at any rate in his philosophical treatment of ethical life, provide an extended discussion of family relations and work relations. The same cannot be said of Bradley. He continues:

> Leaving out of sight the question of a society wider than the state, we must say that a man's life with its moral duties is in the main filled up by his station in that system of wholes which the state is . . .

Without explanation, the family and civil society have dropped out of sight, and Bradley has decided to focus entirely on the state. This focus dominates the rest of the chapter, in which morality is more or less equated with patriotic duty to one's country. This duty is eulogized by Bradley in tones of nationalistic fervour.

> The non-theoretical person . . . sees in the hour of need what are called "rights" laughed at, "freedom," the liberty to do what one pleases, tramped on, the claims of the individual trodden under foot, and theories burst like cobwebs. And he sees, as of old, the heart of a nation rise high and beat in the breast of each one of her citizens till her safety and her honour are dearer to each than life, till to those who

live her shame and sorrow, if such is allotted, outweigh their loss, and death seems a little thing to those who go for her to their common and nameless grave. (V.32.)

This concentration on duties to the state is not justified by Bradley's original argument. I believe that the argument does, however, succeed in showing the ethical importance of the social relations which serve to define the individual, and this is something which can be accepted much more plausibly if we reject Bradley's own narrowing of focus. If we look now at a much wider range of social relations, we can bring out more effectively their importance for ethics.

Let us being at the opposite extreme from Bradley and the state, with very small-scale and short-term relations between people. Consider the problem of the ethics of promising, which has already been so prominent in the last two chapters. We saw that it is difficult to give a purely utilitarian account of the obligation to keep a promise. Utilitarianism, because it concentrates entirely on future good to be achieved, cannot do justice to the way in which a fact about the past, the fact that one has promised, is itself a reason for acting in a certain way; nor can it do justice to the fact that the obligation to keep a promise is an obligation to a specific individual, not an obligation to humanity in general. On the other hand, it is not enough for the deontological moralist simply to assert that we have a duty to keep promises. We want to know *why this should matter*, why such a duty has the ethical significance which it does have. That is a question which utilitarianism purports to answer, though unsuccessfully, but it is not answered by the baldly uninformative and dogmatic assertion that promise-keeping is a duty.

As we saw in the last chapter, Ross gives us an important clue when he points out that utilitarianism 'seems to simplify unduly our relations to our fellows'. Suppose we now ask: what is the nature of the relationship which is involved in the act of making a promise? The answer must surely be that a promise typically creates or presupposes a relationship of *trust*, of *reliance*. This is the crucial fact, whose importance is missed both by the utilitarian account and by most deontological accounts. What is wrong with breaking a promise is that it is a violation of a relationship of trust. We can see this more clearly if we notice that there is nothing vital about the actual *word* 'promise'. If I simply *tell* someone that I will do something and thereby get him to trust me, my breaking that trust is just as much of a wrong, whether or not I actually said, 'I promise'. We could perhaps agree with the utilitarian that to violate a relationship of trust is to harm the other person, and that this is what makes it wrong. What the utilitarian fails to grasp, however, is the quite specific and unique nature of the harm. We can only understand what makes it a harm if we first understand the relationship of trust, and understand what it is to have one's trust betrayed.

Here, then, is a very simple but very important social relation into which people can enter, and which is by its very nature an ethically significant relation. Other similar examples involving small-scale, short-term social relations would be telling the truth, and paying a debt. In these cases too, the relationship of trust is crucial.

Moving now to equally small-scale but more long-term social relations, consider such examples as friendship, or sexual relations, or parent–child relations. Here again the point is that each such relationship carries a specific ethical significance. Loyalty to one's friends, for example, is part of what it is to be a friend. I stand by my friend just because he or she is my friend, and if I did not do so I would not be a true friend. Someone who did not understand this would have failed to understand what is involved in the relation of friendship, and the kind of affection it involves. Similarly, a parent's devotion to a child is part of what is involved in a particular kind of affection, the close and intimate sharing of a life, the particular kind of responsibility which follows from the child's vulnerability, the identification with the child which stems from bringing it up and sharing in its process of growth. Here again, to understand the relationship is to understand its ethical significance. Something like this could also be said of sexual relations. In this case there may be additional complications, but if we can give any real sense to the notion of sexual fidelity, it must be by seeing it as part of what is involved in the intimacy of a sexual relationship.

Notice that, in dealing with these kinds of relations, we are dealing with particular kinds of emotion, and that the character of the relationship is in part a matter of the kind of emotion it involves, the kind of affection or love which is felt for a friend or child or beloved. This does not mean, however, that the loyalty, or care, or fidelity required by the relationship is to be seen simply as the immediate and spontaneous expression of the emotion one happens to be feeling at the time. I may feel infuriated with my friend, or exasperated with my child, and yet recognize that the underlying relationship—my emotional commitment if you like, but not just my transitory feelings—demands of me a certain kind of concern.

Consider now a more large-scale example. Take the case of work relations. Here there is room for considerable complexity. To understand, for example, the ethical notion of 'loyalty to one's colleagues', we have to look at the kinds of relations in which one may stand to those colleagues. One may be sharing with them in a common enterprise, where all participate jointly in the overcoming of common problems. The requirement of loyalty will then be neither a mere instrumental recognition that one's own interests depend on the satisfaction of other people's interests, nor an abstract demand of altruistic duty, but rather the expression of one's identification with the common task and with those who share it. All of this presupposes, however, that the work really is a co-operative enterprise. If one works within a context which is structured entirely in terms of individual career advancement, for example, and if one's colleagues are primarily interested in getting one's job for themselves or using one for their own advancement, then the notion of loyalty will be a hollow mockery. Similarly, if one is working for a wage, one may perhaps also recognize a loyalty to one's employer(s), but to the degree that the relationship is in reality exploitative, such loyalty will be misplaced. Loyalty to one's colleagues or workmates may then actually take the form of solidarity in opposition to one's employers (and one can see how this could be extended to the ethical notion of class solidarity, the solidarity of an exploited class in opposition to its exploiters). The general point here is that the kinds of ethical requirements or loyalties which can be rationally justified, will depend on the kinds of relations in which one stands to others.

With this last example we are coming closer to Bradley's own examples. Bradley, we have seen, focuses entirely on institutionalized relationships, and on the duties which attach to institutionalized social roles. I want to suggest that if we are to understand and justify the moral force which these institutionalized relations have, we must see them as built upon pre-institutionalized relations, loyalties, and commitments. The notion of institutionalized family duties, for example, can be given a rational foundation only in so far as these duties can be seen as a formalization of the pre-institutionalized commitments and loyalties involved in parent–child relations and sexual relations. Similarly, one can provide a rational justification for regarding oneself as bound by the institutionalized duties of one's work or profession only in so far as those duties are grounded in authentically co-operative relations with those with whom, or for whom, one works. Along these lines we might eventually find a rational foundation for Bradley's dominant preoccupation, the idea of duty to one's country. This, however, will require more than simply the assertion that one is a member of a certain nation, and is therefore bound by the duties of that role. We should have to look at the ways in which a sense of commitment to one's country might arise out of various components: an attachment to a certain place, the place where one was born and brought up and which may therefore have very special associations; one's being immersed within a national culture, a language, and a set of literary, artistic, and intellectual traditions which form one's whole way of thinking and feeling about the world; the network of relations and loyalties to innumerable individuals and groups, with all of whom one shares a common nationality. Upon such a foundation the idea of duties to one's country might make rational sense, but the presentation of such duties is often a counterfeit, and without such a foundation it is bound to be.

Bradley's ethics of social relations needs to be revised in this way if it is to be plausible and acceptable. It requires this radical extension of the kinds of social relations to be considered. When thus enlarged, however, it becomes a theory of tremendous importance, and we can begin to appreciate that importance if we think back to the problems which we found in Kant and Mill. The basic problem which they shared was that of providing a rational justification for disinterested altruism. What we learn from their failure (and from the failure of their innumerable successors) is that such a justification cannot be provided by an appeal to purely formal rationality or logic. Kant, we saw, tries to show that obligations to respect the rights or promote the interests of others can be derived from the formal requirement of universalizability. This cannot be done. So long as the universalizability principle is grounded in purely formal rationality, it can legitimately be interpreted as a principle of consistency, and as a principle of the impersonality of reasons, but not as a principle of impartiality. Again, we saw that Mill starts with a notion of the individual desiring his or her own happiness, and suppose that mere logic can show that we all ought to desire one another's happiness. He too is unsuccessful. The transition from individual happiness to the general happiness cannot be made, so long as we start from the idea of the isolated individual. Disinterested concern for others can be exhibited as rational only when we look at the real ties which do in fact bind human beings to one another. That is to say, we have to start not, like Mill, with the asocial individual, but like Bradley, with the idea of the individual as a social being involved in relations which carry with them commitments to others. We can bridge the moral gap between self and others only when we understand the self as a social self. Once we appreciate this, we can provide a refutation of egoism which consists not in adding on something external to self-interest, but in showing that the kinds of things which matter to human beings are not just desires and interests. Relations with others play just as vital a part in human life as the pursuit of interests and the satisfaction of desires, and they are not reducible to the latter.

What we are doing here is not arguing from egoism to altruism, but revealing the inadequacy of the dichotomy

between egoism and altruism. Take the case of loyalty to
a friend. If I give up my time and effort to help a friend in
need, I am not doing it out of long-term self-interest. If
I am a true friend my thought is not, 'Maybe he will do the
same for me some day.' It would be equally inappropriate,
however, to suppose that I am therefore sacrificing myself
to something external. The friendship is an integral part of
my life. Along with all my other commitments and loyalties
to other individuals, and to various human groups, causes,
and institutions, it defines my identity and gives my life its
meaning. As Bradley has it, my self 'is penetrated, infected,
characterized by the existence of others, its content implies
in every fibre relations of community' (V.16). And this is
not to say that when I act on the basis of such loyalties I do
it in order to retain my sense of identity, or in order to give
meaning to my life. Rather it is to say: the fact that these
relations to others are a part of my own identity, and part of
what gives meaning to my life, finds its natural expression
in my willingness to devote myself to these concerns.

Bradley's Self-criticisms

This enlarged reading of Bradley can in part help to answer
his own self-criticisms at the end of 'My Station and its
Duties'. Bradley is aware that the Hegelian position has its
problems and its limits. His criticisms revolve around two
main points: (i) that there are aspects of the moral life which
do not derive from one's membership of any social community (paragraphs 70-2); and (ii) 'that the community in
which he is a member may be in a confused or rotten condition' (69 and 71).

(i) As examples of activity which has a moral aspect but
which 'does not fall wholly within any community', Bradley
cites artistic and intellectual activity (72). 'The production of
truth and beauty', he says, '(together with what is called
"culture") may be recognised as a duty; and it will be very
hard to reduce it in all cases to a duty of any station that
I can see.' Now, what *is* true is that people do not engage in
such activities primarily in their capacity as citizens of the

state (or, if they do, then they are mere propagandists); and the duties which such activities involve are not duties to the state. What makes Bradley's self-criticism seem plausible and necessary, then, is his narrow preoccupation with the state. If we consider a wider range of social relations, it certainly is the case that we engage in intellectual and cultural activities as social beings. Artistic work, for example, necessarily involves a relationship to an artistic tradition. Even the most iconoclastic artist must, if his or her iconoclastic response is to be a meaningful and intelligible one, make some use of an inherited style and an inherited artistic vocabulary. The artist does not work within a vacuum; he or she works within an artistic community, even if no one actually sees his or her pictures, or reads his or her novels. The same is true of the intellectual or scientific worker. The problems he or she works on are problems posed by an existing tradition of scientific or intellectual work. They are the problems created by the science at this stage of its development, and any solution will, by its very nature, have the character of being a contribution to the intellectual or scientific community (again, whether or not it is actually recognized as such).

A more problematic case which Bradley mentions is 'what may be called cosmopolitan morality' (71). Bradley is rather cryptic here, but presumably part of what is involved is the idea of duties to people who are not members of one's own community. Now, in part, the recognition of social relations other than those of the state can help to meet this point too. There are innumerable human beings with whom we do not share membership of the same nation-state, but to whom we may stand in other relations which carry responsibilities with them. We may, perhaps, share with them membership of an intellectual or scientific community which transcends national boundaries; or we may be fellow-participants with them in a political movement which has an international character; or we may be linked with them by direct or indirect economic relations. It may still be felt, however, that this does not take us far enough—that it still leaves unrecognized the moral responsibilities which we have to people to whom we stand in no specific relation at all, responsibilities

which we have to them *simply as human beings*. This idea is
to be found in the Kantian principle of respect for persons.
It is to be found in Mill's insistence that the happiness or
suffering of any human being, just because it is human
happiness or suffering, cannot be morally indifferent to us.
I have been arguing that the Hegelian ethics of social relations
is more successful than Kantian and utilitarian ethics in
justifying concern for others. If, however, the Hegelian
position, because it focuses on social relations, has to stop
short of the universal humanitarianism of Kant and Mill,
that may be felt to be too severe a limitation. We shall have
to consider, in due course, whether the ethics of social
relations can be so extended as to incorporate the idea of
one's moral responsibility to all other human beings. I shall
come back to this question in Chapter 11.

(ii) Bradley's second self-criticism is that the existing moral
world is not as it should be. The actual communities in which
people happen to find themselves are likely to be defective
in one way or another; and then it will not be the case that
in such a community the individual can find self-realization
simply by carrying out the tasks which fall to his lot, and
thereby live a morally good life.

This is undoubtedly true. If, for example, I had lived in
Nazi Germany, it is unlikely that I could have lived either
a fulfilling or a morally decent life by faithfully carrying out
all the duties allotted to me. As before, the point can be
partly, but only partly, met by pointing to social relations
other than those of the state. My resistance to carrying out
the duties imposed on me by a corrupt political state may
in part stem from other social relations in which I am
involved, for example, my solidarity with other social groups
or movements. But though my duties to the state may conflict with the requirements of other social relations, that is
only part of the answer. Other sets of social relations, besides
those of the state, may also be defective or corrupt. And if
that is so, we seem to need some standpoint, independent
of the social relations themselves, from which they can be
assessed.

Where then do we go from here? Bradley moves into the

realm of religion. He asserts, in his Concluding Remarks, that since the moral world is inevitably imperfect, the conflict between the ideal and the real remains an inescapable contradiction in morality. Only in religion, in a condition of oneness with God, are we able to realize a self which is also the ideal self. That at any rate is the claim of religion, and specifically of the Christian religion. Bradley offers no grounds for thinking it to be true. As he explicitly acknowledges, he is simply reiterating what the religious consciousness asserts about itself. Its claim to reconcile what cannot be reconciled in the moral and social world has simply to be taken on faith.

I want to propose a different route out of the difficulty. Bradley's guiding concept has been that of self-realization. Utilitarian and Kantian ethical theories offered an inadequate interpretation of this, because they worked with inadequate notions of the self. 'My Station and its Duties' seemed at first more satisfactory, because it involved an organic and social conception of the self. It turns out, however, that in so far as any existing social community is defective, it will fail to make for the self-realization of its members. Now this suggests that confronted with the imperfection of the social world, we might, instead of abandoning it for the world of religion, ask instead what social relations would have to be like, in order to make genuine self-realization possible. The concept of self-realization would then serve us as the standpoint from which to assess different kinds of social relations. We therefore need to look more closely at that concept.

Self-realization

In Essay II, 'Why Should I Be Moral?', Bradley sets out an extremely abstract argument in defence of the view that self-realization is the ultimate end of moral activity. The argument has a certain similarity to Mill's attempted 'proof' of utilitarianism, in that it appeals to a very general theory of human action. Put very schematically the argument is this:

(i)   All action aims at realizing desire.

(ii) 'In desire, what is desired must in all cases be self.'
(iii) Therefore all action is an attempt at self-realization.

This argument is set out in paragraphs 26 to 32 of Essay II. Proposition (i) may seem plausible, but (ii) looks much more problematic. What could Bradley mean by the claim that all desire is for self? He provides some slight elaboration:

all objects or ends have been associated with our satisfaction, or (more correctly) have been felt in and as ourselves, or we have felt ourselves therein; and the only reason why they move us now is that when they are presented to our minds as motives we do now feel ourselves asserted or affirmed in them. The essence of desire for an object would thus be the feeling of our affirmation in the idea of something not ourself, felt against the feeling of ourself as, without the object, void and negated; and it is the tension of this relation which produces motion. (II.31.)

This is still very vague, and sounds quite compatible with the idea that any satisfaction whatever would count as 'feeling oneself affirmed in something', and would therefore count as self-realization. Bradley seems aware of its incompleteness, for he continues: 'Is the conclusion that, in trying to realize, we try to realize some state of ourself, all that we are driving at? No, the self we try to realize is for us a whole, it is not a mere collection of states' (33).

This idea that full satisfaction is achieved only when the self is affirmed *as a whole* was referred to earlier in connection with Bradley's criticism of utilitarianism, and I shall return to it again. Bradley adds a second requirement. Genuine self-realization requires that the self be affirmed not only as a whole, *but as an infinite whole*. Bradley is here drawing on Hegel's distinction between a true infinity and a false infinity. The false infinite is the popular conception of the infinite, as the constant repetition of the finite. It is the infinite as the unending series, or the indefinitely extended straight line. According to Hegel (and Bradley) this kind of infinite is 'false' because it forms no real contrast to the finite, it simply repeats the finite. We might ask what is wrong with that: why should 'infinite' involve any stronger contrast with 'finite'? But Hegel, I think, has in mind the honorific connotations of 'infinite', especially as a description of God. God is not 'infinite' in the sense of being like the finite but indefinitely more so. What then is the true infinite? It is that which is unlimited, unbounded, because it incorporates everything else within itself. It does not stand over against something else which would thereby limit it. An example would be the infinite character of consciousness. In some sense, perhaps, there is a contrast between consciousness and its objects, but these objects do not limit it, they exist within consciousness, as the content of consciousness, and in that sense consciousness is infinite. By definition, consciousness could never come up against something external which was outside of consciousness and could limit it (for if it were external to consciousness, consciousness could never encounter it). Now, it is in this sense that Bradley thinks that the self to be realized must be an infinite self. It must leave nothing outside it. In particular, it must not leave other selves outside it, for then it would be finite, limited by its opposition to every other self. Here we see, adumbrated in very schematic terms, the subsequent thesis of 'My Station and its Duties', that full self-realization is possible only for the social self.

This, then, is Bradley's abstract argument. It is intended to provide the basis for the subsequent chapters, which are to be read as successive attempts to explain how this self-realization could more concretely be achieved. Although, then, the subsequent chapters make the thesis less abstract, they still depend upon the abstract argument to explain why we should be interested in self-realization in the first place. And the trouble with that abstract argument is that, like all such arguments, it is so general as to admit of innumerable interpretations, and it then trades on that ambiguity. Self-realization, argued for in this way, is so general that it sounds as though it *must* be the aim of all our activity, for what other aim could there be? But, because it is all-embracing, it can then give us no definite guidance as to how we ought to act, and any attempt to make it more specific will inevitably be arbitrary and contentious. This problem is reflected in some of the standard objections to the ethics of self-realization, as we shall now see.

Probably the most common interpretation of self-realization is the idea of *realizing one's potentialities*. It is in this sense that the concept has achieved popularity outside the confines of philosophy. If I am told, however, that I ought to aim at realizing my potentialities, this simply poses the question: which potentialities? I have the capacity to engage in all sorts of different activities, many of which would conflict with one another, and indeed whatever activity I engage in will necessarily realize some potentiality or other. When people talk of 'realizing one's potentialities', they usually have in mind talents and capacities of a kind appropriate to some useful or socially approved career—realizing one's potentialities for being a musician, or an architect, or a gymnast, or whatever. What grounds are there, however, for fastening upon those particular potentialities? The nimble-fingered person who decides to go in for the life of a pick-pocket rather than a concert pianist is just as certainly realizing his potentialities. I may have a remarkable talent for deception, or for practising subtle kinds of cruelty—am I to realize such potentialities? The assumption that certain kinds of potentialities rather than others are the ones to realize can, in the absence of further justification, only appear as arbitrary.

A common suggestion, aimed at meeting this difficulty, is that we ought to realize our *distinctively human* potentialities and our distinctively human selves. This of course takes us back to Aristotle, who is an important source for the idea of self-realization. It also takes us back to familiar difficulties. There is first the problem of determining what these distinctively human potentialities are. The exercise of rationality or creativity is distinctively human, but so is cooking, or waging nuclear war; why should not the latter activities count as 'self-realization' in the required sense? Now this problem is not intractable. We can argue that among the many uniquely human activities, some are more basic than others, and perhaps something like 'rationality' is fundamental to all of them. But even if we solve this problem there remains the question which we came up against when discussing Aristotle. Why do what is distinctively human? What is so great about being human? If a certain activity is unique to human beings, why is that any reason for engaging in it? (Mill, we have seen, has another answer to the question, which I shall come back to in a moment.)

For Bradley the self which we are to realize is not so much the distinctively human self, but rather the *social self*. I have, in this chapter, tried to indicate the merits of this emphasis. The fact is that the specific relations in which we stand to others are a vitally important aspect of our lives, and the recognition of this is essential for ethics. When, however, Bradley tries to elevate the idea of 'realizing the social self' into a comprehensive ideal, it combines the defects of both the previous interpretations. What is the social self? Bradley claims to have shown that the self is permeated through and through by its social character, and that all our ideas and sentiments come to us from society; but in that case everything we do will be 'realizing the social self', and the injunction to realize it (like the injunction to realize our potentialities) will exclude nothing. If, on the other hand, Bradley does want to work with a distinction between the social self and the non-social self, this raises the question: Why realize the social self rather than the non-social? The requirement is as arbitrary and unsupported as the requirement to realize the distinctively human self.

These are standard objections to the ethics of self-realization, and they are cogent ones. They seem to indicate that the concept of self-realization cannot by itself function as the one underlying principle of ethics. By itself it cannot tell us how to act, even when made more concrete. If it is to be of value it will have to be integrated with other ethical concepts. I suggest that at this point we abandon the abstract approach, that is, abandon the attempt at a general *a priori* defence of self-realization as a comprehensive ideal. It will be more helpful if we ask instead: What are the important particular emphases conveyed by the concept? What are the important features of the good human life to which it draws attention? I want to indicate three things which it especially picks out.

(1) *The need for coherence* Recall how Bradley contrasts self-realization with the Benthamite ideal of 'pleasure for pleasure's sake'. He sees that a life may be filled with innumerable particular pleasures, without these pleasurable experiences ever cohering into a self. Of course they belong

to a self in the sense that they are all states of one and the same continuing person, but if the particular pleasures do not have any meaningful relation to one another, they will not give any satisfying overall character to one's life—one will not, in Bradley's phrase, find oneself affirmed in them. This failure of coherence need not be confined to the pursuit of pleasures. In much the same way, one's life may be one in which innumerable particular ambitions are achieved (career ambitions, domestic ambitions, the acquisition of consumer goods), and yet one may have a sense that these various achievements do not hang together, that one's life lacks any overall shape or meaning. Such examples give us a negative contrast with self-realization as coherence. What more positively can we say about it? What can make a human life into a coherent unity? It may be, perhaps, that one's life is given a shape by some dominating aim or object. This may be an involvement in a certain kind of work; or a commitment to a religious or political ideal; or the focus of one's life may be some relationship or set of relationships with other people, family relationships perhaps, or sexual relationships. To give unity to one's life, such a dominating concern will not be all-embracing, but it may be the centre around which everything else organizes itself, so that one may be able to say of it, 'This is what ultimately matters to me', and other independent interests may be integrated into one's life by being brought into relation to this central concern.[1] Bradley puts it like this:

If we turn to life we see that no man has disconnected particular ends; . . . each situation is seen (consciously or unconsciously) as part of a broader situation. . . . I am not saying that it has occurred to everyone to ask himself whether he aims at a whole, and what that is. . . . Nor further do I assert that the life of every man does form a whole; that in some men there are not coordinated ends which are incompatible and incapable of subordination into a system. What I am saying is that if the life of the normal man be inspected and the ends he has in view (as exhibited in his acts) be considered, they will, roughly speaking, be embraced in one main end or whole of ends. . . . You will find that his notion of perfect happiness or ideal life is not something straggling, as it were, and discontinuous, but is brought before the mind as a unity, and, if imagined more in detail, is a system where particulars subserve one whole. (II.36-7.)

Bradley may be too sanguine about the extent to which people are able to achieve this, but he is right that they need to achieve it.

(2) *The need for identity* The concept of self-realization takes up and develops the Kantian idea of persons as ends in themselves. It recognizes that human beings need to have a sense of existing as persons in their own right, with a life of their own and with aims and ideas of their own. There are two important pre-conditions of this sense of identity. The first of these is the *need for recognition*. This is a major theme in Hegel's philosophy—the idea that the individual's consciousness of himself depends upon its being confirmed by others. It is through other people's responses to me, not necessarily positive or supportive responses, but at any rate reactions which take me seriously, that I have a sense of myself as an agent, as a distinct individual, as one whose actions make a difference in the world. This is a further element in the Hegelian stress on the social nature of the individual, and the theme is hinted at in Bradley's long quotation from Hegel (V.35-7). More recently writers on schizophrenia such as R. D. Laing have shown from empirical studies how the constant invalidating or ignoring of a person's actions and utterances, especially within the family, can quite literally produce a loss of any coherent sense of who one is, or of being a person, to the point of mental breakdown.

A second and closely-linked pre-condition of a sense of identity is the *need for self-expression through work*. This too is a point made by Hegel, and it is taken up and developed more extensively by Marx in his discussion of alienated labour. I shall look in the next chapter at Marx's idea that it is through their work on the world that human beings give objective expression to their own identity, in a public and visible form.

(3) *The need for activity* Closely connected with the previous point is the idea that human beings cannot derive full satisfaction from a life of purely passive enjoyment. Bradley says:

Is a *harmonious* life all that we want in practice? Certainly not. . . . It is no human ideal to lead 'the life of an oyster.' We have no right first to find out just what we happen to be and to have, and then to contract our wants to that limit. (II.44.)

Bradley is at one with Mill here. It is the striving for achievement, in activity which makes full use of our faculties, that makes life genuinely rewarding. Normally, other things being equal, as we acquire skills and talents we shall enjoy using them and want to use them—one can see this in the young child learning to crawl, to walk, to talk, and so on. This is the important insight to be retained from the idea of 'realizing one's potentialities'. As we saw earlier, that phrase does not tell us which potentialities to realize. What it does rightly emphasize, however, is that we need to realize *some* of our potentialities, and a substantial set of them at that. Certain kinds of life will make it impossible for us to do this; the life on the assembly line, working at screwing nuts on bolts, or the life of the full-time housewife washing dishes and changing nappies, is therefore likely to be intrinsically frustrating.

The use of the term 'frustrating' is crucial here. In the case of this, and of all the needs which the concept of self-realization points to, I want to suggest that they are genuine needs only because they are, ultimately, *felt* as needs. In this respect I am assimilating the ethics of self-realization to the ethics of Mill, who, it will be remembered, says that the higher pleasures are higher because, in the light of a full and complete experience of them, human beings will prefer them, and be more fully satisfied by them. I contrasted Mill's approach with the Aristotelian essentialist argument, that happiness as rationality is to be sought just because it is distinctively and essentially human. I am now suggesting that it is Mill's approach rather than Aristotle's that we should follow in looking for a viable element in the ethics of self-realization.

Now to say that needs, if they are to count as genuine needs, must be *felt* needs does not mean that they must be blatant and obvious. I do not necessarily mean that self-realization (or the various needs which make it up) is valuable only in so far as it is consciously and explicitly desired. In talking of 'felt needs' we need to recognize the existence of different levels of awareness, and the concealed ways in which needs can be experienced. In many cases, for example, people may think that they have everything they want, they may genuinely believe that they are content and happy, and yet may still feel a vague sense of malaise or frustration which they perhaps cannot explain. We need to recognize too the possibilities of self-deception in this area. People's awareness of their frustration may be manifested precisely by the ways in which they hide it from themselves. An example might be the phenomenon of 'keeping up with the Joneses', living for an endless succession of consumer goods, each of which is pursued as the one thing needed to make one's life complete. The immersion in the pursuit of the next commodity, and the fact that the acquisition of it is immediately succeeded by the emergence of a new desire, may function as a mechanism by which people avoid having to confront the overall nature of their life and its point-lessness. So in speaking of 'felt needs', we should have to draw on a subtle and sophisticated psychology, including the Freudian theory of the unconscious which we shall come to in Chapter 10. The fact remains that self-realization in its various forms can justifiably be regarded as a need only because, at some level or other, it is experienced as a need, and because the achieving of it is experienced as satisfaction.

This way of treating the concept of self-realization brings it closer to that of happiness. Bradley himself is not averse to making this connection. At the end of 'Pleasure for Pleasure's Sake' he says: 'We agree that happiness is the end; and therefore we say pleasure is not the end.' Similarly, at the end of the additional Note to that chapter, he allows that 'if "happiness" means well-being or perfection of life, then I am content to say that, with Plato and Aristotle, I hold happiness to be the end.' Mill likewise is concerned to bridge the gap between 'happiness' and 'self-realization' from the other side. Each concept has something to be said for it. Talking of 'happiness' stresses more firmly that the ultimate test of desirability is the appeal to experience. Talking of 'self-realization' emphasizes more clearly that the accumulation of superficial satisfactions may leave one's life incomplete. The danger with either concept is that it suggests too easily the idea of a single ultimate end, and the assumption that all human activity can be measured on a single scale, according to the degree to which it contributes to that end. There is no one commodity, happiness, which satisfies all human needs. Felt needs may be experienced as a feeling of unhappiness; but human beings also experience boredom, frustration, malaise, anxiety, insecurity, loneliness, emptiness, alienation, and meaninglessness. Possibly we could describe all these as different *forms* of unhappiness; that way of putting it would be appropriate in some cases, less so in others. But they are not all *synonyms* for a single state, unhappiness, varying only in intensity. They are experiences which point to a multiplicity of human needs. The concept of 'happiness' or that of 'self-realization' may equally serve as a *shorthand* to refer to the range of these needs, but neither concept should become a *substitute* for the recognition of their multiplicity.

Finally, having allowed something of a *rapprochement* between the concepts of 'happiness' and 'self-realization', we should remind ourselves of the two crucial ways in which Bradley's conception of self-realization differs from the utilitarian conception of happiness.

(a) Traditional utilitarianism employs an additive, cumulative conception of happiness. Whether one's life is happy is determined by putting together individual units of happiness, adding up experiences of pleasure and subtracting pains. Mill, we saw, breaks only tentatively with this conception. Bradley breaks with it decisively. The Hegelian vocabulary of 'organic unities' provides a clear alternative to the Benthamite vocabulary of addition and subtraction, and indicates effectively that self-realization has to do with the character of one's life as a whole.

(b) The two conceptions differ in where they locate relations to others. The utilitarian approach is to extend the concept of happiness, from the individual to the general happiness. The utilitarian starts with the idea that it is rational for the agent to pursue his/her own happiness, and then adds on, *externally*, the requirement that the agent must also aim at everyone else's happiness. For Bradley, commitments to others are *internal* to self-realization, because they are internal to the self.

Postscript to Part Two

The contrast I have stressed between the Ancients and the Moderns is that the latter place altruistic concern for others at the centre of their ethics. I have argued that Hume, Kant, and Mill fail to provide an adequate rational justification for this. Bradley fares better, by developing the ethical significance of social relations. The 'social relations' approach then leaves us with the question: can we justify not only specific concerns stemming from specific relations to others, but also a generalized humanitarianism—a concern for the needs of all human beings?

I shall return to this question in Chapter 11, but there are other problems which I want to look at first. Bradley has focused our attention on social relations, but in an idealized form. When confronted with the imperfection of existing social relations, he abandons the social realm altogether. I suggested that this is too hasty, and one of the tasks we have already set ourselves is to look at the problems of existing social relations in the light of the ideal of 'self-realization', or 'the fully human life'. In the next two chapters I shall look at some aspects of existing social institutions, their implications for human psychology, and their relevance for ethics. In doing so, I hope to throw further light also on the concept of self-realization.

Notes

1   A very valuable treatment of such matters is Bernard Williams's discussion of what he calls 'ground projects' in his article 'Persons, Character and Morality', especially pp. 207–15, in Amelie Oksenberg Rorty (ed.): *The Identities of Persons* (Berkeley, 1976).

PART III

Contemporary Themes

9 Ethics and Marxism

Reading: There is no one text which provides a com-
prehensive view of the Marxist approach to ethics,
but the two writings most useful for this chapter are:
Karl Marx: 'Alienated Labour' in *Economic and
Philosophical Manuscripts* of 1844;
Karl Marx and Friedrich Engels: *The German Ideology*
Part I. Another of the 1844 Manuscripts, on 'Private
Property and Communism', is also very relevant,
though rather difficult. All of these writings are
available in the following anthologies: *Karl Marx:
Selected Writings*, ed. David McLellan (Oxford),
1977; *The Marx–Engels Reader* (2nd edition), ed.
Robert C. Tucker (New York), 1978.
Part I of *The German Ideology* is incomplete in
McLellan but is supplemented with useful extracts
from Part II. Paragraph numbering in *The German
Ideology* is impossible because of the chaotic state
of the text and the variations between editions.
I shall therefore give all references, wherever possible,
as page numbers in McLellan and in Tucker (referred
to as 'M' and 'T' respectively).

Alienation and Self-realization

At this point an orthodox history of ethics would turn to
the consideration of twentieth-century academic moral
philosophy, beginning with the reaction against Hegelian
idealism in British universities at the turn of the century.
In Chapter 11, I shall look briefly at some of these develop-
ments. I have, however, already indicated in Chapter 1 that
I believe the ideas of Marx and Freud to be at least as important in developing further the Western ethical tradition,
and it is to them that I turn first. The claim for their importance is one which I shall have to make good in this chapter
and the next. Meanwhile, if some preliminary justification
is needed for looking at Marx, I can point to a straightforward historical continuity beteen Hegelian and Marxist

philosophy. As a student, Marx was strongly influenced by Hegel's philosophy, which was dominant in Germany in the years after Hegel's death. Then, in the early 1840s, Marx was closely associated with the Young Hegelian movement. Although he became strongly critical of Hegel's idealism, Marx remained, as he declared himself to be in *Capital*, 'the pupil of that mighty thinker' (M 420, T 302).

In his early writings Marx's most important debt to Hegel is his use of the concept of 'alienation'. This concept does not feature significantly in Bradley's version of Hegel, but is is central to one of Hegel's major works, *The Phenomenology of Mind*. Hegel uses it to refer to the way in which the products of reason or mind are not recognized by consciousness as its own creation, but rather are experienced as alien forces set over against consciousness. He applies it to ways of experiencing, for example, the products of physical work, the power of the state, the creation of wealth, and the remoteness of God. Since, for Hegel, the whole of reality is ultimately to be understood as the externalization of spirit, the final overcoming of alienation consists in the ascent of consciousness to the philosophical recognition of its unity with absolute spirit and therefore with all reality. Marx repudiates these idealist underpinnings of the concept, but employs it in a more concrete and empirical way to illuminate the experience of work, and especially of wage labour, which he takes to be the most fundamental form of alienation. His best treatment of the subject is in the early and incomplete essay 'Alienated Labour', one of the so-called *Economic and Philosophical Manuscripts* of 1844, which were not published until long after Marx's death, in the 1930s.

I said that Bradley makes no explicit use of the concept of 'alienation'. Nevertheless, coming to Marx from Bradley, we can usefully understand alienation as the obverse of self-realization. For Marx self-realization is located, above all, in the process by which human beings objectify themselves through their work. It is in work upon the world, in productive activity, that a human being affirms himself or herself as human.

Through it nature appears as his work and his reality. The object of work is therefore the objectification of the species-life of man; for he duplicates himself not only intellectually, in his mind, but also actively in reality and thus can look at his image in a world he has created. (M 82, T 76.)

When work has this character, when it is meaningful, creative, and self-expressive, it embodies the three aspects of self-realization which we noted in the previous chapter.[1] It constitutes the organizing centre of a person's life, it gives the individual a sense of his or her own identity, recognized and confirmed by others, and it calls forth his or her energies and capacities. Alienated labour lacks these qualities. It lacks them when it becomes simply the earning of a wage, with no intrinsic significance for the worker, an activity over which he has no say and into which he puts nothing of himself. Work takes on this character within an economic system based on private ownership of the means of production. Society is then divided into two main classes, those who own capital and therefore own the means of production, and those who own only their labour-power. For the latter, work must necessarily take the form of work for another, work for the capitalist, as a means of earning a wage. It is therefore alienated labour. Marx distinguishes four aspects of this alienation.

(i) The worker is alienated from his product. Quite literally, it does not belong to him, and its particular qualities are of no concern for him. He could be producing absolutely anything so long as it provided him with a wage.
(ii) He is alienated from his own productive activity. He has no control over that activity, it is not the expression of his own ideas and projects, it is something imposed on him, which he is simply ordered to perform. The extreme case of this is mechanized labour in the factory.
(iii) He is alienated from his species-being, that is, from those of his qualities which make him distinctively human. The human species is distinguished from other species by its capacity for free, conscious, and creative productive activity. Alienated labour reduces a human being to the level of an animal.
(iv) He is alienated from other human beings. When work is

simply the means to one's own individual wage, it does not have the significance of an activity shared with other human beings, in a co-operative project.

All of this is clearly and eloquently set out by Marx. I do not want to elaborate it, but rather to stress its continuity with the ethical tradition which we have been following. Not only does it take up and give a new emphasis to the Hegelian notion of self-realization. More generally, Marx offers an account of that ideal of the 'fully human life' which we have found to be the continuing theme in Plato and Aristotle, Kant and Mill, as well as in Hegelian ethics. Like them, Marx has a view of those activities and capacities which are distinctively human, and asserts that a life which gives full play to these is the best kind of life for human beings. His predecessors had all, in one way or another, picked out the possession of intellect, the capacity for conscious and rational thought, as the distinctive feature of human beings. Marx partly concurs, but with a new emphasis. What is essential is not just consciousness, but the capacity for conscious work, conscious vital activity. By 'vital activity' Marx means that activity which the human species or any other species engages in to maintain its own life. In the distinctive character of this 'vital activity' we can see the distinctive character of the species. Marx spells this out in the important passage (M 81–2, T 75–6) where he talks about man as a 'species-being', i.e. a being which is conscious of belonging to a certain species (a notion which he takes from Feuerbach).

Human beings are distinguished from other species by their capacity to distance themselves from their vital activity, to think about it and adapt it to varying purposes, and to assess it in accordance with standards and principles. And it is this capacity that is thwarted in the condition of alienation.

I distinguished in earlier chapters between two kinds of ethical appeal to human nature: the essentialist argument of Aristotle, that certain activities ought to be engaged in, just because they are distinctively human, and the empirical approach of Mill, according to whom the reason why human beings ought to engage in such activities, is that they will be frustrated and dissatisfied if they fail to make full use of their capacities. In the passage on man as species-being, Marx may seem to incline towards Aristotle's essentialism, but on the whole his position is, like Mill's, empirically grounded. This is particularly clear in the following passage:

What does the externalization of labour consist of then? Firstly, that labour is exterior to the worker, that is, it does not belong to his essence. Therefore he does not confirm himself in his work, he denies himself, feels miserable instead of happy, deploys no free physical and intellectual energy, but mortifies his body and ruins his mind. Thus the worker only feels a stranger. He is at home when he is not working and when he works he is not at home. His labour is therefore not voluntary but compulsory, forced labour. It is therefore not the satisfaction of a need but only a means to satisfy needs outside itself. How alien it really is is very evident from the fact that when there is no physical or other compulsion, labour is avoided like the plague. External labour in which man externalizes himself, is a labour of self-sacrifice and mortification. . . . The result we arrive at then is that man (the worker) only feels himself freely active in his animal functions of eating, drinking, and procreating, at most also in his dwelling and dress, and feels himself an animal in his human functions. (M 80–1, T 74.)

Marx's critique of alienated labour is here firmly based on the facts of how such labour is actually experienced.

If Marx is to rely on empirical rather than essentialist arguments, he must provide empirical grounds for the claim that work is so important for self-realization. It is not enough to appeal to the fact that the nature of their work distinguishes human beings from other species. Why, then, is the quality of people's work crucial to their experience of the quality of their lives as a whole? Marx does not have clear answers but, building on his account, we can suggest some considerations. There is, first, the sheer quantitative dominance of work in relation to other activities. The work which people do to maintain themselves and their dependents engages a great deal of their time, and because it bulks so large it does more than anything else to shape the general character of their lives. Then there is its inescapability. Other activities which people perform are largely a matter of individual choice, but work is the one activity which almost all human beings (other than the young, the old, or the excessively privileged) have to perform in order to maintain themselves. For this reason too it forms the common core of people's lives, which sets the pattern for their general character. Finally, there is the fact that people's work is the most clearly public aspect of their lives. It is their work above all that defines them in the eyes of others—and I have stressed previously the importance of being recognized by others as an aspect of self-realization. Putting all of this together, we can say that what you are is primarily a matter of what you do, and what you do is primarily a matter of what work you perform. This is not to deny that people whose work is boring and soul-destroying may, in their spare time, pursue all sorts of intensely absorbing leisure activities, and that their doing so may be absolutely essential to their overall happiness. The fact remains, however, that these activities do indeed belong to 'spare time', that they are peripheral, and can at best compensate for the central experience of alienated work. For these reasons, then, Marx can claim that his theory of alienated labour is not just one particular application of the concept of self-realization, but that it identifies the crucial and essential features of the fully human life.

It may be objected that the reasons just given for making work so central are, in fact, historically transitory. It may be argued that with increasing automation the production of material necessities requires less and less labour time, and that there is a real prospect that in the future people may need to devote only a small portion of their time to their work. Marx himself looks forward to the shortening of the working day, as the pre-condition for the human ascent from the realm of necessity to the realm of freedom (T 441). It is difficult to predict what the realistic possibilities are in this area. I would suggest, however, that even if the average working day were halved (a prospect which seems to be still largely confined to utopian speculations about the future), work would still play a large part in people's organization of their time, quite apart from the other reasons I have given for its centrality. More telling, perhaps, is the objection that work has, historically, been given its present quantitative and qualitative importance only in modern industrial societies;

that in non-industrial societies both past and present, working time has been kept to a minimum, and the socially shared activities to which the greatest value has been attached have been quite other than those of work.[2] Again I am unsure of the facts here. It may be that the need for self-realization through work is indeed historically and culturally specific. Even so it can still be maintained, at the very least, that within our own society the need is a real and objective one. The idea that one's work determines one's identity, and the stimulus to invest one's energies in that work, are so deeply embedded in our culture that no one could now find full satisfaction in a life which did not contain its component of meaningful work.

How, then, is this need to be satisfied? How is the alienation of labour to be overcome? Here we are brought to Marx's second decisive innovation in our understanding of the fully human life. If the first was the insistence that the quality of work is central to self-realization, the second innovation is the claim that self-realization through work can be made possible only by a radical change in the economic structure of society. The essay on 'Alienated Labour' diagnoses alienation as being inextricably linked with the existence of private property in the means of production. 'If the product of labour does not belong to the worker but stands over against him as an alien power, this is only possible in that it belongs to another man apart from the worker' (M 84, T 78). Consequently, work can lose its alienated character only when the means of production are brought under the ownership and control of the workers themselves. Only then can work be experienced by the workers as the putting into effect of their own communally formulated projects and aspirations. Only then can it be experienced as an activity in which each individual finds his own identity confirmed by others in a shared enterprise. This vision of communism as the overcoming of alienation is further elaborated in the 1844 manuscript on 'Private Property and Communism' (and it goes without saying that the vision is markedly different from the reality of any of the 'communist' societies presently in existence[3]). Once again we can bring out the significance of Marx's account by comparing it with Bradley's. We saw that Bradley argues that self-realization depends on the social nature of the individual, but then, recognizing the imperfection of existing social relations, he asserts that full self-realization must take us beyond the limits of social life. Marx agrees with Bradley that 'it is above all necessary to avoid restoring society as a fixed abstraction opposed to the individual. The individual is the social being' (M 91, T 86, in 'Private Property and Communism', which is good on this). But Marx's response to the imperfections of existing society is to assert that human self-realization requires changed social relations. It requires the abolition of private property in the means of production, it requires that form of communism in which individuals can fully and authentically experience their existence as social beings.

Morality as Ideology

So far I have been reading Marx as having a positive ethical theory which places him within the broad tradition of Western ethical philosophy. That interpretation, however, comes up against a major obstacle, and the obstacle is Marx's theory of history. I am not going to set out the theory in full. That is admirably done by Marx and Engels themselves in Part 1 of *The German Ideology*. I shall focus on the problem which the theory poses for the idea of a Marxist ethics. The problem is revealed in passages such as the following:

We set out from real, active men, and on the basis of their real life-process we demonstrate the development of the ideological reflexes and echoes of this life-process. The phantoms formed in the human brain are also, necessarily, sublimates of their material life-process, which is empirically verifiable and bound to material premises. Morality, religion, metaphysics, all the rest of ideology and their corresponding forms of consciousness, thus no longer retain the semblance of independence. They have no history, no development; but men, developing their material production and their material intercourse, alter, along with this their real existence, their thinking and the products of their thinking. Life is not determiend by consciousness, but consciousness by life. (M 164, T 154.)

This seems to deny morality or ethics any independent

rational status. The assumption behind ethical thought is that human beings are capable of distinguishing between better and worse kinds of life, better and worse kinds of society, and are capable of acting to change their lives and their society. Marx and Engels seem to imply that this is impossible, that society changes only under the impact of economic necessity and that ethical and moral ideas are mere 'reflexes and echoes', rationalizations of changes which are already under way.

Let us see if we can make any progress towards the resolution of the problem by examining more closely the position which Marx and Engels take in this and the preceding paragraph. Note first that, though they are not entirely clear on this, they seem to distinguish between 'ideas' or 'consciousness' in general, and 'ideology' as a specific kind of consciousness. It is ideology that is said to be a mere 'reflex' and 'echo', a 'phantom' and 'sublimate'. Consciousness in general, on the other hand, though it too is said to be necessarily linked to men's 'real life-process', is not given this merely derivative status. What is said, rather, is that 'the production of ideas, of conceptions, of consciousness, is at first *directly interwoven* with the material activity and the material intercourse of men' (my italics), and that 'consciousness can never be anything else than conscious existence'. Up to a point we can compare what Marx and Engels are saying here with the view which we found in Bradley. Like Bradley, they maintain that 'consciousness is . . . from the very beginning a social product, and remains so as long as men exist at all' (M 167, T 158). Like Bradley, they suggest that the social character of consciousness follows from its being embodied in language. 'Language is as old as consciousness, language is practical consciousness that exists also for other men, and for that reason alone it really exists for me personally as well; language, like consciousness, only arises from the need, the necessity, of intercourse with other men'. (Ibid.) Marx and Engels, however, emphasize more strongly than Bradley the interconnection of consciousness and activity. It is not that human beings are born and brought up in a society, acquire a language and with it a system of concepts, and *then* are able to apply these to their life and activity. Rather, learning the concepts of a language, and learning to engage in the activities in which these are used, are inseparable aspects of one and the same process.[4]

There is no suggestion, then, that consciousness as such is necessarily illusory and derivative. That is true only of ideology as a particular kind of consciousness. In a letter written much later, Engels defined ideology in this way:

Ideology is a process accomplished by the so-called thinker consciously, it is true, but with a false consciousness. The motive forces impelling him remain unknown to him; otherwise it simply would not be an ideological process. Hence he imagines false or seeming motive forces. Because it is a process of thought he derives its form as well as its content from pure thought, either his own or that of his predecessors. He works with mere thought material, which he accepts without examination as the product of thought, and does not investigate further for a more remote source independent of thought. (Letter to Franz Mehring, 14 July 1893, T. 766.)

The three distinguishing features of ideology, then, are: (a) it is *false* consciousness; (b) it is the product of motives which remain unrecognized by the thinker himself; (c) it is mistakenly supposed by the thinker to be the product of pure thought. In other words, whereas all consciousness is inseparably interwoven with material life, ideology typically conceals this interweaving.

This is still rather obscure, but I think we can begin to make some sense of it if, guided by it, we look for some ideological components in moral systems and beliefs. Consider, for example, Marx's frequent attacks on the ideological equation of freedom with 'free trade', 'free competition', and the supposedly 'free contract' between worker and employer (e.g. *Communist Manifesto* M 233, T 486; *Grundrisse* M 372; *Capital* M 455, T 343). Here we have all the distinctive features of ideology. It is, in the first place, a 'false' consciousness in the straightforward sense of being a hopelessly distorted view of the real nature of freedom. Not only is it, as Marx says, an 'absurdity' to regard free competition and the like as 'the final development of human liberty'; far from exhausting the concept of freedom, they do not genuinely qualify as instances of freedom at all, for the individuals engaged in such activities (for instance, the worker who makes a contract of employment) are constrained by economic forces which leave them little or no real choice. Second, this ideological view of freedom is the product of concealed motives. Its function is to legitimate the unrestrained competition and exploitation in a capitalist economy by dignifying it with the honorific title of 'freedom'. This leads directly to the third feature. The ideology of 'free competition' and 'free contract' is presented as the application of a timeless universal ideal of freedom, the product of pure thought, whereas it is in reality a product of, and a rationalization of, very specific historical and social conditions.

Examples of ideology are to be found not only, as here, in popular moral discourse, but also in the thought of the moral philosophers. In an interesting passage on Kant in *The German Ideology*, Marx and Engels see his moral philosophy as a reflection of the backwardness of the German middle class, in comparison with its English, French, and Dutch counterparts. Liberal ideas, when they spread to Germany, did so in advance of the material conditions to which they corresponded, and therefore found their natural expression in Kant's *a priori* ethics, abstracted from any consideration of empirical consequences and inclinations. It is in this light that we are to understand Kant's treatment of 'autonomy', 'respect for persons', and 'the kingdom of ends' as formal principles of reason rather than as concrete organizing principles of social life.

Compare this with Marx's and Engels's comments on Bentham. As a representative of the more advanced English middle class, Bentham's ethical theory is more securely rooted than Kant's in the empirical realities of material life. For that very reason it is a cruder and more direct expression of capitalist economic relations.

The apparent stupidity of merging all the manifold relationships of people in the one relation of usefulness, this apparently metaphysical abstraction arises from the fact that, in modern bourgeois society, all relations are subordinated in practice to the one abstract monetary-commercial relation. (*The German Ideology*, M 185).

Bentham's egoistic theory of human nature, in which each

individual is related to others solely as means to his own utility, exactly reflects bourgeois social relations of mutual exploitation. Marx and Engels see this as a classic case of ideology rationalizing historically specific social phenomena as universal truths.

one sees at a glance that the category of 'utilization' is first of all abstracted from the actual relations of intercourse which I have with other people (but by no means from reflection and mere will) and then these relations are made out to be the reality of the category that has been abstracted from them themselves, a wholly metaphysical method of procedure. (M 186.)

We could find further examples of ideology in the other philosophers we have dealt with in this book. Consider, for example, Plato's and Aristotle's contempt for manual work (e.g. *Republic* 590b), their assumption that it can have no value as an activity in its own right, and that the highest human activity is that of leisured contemplation. Or consider Aristotle's depiction of the 'great-souled' man's preoccupation with the proper observance of social distinctions; or his assertion that women and slaves are by nature born to be subordinate. All of these we can see as the self-legitimating attitudes of a male, slave-owning aristocracy, presented in the guise of permanent human values. Hume's automatic equation of justice with the protection of private property is likewise distinctive of a class which maintains itself through its ownership of the means of production, rather than through its own labour. Or consider Bradley's previously-noted elision of all social relations into the relation of the citizen to the state, and his consequent glorification of patriotic self-sacrifice. These features of Bradley's ethics are more an unacknowledged reflection of late Victorian imperialism than a product of rational argument.

With such examples we can make sense of, and see the force of, the Marxist concept of 'ideology'. We have not yet, however, solved our original problem. So far we have picked out, as examples of moral ideology, specific elements of moral theories. The implication of this procedure is that other elements of these moral theories are untainted with ideology—that within Plato's, or Aristotle's, or Kant's, or any other major moral theory, we can distinguish between ideological and non-ideological components. Our problem is, however, that Marx asserts *all* morality, morality *as such*, to be ideology.

One possible and widely maintained interpretation of this assertion would be to understand Marx as holding a positivist theory of knowledge—holding, that is, that the only authentic knowledge is science, understood as the purely neutral description and explanation of natural and social phenomena. On this view all value-judgements would be regarded as non-scientific and, as such, ideological. There are indeed occasions when Marx and Engels do appear (though never unambiguously) to maintain such a position. They sometimes seem to assert, for example, that their theory of communism is not intended as an account of a better, more desirable society, but simply a neutral scientific prediction of the direction in which history is inexorably tending. An example is the statement in *The German Ideology* that

Communism is for us not a state of affairs which is to be established, an ideal to which reality will have to adjust itself. We call communism the real movement which abolishes the present state of things. (M 171, T 162.)

A more extended example is Engels's later work *Socialism Utopian and Scientific,* which is as pervasively ambiguous as I take the above quotation to be. Now certainly such passages *can* be read in a positivist way. But such a reading does not, I think, do justice to the overall character of Marx's thought, not only that of his early writings, but also his later works. Consider the following passage from Volume I of *Capital.*

Within the capitalist system all methods for raising the social productiveness of labour are brought about at the cost of the individual labourer; all means for the development of production transform themselves into means of domination over, and exploitation of, the producers; they mutilate the labourer into a fragment of a man, degrade him to the level of an appendage of a machine, destroy every remnant of charm in his work and turn it into a hated toil; they estrange from him the intellectual potentialities of the labour process in the same proportion as science is incorporated in it as an independent power; they distort the conditions under which he works, subject him during the labour process to a despotism the more hateful for its meanness; they transform his lifetime into working-time, and drag his wife and child beneath the wheels of the Juggernaut of capital. (Ch. XXV, Section 4, M 482-3, T 430.)

This is hardly a neutral description. On the other hand it is not a merely incidental and self-indulgent passage of rhetoric. It is central to Marx's analysis of capitalism. He is here stating what he calls 'the general law of capitalist accumulation', and his analysis is essentially an analysis of capitalism as exploitation. *Capital* is both a scientific analysis and a critical evaluation of the workings of a capitalist economy, and the two aspects are inseparable. It hardly seems plausible, then, to attribute to Marx the view that science excludes all evaluation and that value-judgements are therefore intrinsically ideological.

A second possible interpretation of Marx is what we can call the relativist interpretation.[5] On this view all value-judgements reflect the interests and perspective of a particular class, and as such are ideological. Marx is indeed committed to a critical evaluation of the capitalist economy, but this is because he analyses it from the standpoint of the proletariat. His condemnation of it reflects the interests of the proletariat. From the standpoint of a different class, a different evaluation would be appropriate. But there is no objective standpoint, independent of classes, from which a rationally objective value-judgement could be arrived at, on this or on anything else. Hence the characterization of all morality as ideology.

Once again there is evidence to support this interpretation, though less in Marx than in Engels (cf. the latter's *Anti-Duhring* Part 1, Ch. IX, T 725-7). Once again, however, it fails to do justice to the representative passage which I quoted from *Capital*. That passage certainly reads as an objective condemnation of capitalism, not just an appeal to the values of a particular class. And quite generally Marx identifies the cause of proletarian emancipation with that of human emancipation. The society which he envisages for the future would be in the interests not just of the proletariat, but of human beings in general, it would be the kind of society most capable of satisfying general human needs. Certainly Marx recognizes that not everyone in capitalist society can be expected to welcome its demise. Individual members of the bourgeoisie may recognize the objective grounds for the creation of a different kind of society, but in general the bourgeoisie as a class is bound to resist it, since it is contrary to its most immediate and obvious economic interests. Nevertheless, the fact remains that the society which Marx envisages would be, in his view, a society which would satisfy the essential human needs of everyone.

Where then do we go from here, if neither the positivist nor the relativist solution seems adequate? The most promising answer seems to me to be that suggested by Anthony Skillen in his recent book *Ruling Illusions*. Here is his statement of the problem, and his proposed solution:

Marx spoke with contempt of morality, is said to have burst out laughing at the mention of the word, and claimed (in *The German Ideology*) 'the Communists preach no morality at all'. Yet it is obvious that Marx knew capitalism to be a vicious social order, at best transitionally necessary, in favourable conditions to be overthrown and replaced by a better one, socialism, which would in turn evolve into communist society. Most commentators have seen inconsistency here. . . . but it is possible to see that Marx's condemnation of capitalism is quite consistent with his contempt for morality. . . . Marx appears to have had a quite specific conception of morality; he did not see the term generically as embracing the 'norms and values' of any historical society. For him, morality was an historically fairly specific ideological institution, functioning to mystify and discipline people in accordance with the oppressive needs of class society.[6]

In other words, morality is not to be equated with just any kind of evaluation. It is a specific mode of evaluative discourse, defined not so much by its content but rather, Skillen suggests, by its characteristic psychological form or structure, and it is this structure that makes it intrinsically ideological. This intepretation cannot, I think, be unequivocally offered as 'what Marx really meant', for Marx himself is simply not sufficiently explicit or consistent for that. It does, however, seem to me to be the position which can best do justice to Marx's most important insights, and work them into a coherent form. In elaborating it further I draw heavily on Skillen's discussion, though with the usual proviso that what I say is not to be taken as a reliable guide to his views; the reader is urged to consult them directly.

What are the specific features of morality which distinguish it from other modes of evaluation and make it essentially ideological? Three features seem to be crucial.

(a) Morality is premissed on the assumption of individual responsibility. It addresses itself to the individual, focuses on individual actions, and requires the individual to improve his or her life through his or her own individual efforts. The moral response to the problem of alienation, for example, would be to say: You ought to live a less alienated life, you ought to engage in meaningful and creative work, you ought to develop your talents and capacities more than you do at present. This kind of moral injunction, calling on individuals to change themselves so as to live a more worthwhile life, ignores the objective conditions which preclude such a life. It ignores the pressure of existing social relations; if the prevailing economic relations are such that work is predominantly wage-labour, over which individuals have no effective control, then I cannot make it more fulfilling and creative simply by my own individual willing. It ignores the pressure of sheer physical needs. I could perhaps decide to develop my talents and devote myself to something worthwhile, by working at the making of hand-carved furniture or the writing of lyric poetry, but if in so doing I deprive myself of the means of physical survival, that is no real option. I could enrich my life by cultivating harmonious and living relationships with everyone around me, but if I thereby do myself out of a job in a competitive economy, and reduce myself to poverty or starvation, I shall be that much less capable of having fruitful relationships with anyone. In short, the necessary condition for a worthwhile life may be not action by individuals to change themselves, but collective action to change existing social structures. Moreover, this collective action for social change may have to violate precisely those values which are eventually to be realized in the new society. In order to create a society in which all individuals can be respected as autonomous persons, putting into effect 'the categorical imperative to overthrow all circumstances in which man is humiliated, enslaved, abandoned, and despised' (M 69, T 60), it may be necessary to take political action which does *not* respect all persons as ends in themselves, for it may be necessary to use violence and coercion against the guardians and beneficiaries of the existing exploitative and depersonalizing society. Thus the morality of 'respect for persons', addressing itself to the actions of individuals, may be one of the principal obstacles to the political creation of a world in which persons enjoy authentic respect.

(b) Morality is further defined by its alienated character. It is typically expressed as a set of external requirements to which the individual must conform. The classic formulation of this is the idea of morality as *law*, as that which must be *obeyed*. Kant's moral philosophy epitomizes this aspect of morality, with its talk of 'the moral law', and of 'commands' or 'imperatives' which typically oppose themselves to our inclinations. We have seen that there is another side to Kant's ethics, that the moral law is not for him purely external, but is also something which we ourselves legislate in our capacity as rational beings. In this too, however, he is faithful to the idea of morality. If morality were *purely* external it would not be morality (but rather social pressure, or law in the strict sense). Morality is thought of as an inner voice, the voice of our own conscience, and yet at the same time a voice which speaks with an external authority, and commands us to obey. Thus 'Kant's dualism powerfully reflects and firmly captures key elements in the prevailing idea of what morality is, and especially the sense . . . that a distinctly Moral appeal is an appeal that is from within, yet from outside, and yet again from above' (Skillen, p. 138). In the next chapter we shall look more closely at the psychological mechanisms that are involved here.

This aspect of morality helps to explain Marx's frequent description of all ideology as an *inversion* of reality, his claim that 'in all ideology men and their circumstances appear upside-down as in a *camera obscura*' (*German Ideology*, M 164, T 154). He derives this language of 'inversion' from Feuerbach's theory of religion. According to Feuerbach the idea of a divine being is derived from the essential attributes of human beings, but these qualities are then projected into the beyond as attributes of an alien being who stands over and above human life. Marx retains this view of religion, but adds that this religious self-alienation must be further explained by the actual social conditions which give rise to it; 'that the secular basis detaches itself from itself and establishes itself as an independent realm in the clouds can only be explained by the cleavages and self-contradictions within this secular basis' (*Theses on Feuerbach* M 157, T 144). The Feuerbachian view of religion as a topsy-turvy mirror image of the real world serves Marx as a model for ideology in general, and morality qualifies as ideology partly because it shares this feature. The real needs and strivings by which human beings are exercised, the actual social relations which form the content of their lives, are transformed by morality into other-worldly ideals, and in this estranged form they then exact obedience. For example, the concrete relations of co-operation, of solidarity, and of love in which people are involved, and by which they are sustained in their daily lives, are transformed by morality into an abstract ethics of altruism, of unselfishness, which then, as an external demand, requires of them an irrational self-sacrifice and self-impoverishment.

(c) The third feature of morality follows closely upon this and helps to explain it. Morality presupposes what Marx calls 'the illusory community'. Morality is typically thought of as defined by its requirement of altruism. (Whenever I have asked people for an example of a morally good action, they have invariably replied: 'Helping an old lady across the road.') Why is this? Marx stresses the divisive nature of capitalist social relations, which separate people from one another in antagonistic and competitive ways. They set class against class, and they engender conflict within classes. Within the capitalist class economic competition holds sway. Within the professional middle class, competitive career structures keep people upon the road of individual ambition and self-advancement. Members of the working class are compelled to compete with one another for scarce jobs. However, if a capitalist society is to maintain itself as a viable social order, limits must be set to this divisiveness. 'Just because individuals seek only their particular interest, which for them does not coincide with their communal interest, the latter will be imposed on them as an interest "alien" to them, and "independent" of them, as in its turn a particular, peculiar "general" interest; . . . the practical struggle of these particular interests, which constantly really run counter to the communal and illusory communal interests, makes practical intervention and control necessary through the illusory "general" interest in the form of the State' (*German Ideology* M 170, T 161). Marx stresses particularly the role of the state here, but the morality of abstract altruism plays an equally vital role. Skillen describes that role eloquently.

Our society divides people up and presents this atomisation as the human condition; it pits them into competition with each other and calls this human nature; it demands the suppression of impulses and calls these humanity's enemy. Deficient in positive bonds, society, and even the lives of individuals, need to be held together and prevented from erupting into chaotic orgies of decadence and violence by external and internal police. If the state is God's march on earth, morality is his parade in the spirit. In the absence of positive cooperative ties and positive motives to work and create, the capitalist system requires 'specialist' forces of control, armed men and harsh consciences, bullies to make us do what money alone cannot bride us to do.[7]

But this 'general interest' imposed by the state and by morality is a spurious general interest. Since its function is to sustain in being a particular social order, it is in reality the interest of a particular class, that class which benefits from the existing social order. Consequently, the members of other classes who are exploited or oppressed by that social order have no rational grounds for sacrificing themselves to this spurious general interest. This is not to say that Marx counter-poses to the morality of altruism an attitude of egoism. The appropriateness of either altruism or egoism depends upon the real and specific nature of people's relations with one another. Marx looks to the possibility of a system of social relations which would overcome the dichotomy of egoism and altruism—not, of course, to the elimination of all conflicts between people, but to an authentically communal social life, based on shared work, which would no longer have pervasive antagonisms built into its very structure, and would therefore no longer require an abstract and external morality to counteract them. In the absence of such a society, egoistic and 'immoral' behaviour may sometimes be the only rationally appropriate response.

> The communists do not preach morality at all. . . . They do not put to people the moral demand: love one another, do not be egoists, etc; on the contrary, they are very well aware that egoism, just as much as self-sacrifice, is in definite circumstances a necessary form of the self-assertion of individuals. . . . They know that this contradiction [between general interest and private interest] is only a seeming one because one side of it, the so-called 'general', is constantly being produced by the other side, private interest. . . . Hence it is not a question of the Hegelian 'negative unity' of two sides of a contradiction, but of the materially determined destruction of the preceding materially determined mode of life of individuals, with the disappearance of which this contradiction together with its unity also disappears. (*German Ideology* M 183.)

The Limits of Amoralism

The above account is, I think, not only the best interpretation of Marx but also a substantially correct criticism of the traditional conception of morality. This is not to say that we have to jettison all previous morality, still less all previous moral philosophy. The ethical thought of Plato, Aristotle, and Hume is not on the whole cast in the form of a 'morality' in the narrow sense. The theories of Kant, Mill, and Bradley do perhaps have a more distinctively moral character, but this still does not imply, of course, that if we are convinced by the critique of morality, we have to abandon everything in Kant, Mill, and Bradley. What it may imply is that we need to recast it in a non-moral form, as a theory of the human good rather than specifically a theory of morality.

It may be thought that Marx understands the term 'morality' in too narrow a sense. It may be said that what he attacks is just one particular conception of morality, and that it is a mistake on his part to present the critique as an attack on morality in general. So it may be that we need to hang on to the idea of 'morality', while interpreting it in a wider sense. The crucial question here is not the pragmatic question of whether we can successfully detach the word 'morality' from its narrow associations, and give it a larger meaning, but the more substantial question of whether, if we were to abandon the concept, we would be in danger of missing something important. I think that there are such dangers, and I think that they can be brought out by the following quotation from Lenin. Lenin's major claim to fame is his having been one of the leaders of the first successful Marxist-inspired revolution, but he also wrote extensively on all aspects of Marxist theory including philosophy, and the following quotation is from a speech on communist ethics addressed to a Congress of the Russian Young Communist League:

We reject any morality based on extra-human and extra-class concepts. . . . We say that our morality is entirely subordinated to the interests of the proletariat's class struggle. Our morality stems from the interests of the class struggle of the proletariat. . . . Morality is what serves to destroy the old exploiting society and to unite all the working people around the proletariat, which is building up a new, a communist society. Communist morality is that which serves this struggle and unites the working people against all exploitation. . . .[8]

I doubt whether the position which Lenin formulates here is one which Marx would endorse. Moreover, it is not so much a repudiation of morality, but rather a radical redefinition of it. Nevertheless, it will serve us as an example with which to sound some cautions about the rejection of morality.

(i) Lenin says nothing about what justifies the class struggle of the proletariat to create a new society. If morality is 'subordinated to' and 'derived from' that struggle, then the justification for the struggle cannot itself be a justification from the standpoint of morality. Yet it certainly stands in need of some justification. Even if the struggle to create a new society is justified simply as being in the interests of the proletariat, something needs to be said about the nature of those interests, for their nature is not self-evident. If they are taken to be simply basic physical needs, for food, clothing, shelter, etc., then they would certainly furnish a case for the creation of a new society, but it could also be argued that, at least for some sections of the proletariat, an advanced capitalist society could satisfy those needs just as effectively.

If, on the other hand, the interests of the proletariat are also taken to include needs for meaningful unalienated work and free all-round development, this would not only strengthen the case for a new society but might also lead to a very different idea of the form the society ought to take. Marx however does not, I have claimed, want to justify the creation of a communist society simply as being in the interests of the proletariat. He sees such a society as being one which would most effectively satisfy the needs of human beings in general, so that the struggle for proletarian emancipation is the struggle for human emancipation. Such a claim all the more clearly has to be backed up by a theory of human needs and interests.

Now the danger of simply replacing the idea of morality with the idea of politics, or of subordinating the former to the latter, is that any such justification may then be forgone. We may then end up with the idea of a commitment to a political cause as an entirely arbitrary, non-rational commitment. One would then have to say that one just happened to be committed to the struggle for a communist society (or a fascist society, or whatever), either as a result of one's class position or the quirks of one's individual psychology, that one's own and other people s actions could be assessed solely according to whether they furthered this struggle, and that the struggle itself could not be rationally assessed, justified, or criticized. Such a conception of politics, as entirely autonomous and non-rational, would be a debased conception.

(ii) The rational justification of a political struggle not only has to show that that struggle will create a better society. It also has to show that individual agents are rationally justified in participating in such a struggle. I distinguished previously between the individual action on which morality focuses, and the collective action which is needed to create a better society. That distinction is vital, but it is also true that collective action is itself ultimately composed of the actions of individuals. Certainly, individuals who act collectively are acting very differently from how they would act if they acted simply as individuals. Nevertheless, any justification of collective action must, in the end, justify it to the individuals who are to engage in it. Thus, even when it is shown that collective political action could create a society in which all human beings enjoyed free, satisfying, and meaningful lives, the individual agent might still legitimately ask: 'What is that to me?' The question may well be answerable, and the answer does not have to be an egoistic one. It may be answered by pointing out that even though that particular individual may never enjoy the fruits of the struggle, his or her children may do so; or by appealing to his or her identity as a member of a certain social group or class, with ties of loyalty to that group; or by appealing to a generalized humanitarianism on his or her part (and in this book we have still to consider how rational a justification that would be). But *some* such justification must be forthcoming. Decisions ultimately are made by individual human beings (whether in isolation or in co-operation with others), and morality's emphasis on individual responsibility, misstated though it may be, draws attention to this inescapable fact.

That fact has a further important corollary. Political change takes time, fundamental changes in a social structure can be brought about only by continuing action over many decades, and a political movement whose ultimate success may be highly desirable from the point of view of humanity in general may have a less compelling claim on those individuals who will not live to see that eventual success. The individual agent may quite rationally say something like this: 'I accept that this struggle for social change will eventually, if successful, enable future generations to live more worthwhile and satisfying lives. But its outcome is uncertain, and my own participation in the struggle, though it might be of some assistance, could make only a slight difference one way or the other. Meanwhile I have my own life to live, I have my own more immediate commitments to those around me, I have my own work to do, in which I can achieve something more directly. I have to make sense of my own life, here and now, not in some future world which I shall never know.' Now there may not necessarily be this dichotomy between what is of immediate personal significance

and the claims of a long-term political struggle. One's relationship to a historically developing social movement may be
a vital element in one's overall conception of one's own life.
Moreover, some political movements have consciously set
out to overcome the division between the personal and the
political, by searching for forms of action which will combine long-term effectiveness with a more immediate personal
significance for the lives of the participants (certain tendencies
in the contemporary feminist movement are an example).
Nevertheless, the dichotomy is a possible one, and it arises
from the fact that political action which is justified from
a political perspective may not thereby be automatically
justified from the standpoint of the individual agents who
have to decide what to do. However limited individual
action may be, it *can* have *some* effect in making one's
life more worthwhile and fulfilling, and in some cases this
possibility may take precedence over the demands of the
need for political change.

(iii) Returning to the quotation from Lenin, we notice
further that by subordinating morality to the struggle of the
proletariat for a new society, he rules out the idea that
distinctively moral considerations might be relevant to the
question of what methods should be adopted in that struggle.
The implication is that anything goes, that absolutely any
means may be adopted, provided that they will lead to the
ultimate success of the struggle. One way in which the
relation between morality and politics has traditionally been
conceived is that, however admirable the goals of a political
movement may be, there are certain moral constraints on
the means which may be adopted in pursuit of those goals.
On such a view it might be said, for example, that a desirable
political end may not be pursued by the large-scale infliction
of suffering and death on innocent human beings. Lenin is
bound to repudiate such a view, and to subscribe instead to
the principle in which the repudiation of it has traditionally
been formulated, the principle that *the end justifies the
means*. For Lenin, on the strength of the above quotation,
this would imply that the only question to be raised about
the means to be adopted in the political struggle would be

whether they will lead to the success of the struggle. This would logically commit him to the view (which I certainly do not want actually to ascribe to him) that if, by initiating a war which would wipe out half of humanity, we could ensure that socialism would be adopted by the remnants of human civilization, we would be justified in doing so.

One way of refurbishing the principle that the end justifies the means, so as to avoid this kind of conclusion, would be to say that the relevant end to be considered is not the intermediate political end of creating a certain kind of social structure, but the underlying human end, the satisfaction of human needs, and the elimination of human suffering. The principle would then amount to the statement of a utilitarian standard: all means are to be assessed in terms of their promotion of that underlying end of human well-being. On this view, if it can be shown that a certain kind of political change will, in the long run, contribute enormously to that aim, then such action will be justified even if, in the short term, the measures involved in the upheavals of revolution may produce a temporary increase in suffering. The trauma of revolutionary violence and coercion will then be justified by the eventual amelioration of the human condition. But such an end will not, of course, justify measures so harsh and extreme that the suffering they involve outweighs the eventual good to be achieved. Consequently, certain kinds of political means may indeed be ruled out (as in our imaginary example above).

This reinterpretation of the principle that the end justifies the means changes if from an absurdity to a highly plausible principle. Its plausibility is the plausibility of utilitarianism, and those Marxists who have defended it (such as Trotsky, the other great leader of the Russian Revolution) have in effect been defending utilitarianism. This, however, still leaves us with problems, as I hope that my Chapter 7 will have shown. Consider, for example, the criticism discussed there that utilitarianism fails to recognize the ethical significance of specific social relations. Consideration of these may be relevant to the question of political means. Certain kinds of political methods, employing violence, coercion, and deception, will thereby involve the violation of relations of trust and co-operation. It may be said by Marxists that such methods are legitimate in dealing with the oppressor class, with whom no such relations of trust and co-operation obtain, but impermissible when used by a revolutionary movement against the oppressed class, since revolutionary action requires the free participation and trust of that class. However, class relations are not the only ethically significant social relations. Deception, violence, and coercion against the class enemy will sooner or later involve deception, violence, and coercion against those 'enemies' who are in other respects friends, comrades, colleagues, or to whom one has other kinds of loyalties. In such cases one can, I think, legitimately speak of a conflict between 'moral constraints' and the requirements of a political struggle. There is no simple principle for the resolution of such conflicts. My argument in Chapter 7 was that when the pursuit of desirable ends involves the violation of ethically significant relations, there can be no simple utilitarian calculus of addition and subtraction to resolve the conflict. It cannot be said that the violation of such relations is *never* justified, for that would mean accepting existing widespread suffering and oppression as morally unalterable; nor can it be said that the violation of such relations is *always* politically justified, for that would be to deprive them of any real ethical significance. All one can say in general terms is that political action, if it has a reasonably predictable prospect of producing a *large-scale and permanent* increase in human well-being, may justify the betrayal of ethical ties and loyalties. Nevertheless the fact would remain, I think, that the violation of those relations would have an independent significance as the violation of *moral* constraints—thus qualifying the Marxist critique of morality.

I want to mention briefly two other doubts about the principle that the end justifies the means, when employed in a political context. First, it is important to remember that the ends to be produced by political change are certain kinds of social *institution*, and that social institutions ultimately consist in certain kinds of human *activities*. Thus 'ends' of this sort do not have the kind of finality which may belong to other sorts of ends. The often-invoked metaphors of 'building' and 'construction', for example, the talk of 'building socialism', can be very misleading. In the case of building a house there is a clear separation between the activity of building and the object which is created by that activity, but where the object to be created is itself a set of human activities, the separation is much less clear. In the case of the house, for example, there is a definite point at which one can say that the end has been achieved and the house is finished, but it is doubtful whether one could ever say with the same decisiveness that the creation of socialism (or any other social structure) had been finally and securely achieved. Socialism, understood as the free communal ordering of economic and other activities, will always be in conflict with other tendencies in human activity. Consequently the principle that the end justifies the means, if used to justify 'temporary' violence and coercion 'until socialism has been secured', may be a recipe for perpetual tyranny.

My second point is really the converse of the previous one. If we have to remember that the institutions to be created by political change are themselves modes of human action, we also have to remember that the political action to create them involves certain kinds of institution. In talking about the means to be adopted in a political struggle, we are also talking about the kind of institutional structure to be given to a political party or movement. A party which decides to adopt coercive and authoritarian measures as its standard mode of operation has thereby decided to constitute itself as an authoritarian institution. Again this makes it much more difficult to separate ends and means in a political context. The attempt to justify violent and coercive measures as means to a free and humane society has to depend heavily on a belief in the good intentions of those who employ such measures, an assumption that they will abandon them when these methods are no longer necessary. If we have learned anything at all from Marx's understanding of the way in which human behaviour is formed by its institutional setting, we are bound to be sceptical of such an assumption. A political party which sets itself up as an instrument of violence and coercion will produce political cadres for whom such methods become second nature, and if they become the new political leaders of their society they will not easily abandon their chosen means. Rather, we can envisage the familiar scenario in which demands on the leadership to abandon such methods now that the revolution has succeeded will be regarded as a threat to the new regime, and be met with intensified repression, thus initiating a vicious circle. Recent history has provided examples, more or less extreme, of this tendency. Those who have learned from history have recognized that it can be avoided only by a political movement which aims at a continuity of ends and means, attempting to prefigure, in its own ways of working, the kind of society which it is trying to create.

Strictly speaking, these last two points could be accommodated within the principle that the end justifies the means. They could be said to show that if means are adopted whose character is entirely antithetical to the end at which they are directed, they will not after all produce the desired end. The lesson to draw, it may be said, is simply that, despite appearances, a wholesale reliance on violence and coercion is *not* an effective means to the end of a free and humane society. Nevertheless, I also want to suggest that the two points exhibit the dangers of thinking too exclusively in terms of political ends and means, with the implied separation of the one from the other. They reveal the inadequacy of a position like Lenin's, which simply subordinates morality to a doctrine of political success. More generally, I conclude from this section that however powerful the Marxist critique of morality, it will not do simply to replace morality with politics. Whether or not we call it morality, what we certainly need to retain is a rational theory of the human good which is more basic than a commitment to any political movement, and in terms of which one will have to assess the aims of any such movement, the methods it adopts, and one's own attitude towards it. I have also suggested that, in considering the problem of political means, we may find inescapable the notion of distinctively moral constraints which may conflict with political effectiveness.

Nevertheless, Marx's recognition that the human good requires not just individual action but political change remains of very great importance. We have found this following from the two themes which we have explored in Marx's philosophy, his account of human needs and his critique of morality. In the next chapter we shall consider the further development of these themes in the work of Freud.

Notes

1 Marx does not use the term 'self-realization' in 'Alienated Labour', but, for instances of it, see the 1844 manuscript 'Private Property and Communism' (e.g. M 91, 92 and 94, T 87, 88 and 91) and the *Grundrisse* (e.g. M 368).

2 Both this and the previous claim are advanced in Ch. 7 of Frithjof Bergmann: *On Being Free* (Notre Dame, 1977).

3 Because the word 'communism' has been so largely pre-empted by the regimes of the Soviet Union and Eastern Europe, I shall, when not quoting Marx, speak of 'socialism' rather than 'communism'.

4 Such a view of the interrelationship of consciousness, language, and activity is worked out much more fully by the twentieth-century philosopher Ludwig Wittgenstein in his *Philosophical Investigations* (Oxford, 1963).

5 A version of this can be found in the chapter on Marx in Alasdair MacIntyre's *Short History of Ethics* (New York and London, 1966).

6 Anthony Skillen: *Ruling Illusions* (Hassocks, 1977), pp. 129–30.

7 Ibid., p. 157.

8 V. I. Lenin: *Selected Works in Three Volumes* (Moscow, 1976), Vol. 3, pp. 420–2.

10 Ethics and Psychoanalysis

Reading: Sigmund Freud:' "Civilized" Sexual Morality and Modern Nervous Illness' (a short essay first published in 1908, and available in Volume IX of *The Standard Edition of the Complete Psychological Works of Sigmund Freud*.);
Sigmund Freud: *Civilization and its Discontents* (first published in 1930, readily available in various editions, and included in Volume XXI of the *Standard Edition*).
The Essay ' "Civilized" Sexual Morality . . .' will be referred to as CSM, and references will be to numbered paragraphs. There are 41 paragraphs. Paragraphs 26, 27, 28, and 29 consist of one sentence each. *Civilization and its Discontents* will be referred to as *CD*, and references will be to numbered paragraphs within each chapter.
I shall also be referring to the work of Erich Fromm, and specifically to his books *Man for Himself* (New York, 1947), and *The Sane Society* (London, 1956). The most useful sections to read, in an appropriate sequence, would be:
Man for Himself ch. II;
The Sane Society ch. 3;
Man for Himself ch. III.2 b.(3);
Man for Himself ch.IV.1, 2, 3a–b, 5a–b.

Needs and Mental Health

From Marx we derived, on the one hand, insights into the nature of human needs, and, on the other hand, doubts about the nature and relevance of morality. My discussion of Freud and the psychoanalytic tradition will deal with the same two themes, and in that order.

Chapter 2, on Plato, included a consideration of the concept of 'mental health' as a possible basis for ethical conclusions. In the present chapter I turn to a modern theory of mental health and examine its ethical implications. Freud's is not the only contemporary theory of mental health and illness, nor even the most widely accepted. Indeed, within orthodox psychiatry it is still regarded with some suspicion. It is, however, the approach to mental health and illness which incorporates the most comprehensive and interesting theory of the human personality, which has had the greatest impact outside the psychiatric profession, and which has the most important implications for ethics.

It is, of course, on the ethical implications that I shall concentrate. I must stress that I have no special expertise in relation either to psychiatry in general or to psychoanalysis in particular. Freud constantly stressed that his theories were based on the evidence which he derived from the clinical diagnosis and treatment of cases of mental illness. I am in no position to assess that evidence. Consequently, in the present chapter I have a particularly strong sense of rushing in where angels fear to tread. Nevertheless, since Freud himself was prepared to venture outside his own speciality and to grapple with more general philosophical questions, the layman may reasonably attempt to meet him on that ground.

The ethical implications of psychoanalysis are effectively illustrated by Freud's early essay ' "Civilized" Sexual Morality and Modern Nervous Illness'. He there argues that, contrary to the requirements of conventional sexual morality, a substantial degree of sexual fulfilment is an essential human need, and a necessary condition of mental health. The sexual code of his day, which restricts sexual activity to the purposes of reproduction within legal marriage, and condemns as immoral not only the perversions and homosexuality but also heterosexual intercourse outside marriage, is, Freud claims, harmful and self-defeating. The institution of marriage, for whose sake these restrictions are imposed, is itself impaired, for the wholesale inhibition of the sexual instinct before marriage makes it all the more difficult for husband and wife to achieve sexual satisfaction within marriage, with the result that their relationship deteriorates. Nor does the restriction on sexuality, beyond a certain point, succeed in liberating energy for the other aims of civilized life such as work and cultural activity. On the contrary, the energy that is consumed in the struggle with a powerful instinct has a generally enervating effect, and the strength of the inhibitions is calculated to produce a docile rather than an independent and vigorous character. Most important of all, the excessive suppression of the sexual instincts leads to nervous illness. Suppression is possible only to a certain degree. When it is carried further, the mental conflict between the instincts and the repressing forces continues at an unconscious level, and the repressed instincts find other outlets, especially in the form of the symptoms of nervous illness which serve as substitute satisfactions. These symptoms may be totally incapacitating. In the case of the nervous illness known as hysteria, they may take the form of the paralysis of a limb, or loss of speech, or severe physical pain. In other kinds of illness, such as obsessional neurosis, the symptoms may be psychologically rather than physically paralysing, involving obsessions and anxieties which dominate and distort the patient's emotional life, rendering him or her quite incapable of functioning effectively in everyday life.

It is important to do justice to the complexity of Freud's thesis. He is not committed to a simplistic claim that sexual abstinence always causes mental illness. Such a claim would be easily refuted by the plentiful examples of individuals who live apparently fulfilling lives of total celibacy. Freud recognizes that the strength of the sexual instinct varies significantly between one individual and another (CSM 16, and 21). He recognizes that individuals vary in their capacity for sublimation (channelling sexual energy into other activities, cultural, or intellectual, or spiritual, which provide a substitute satisfaction). His general thesis is therefore stated with caution. 'A certain amount of direct sexual satisfaction', he asserts, 'seems to be indispensable for most organizations, and a deficiency in this amount, which varies from individual to individual, is visited by phenomena which, on account of their detrimental effects on functioning and their subjective quality of unpleasure, must be regarded as an illness' (CSM 16). The impact of the claim is, however, all the greater for its caution. The fact is that for most people some degree of sexual satisfaction is a fundamental need, and this can be shown, objectively, from an understanding of the causes of mental illness. Sexual satisfaction is as much a necessary condition of mental health as a balanced diet, with the right quantities of proteins and vitamins and minerals, is a necessary condition of physical health. And since mental illness can be just as incapacitating, just as much an impediment to the effective functioning of the human being, as physical illness, the conditions of both physical and mental health can be regarded as basic human needs. Thus Freud's enterprise, though less ambitious, is essentially the same as Plato's. He is using the concepts of mental health and mental illness to provide naturalistic grounds for ethical conclusions about the constituents of a good human life.

I shall consider in due course how far this approach can be extended, and whether it can provide similar grounds for identifying other basic needs. First, however, I want to examine more closely the conceptual structure which Freud employs in his discussion of sexual needs. Crucial here is the question of his *instinct theory*. Freud has frequently been accused of 'pansexualism'—of attempting to explain all human behaviour in terms of the sexual instincts. His defenders have rightly replied that Freud always recognized other instincts besides the sexual instinct. In his early theory of instincts, he postulated two main groups of instincts, those of *self-preservation* and the *sexual* instincts. Subsequently, as he recounts in Chapter VI of *Civilization and its Discontents*, he revised this theory, and came to think that the instincts of self-preservation could be assimilated to the sexual instincts under the general heading of 'libido'. Nevertheless, he still retained the conviction that not all instincts could be of a single type. His awareness of the fundamental role of *conflict* in mental life apparently deterred him from such a conclusion. In place of the earlier duality of sex and self-preservation, he introduced a new duality, between Eros (his new term for the sexual instincts) and what he called the 'death instinct'. The latter he saw as an instinct towards destruction, manifesting itself both as an in-turned masochistic tendency to self-destruction and as an outwardly-directed tendency towards aggression. In both these manifestations the death instinct is to be contrasted with the tendency of the erotic instinct towards the preserving and merging of organic life, rather than its dissolution.

Strictly speaking, then, Freud cannot justly be accused of reducing all human behaviour to the operations of the sexual instincts. Nevertheless the underlying spirit of that criticism might be retained and reformulated. It might be said that the real trouble with Freud's theory is his general inclination to explain the variety and complexity of human actions by reference to a relatively small set of basic instincts. The fact that Freud recognizes two main classes of instincts, rather than one, would be no answer to this more general criticism. What is now in question is the very fact of Freud's reliance on an instinct theory as his dominant mode of explanation. Freud does indeed seem to me to be mistaken in according this dominant role to the instincts, and to see why this is so, we need to look more closely at the concept of 'instinct' and its place in the explanation of human behaviour.

Freud's underlying picture of the relation between the sexual instincts, repression, and mental illness has often, and with good reason, been described as a 'hydraulic' model. He tends to depict the repressing of the instincts as though it were like the damming up of water within a closed system. If the damming up is excessive and not enough water is released, the pressure will build up, and since the normal outlet is closed, other weak points in the system will come under pressure, until they eventually give way and the water floods out, creating havoc. The implication of this model is that the normal release of sexual energy would be simply like the turning on of the tap, or the opening of the dam gate, enabling the water to flow out in the proper manner. Strict application of the analogy would suggest that sexual release involves nothing more complicated than the emission of semen (a revealingly male-oriented picture). Even if that suggestion were to be disavowed (as it surely would be by Freud), the clear implication of the 'hydraulic' model is that the satisfaction of the sexual instincts is a purely physiological matter, the experiencing of a purely physical release of tension. Now if that were the case, there would be no problem of nervous illness resulting from the frustration of the sexual instincts, for the satisfaction of these instincts would be a simple matter. Masturbation would be the typical and sufficient means of obtaining sexual release; or, if it failed to provide quite the right kinds of physical sensations, modern sexual technology would certainly do so. In fact, of course, as Freud's own studies and examples make abundantly clear, the need for sexual satisfaction involves much more than this. It is a need to experience certain kinds of emotion, to be the object of certain kinds of emotion and to experience certain kinds of relationships with other people. And the distinctively physical aspect of sexual satisfaction, though indeed crucial, is inseparable from this emotional and relational context. How the physical gratification is obtained, with whom, with what degree of mutuality, with what qualities of tenderness or affection— all of these factors go to determine whether the result is sexual fulfilment or frustration. Moreover, what counts as sexual satisfaction will vary considerably from culture to culture—think, for example, of the well-documented differences between ancient Athens, medieval courtly love, the Trobriand Islanders, and nineteenth-century Christian Europe. Consequently, the achieving of sexual satisfaction also involves having certain beliefs—beliefs derived from one's culture about what constitutes sexual fulfilment, and beliefs that the relevant conditions obtain in one's own case (a belief that one is in love and is loved by the other person, or whatever).

The upshot of all this is that it begins to seem most implausible to regard the achieving of sexual satisfaction as the expression of an *instinct*. To speak of an 'instinct' is to speak of something which manifests itself in a set pattern of physical behaviour. The vocabulary of 'instinct' is clearly appropriate when applied to the sexual behaviour of other animal species. The mating of animals, though it may involve relatively elaborate courtship rituals, consists in behaviour which is standardized, and can be described entirely in physical terms. The enactment of this standardized behaviour is all that is needed for sexual satisfaction, and this is why the urge towards such satisfaction can be described as 'instinctive'. By the same token, human sexual satisfaction, with its complex intertwining of emotions, beliefs, attitudes, and physical acts, cannot appropriately be explained as the manifesting of an instinct.

In Freud's defence it has been said that he does justice to the complexity of human sexual behaviour by postulating a plurality of sexual instincts, rather than a single sexual instinct; hence he can account for the fact that no one standardized pattern of behaviour constitutes human sexual satisfaction. This is true, but the complexity which it introduces is of a limited kind only. To talk of 'instincts' still implies that the behaviour in question is relatively automatic, that its frustration is to be thought of as some kind of physical blockage, and that the frustration is dealt with simply by some kind of displacement or substitution as between the various sexual instincts. Merely emphasizing the plurality of the sexual instincts cannot do justice to the cognitive and emotional aspects of human sexual fulfilment which Freud himself comprehensively documents.

The argument can be extended to cast doubt not just on the description of sexuality as an instinct, but on the very idea of applying the concept of instincts to human behaviour. Consider the cases of hunger and thirst. Food, drink, and sex are often classed together as a basic trio of physical desires. Now, some of the points I have been making about sexuality could be made by saying that sex is importantly different from hunger and thirst. The satisfaction of hunger and thirst *is* simply a matter of providing the appropriate physical requirements. Of course, eating and drinking can be made into elaborate social activities, and thus become the occasion for emotional and relational satisfactions—the dinner party, the soirée à deux, the evening at the pub, and so forth. But hunger and thirst in themselves demand purely physical satisfactions. In that respect, then, they can, in contrast to sexuality, be described as physical needs. This, however, is still very different from saying that they are instincts. There is no set form of physical behaviour which constitutes satisfying hunger or thirst. This is as true of the non-human animals as it is of humans. What *can* be said of the animals is that hunger and thirst are physical needs, and that certain instinctive forms of behaviour bring about the satisfaction of these needs. In other words, the relevant instincts are not 'hunger' and 'thirst', but 'browsing', 'stalking', etc. In the case of humans, on the other hand, not only are hunger and thirst not instincts; neither are the activities which satisfy them. Human actions to obtain food and drink are purposive and adaptive, involving the conscious selection of appropriate means according to the circumstances. Animals' instinctive actions are not (or not to the same degree) purposive and adaptive. The animal does not adopt a certain kind of behaviour *in order to* satisfy a certain need. Rather, the behaviour is triggered off by the appropriate stimulus, and *as a matter of fact* makes possible the satisfaction of the needs. The non-adaptive character of the behaviour is apparent in the fact that it can be produced by a particular stimulus in the absence of the relevant need or in a context where it will not satisfy a need. Think of the way in which a cat will stalk not only a mouse but any small jerkily-moving object. These, then, are the characteristic features of instinctive behaviour, and they apply to the classic examples such as bird migration, nest building, animals storing food for hibernation, and so on. The behaviour follows a standardized pattern, it is produced as an automatic and innate response to a specific kind of stimulus, and although it serves to satisfy a need, the behaviour is not modifiable in response to changes in the nature of the need, and will be produced even in the absence of the need if the appropriate stimulus is present. I have said that such behaviour is not purposive. That is an over-simplification. There is no hard and fast line to be drawn between purposive and non-purposive behaviour, but rather a continuum. The behaviour of a tiger stalking its prey is, for example, more purposive than that of a fish snapping at a fly. Whereas the latter involves a single simple movement, the former involves the co-ordination of many different kinds of movements into a complex pattern, and hence there is more inclination to say that the movements are so organized as to be directed towards an end. Yet this in turn contrasts with the vast range of human actions which can count as earning a living, buying food, cooking, all of them linked to, and chosen as means to, the goal of satisfying hunger. And the point is that the more appropriate it becomes to describe behaviour as purposive, the less appropriate it becomes to describe it as instinctive.

Is there any human behaviour at all which is the product of an instinct? An example might be the new-born baby's act of sucking at the breast, not only because the behaviour has clearly not been learned, but because it exhibits the qualities just discussed. It serves a purpose, of course, that of nutrition, but it is not in the full sense purposive. The baby does not suck in order to feed itself, it simply sucks, as one quickly discovers when one holds a finger-tip to the baby's mouth. The behaviour is an automatic response to a particular stimulus. And presumably some human behaviour must necessarily be of this instinctive kind, for the process of learning new kinds of behaviour could never get started without some such instinctual basis. Fortunately, however, we need not attempt to answer the question, how much of human behaviour is or is not instinctive. It is sufficient for our purposes to claim that the frustration of sexual fulfil-ment, which Freud identifies as a source of mental illness, is better described not as the frustration of an instinct but as the frustration of a need.[1] And the significance of this redescription is that it opens up the way for us to identify other needs as having the same kind of status, needs which we would be prevented from recognizing if we were to confine our search to what could be described as instincts.

Within the psychoanalytic movement Freud's theory has been criticized, in terms similar to the above, by a group sometimes referred to as 'the neo-Freudians'. Most important of these, from the point of view of ethics, was Erich Fromm, a German psychoanalyst who settled in the United States, and who wrote extensively on ethical, political, and cultural questions from a broadly psychoanalytical perspective. Fromm argues that the needs of human beings include not only the physical needs which are shared with other species (and which he lists in traditional fashion as food, drink, and sex), but also distinctively human needs which stem precisely from the fact that human beings cannot rely on instincts to govern their lives. Inescapably, they have to make use of their capacities for rational thought and conscious choice in order to survive and to act effectively. They may find it difficult to cope with the insecurity, perplexity, and fear which this carries with it, and may attempt to escape from their individuality and responsibility, and to restore their lost unity with nature through fixation on a parent-figure, submission to a charismatic leader, or losing their own identity in that of a group. Such attempts, however, are doomed to futility. Human beings are compelled to face the inescapable fact that they must make decisions for themselves, using their own reason, and that they must therefore create meaningful lives for themselves upon that basis. The pre-conditions of their doing so are what constitute distinctively human needs, and Fromm lists these as the following.[2]

(i) The need for relatedness—the need to escape from the 'aloneness' and separateness which one experiences through one's possession of reason and imagination, by sharing one's life with other human beings. 'This need', says Fromm, 'is behind all phenomena which constitute the whole gamut of intimate human relations, of all passions which are called love in the broadest sense of the word'. (*The Sane Society* p. 30.)

(ii) The need for transcendence and creativeness—the need to use one's reason and imagination in an active way, to create and thereby to transcend the passive role of a mere creature.

(iii) The need for rootedness—the need to feel at home in the world, to overcome its alien and threatening character through the solidarity of a co-operative human community.

(iv) The need for a sense of identity and individuality—the need to be aware of oneself as an active subject, to experience one's actions as constituting a unique, authentic, and coherent self.

(v) The need for a frame of orientation and devotion—the need to understand one's world and to make sense of it, to form a picture of it which renders it meaningful and identifies purposes worth living for.

The list of needs has clear affinities with the ethics of self-realization, and Fromm throughout his work draws heavily on that tradition, and especially on the philosophies of Hegel and Marx, to supplement what he takes from Freud. What Fromm adds to the self-realizationist tradition is the attempt to link it to the concept of mental health. The assertion that these needs are basic and essential requirements for any human being can be given an objective validity, if it can be shown that they are necessary pre-conditions of mental health. Fromm claims that this is indeed the case, and his claim has considerable plausibility.

I want to suggest, then, that Fromm develops Freudian theory in directions which are exceedingly fruitful for ethics, and especially for our understanding of human needs. Now it may be thought that in abandoning the Freudian instinct theory we have abandoned the very essence of Freudianism. The orthodox Freudians would certainly say so. They would argue that in rejecting Freud's account of the exclusively sexual causation of the neuroses, one is removing a crucial component of psychoanalytic theory. Nevertheless, it seems to me that other essential components of the theory remain and that they can survive the separation. We can retain the concepts of the unconscious, of repression and its role in the causation of mental illness, and of neurotic symptoms as the substitute satisfaction of repressed desires. All of this is essential for an adequate theory of human needs. I would add that we should retain also Freud's recognition that sexual fulfilment is, if not of exclusive importance, at any rate a major pre-condition of mental health and therefore an important need. Fromm tends to be rather dismissive of it. On the one hand, as we have seen, he links it with the needs for food and drink as a purely physiological need. As such he seems to regard it as having little relevance to the problem of mental health. By implication he treats it as merely a biological necessity, and in this respect his view of sexuality is even more reductionist than Freud's. On the other hand, in so far as he does link the question of sexual satisfaction with that of mental health, he gives it a purely *symbolic* significance. He suggests that Freud's notion of the 'genital character' and of sexual satisfaction can be usefully treated as a symbol of the full utilization of one's productive capacities (*Man For Himself*, pp. 84 and 219). This suggestion is hardly adequate. Freud has surely demonstrated that sexual satisfaction is a vital need in its own right, not just a symbol for other needs, and that it includes the need for physical satisfaction. I have argued that it cannot be properly understood as a *purely* physical (still less physiological) need. I have also maintained that it is not of exclusive importance for mental health (and recognizing other needs may help us to explain, more satisfactorily than Freud can, how fulfilment in other areas of a person's life may compensate for the absence of sexual fulfilment). Nevertheless it *is* a need, and we can perhaps put the point by saying that Fromm's 'need for relatedness' is incomplete unless it includes the need for sexual and physical relatedness.

Morality as Repression

I turn now to the ways in which the work of Freud, like that of Marx (though less explicitly), calls into question the traditional concept of morality. In the last chapter I stressed, as one of the definitive features of traditional morality, its *alienated* character, the fact that morality is experienced as a set of requirements which impose themselves on the individual, and to which he or she must conform. Freud throws considerable light on this aspect of morality in his theory of the 'super-ego', which is clearly and concisely presented in chapter VII of *Civilization and its Discontents*. The term 'super-ego' is employed by Freud to refer to the phenomenon of conscience, especially in its negative aspect as forbidding certain kinds of actions and producing in us a feeling of guilt when we perform these actions. Freud's theory helps to explain why the voice of conscience is experienced as an inner voice and yet as one which commands us and which we have to obey—why, in other words, it is the voice of one's own self from which one is nevertheless alienated. The super-ego is, according to Freud, the internalization of external authority. It is formed in the young child from the commands and wishes of his or her parents, whom the child obeys out of a fear of forfeiting their love. As the child comes to identify with the parents, their wishes come to be felt as commands issuing from within the child's own self, and conflicting with his or her own inclinations. The aggressiveness with which the super-ego combats these inclinations is fuelled by the hostility which the child feels as a result of these frustrations, and which, since its outward expression is blocked, is turned inward against the inclinations themselves. The gnawing or agonizing sense of guilt which one feels when contemplating or committing morally forbidden actions is thus an anxiety traceable to one's ambivalent childhood feelings of love and hostility towards one's parents.

I shall not dwell on the details of Freud's account, which he himself supplies. Nor shall I dwell on the question of the validity of the theory as a psychological explanation, other than to remark that the confirmatory evidence comes not just from Freud's clinical experience but, more importantly, from everyday experiences of parent–child relations which are familiar enough to all of us, and which the theory makes good sense of. What I want to stress is that the theory exhibits conscience as an essentially irrational phenomenon. The deliverances of conscience which have traditionally been thought of as constituting some kind of moral insight turn out to be nothing more than feelings of fear and anxiety. Moreover, the anxiety is itself irrational in so far as it has been detached from its original objects, and is now a free-floating anxiety, a fear which does not know what it fears and whose real nature is therefore concealed from consciousness. And the conclusion which then suggests itself is that, in so far as we aspire to live rationally and to be honest in our self-knowledge, we should aim to free ourselves as far as possible from the morality of 'conscience'.

Freud does not draw this conclusion. He believes that the morality of the super-ego, though indeed a form of irrationality, is nevertheless a necessary and inevitable feature of human life. To understand his reasons for thinking this, we must turn again to his theory of instincts. We saw that in his later instinct theory Freud classified the instincts under the two headings of Eros and the instinct of death or destruction, and that the latter may express itself either self-destructively or by being directed towards the external world as an instinct of aggression. It is this inclination to aggression, as 'an original, self-subsisting instinctual disposition in man', that Freud regards as 'the greatest impediment to civilization' (*CD* VI.6).

men are not gentle creatures who want to be loved, and who at the most can defend themselves if they are attacked; they are, on the contrary, creatures among whose instinctual endowments is to be reckoned a powerful share of aggressiveness. As a result, their neighbour is for them not only a potential helper or sexual object, but also someone who tempts them to satisfy their aggressiveness on him, to exploit his capacity for work within compensation, to use him sexually without consent, to seize his possessions, to humiliate him, to cause him pain, to torture and to kill him. (*CD* V.8.)

Clearly, such dispositions constitute a massive threat to the cohesion and viability of any human society. Freud claims that since they are ineradicable features of the human instinctual constitution, they cannot be eliminated by alternative social arrangements such as those of communism (*CD* V.10). The abolition of private property would not take away men's reasons for aggressiveness, it would simply divert that aggressiveness in other directions. The only way in which it can be countered is by other psychic forces which oppose or neutralize it. This is where the existence of the super-ego becomes vital.

What means does civilization employ in order to inhibit the aggressiveness which opposes it, to make it harmless, to get rid of it, perhaps? . . . His aggressiveness is introjected, internalized; it is, in point of fact, sent back to where it came from—that is, it is directed towards his own ego. There it is taken over by a portion of the ego, which sets itself over against the rest of the ego as super-ego, and which now, in the form of 'conscience', is ready to put into action against the ego the same harsh aggressiveness that the ego would have liked to satisfy upon other, extraneous individuals. (*CD* VII.2.)

The super-ego thus counters the aggressive instinct in two ways, both by directly inhibiting it, and by itself utilizing that aggressiveness and directing it back against the self. According to Freud, no other psychic expedient will do. The aggressive instinct is too powerful to be rationally controlled by a conscious awareness of its dangerous and destructive consequences. Hence the morality of the super-ego is necessary and inevitable if human beings are to live together in society.

In order to decide, then, whether human behaviour is bound to be dominated by an alienated morality, we have to examine Freud's assertion of the existence of an independent aggressive instinct. How are we to assess this claim? Such large-scale theses about human nature are notoriously difficult to evaluate. As an empirical claim it cannot be fully assessed simply by *a priori* philosophizing, yet it seems too vague and general to be adequately dealt with by any of the specialist empirical sciences, such as psychology or sociology. The evidence of comparative anthropology might help, for the existence of cultures (such as that of the Pueblo Indians) where aggressive behaviour seems to be minimized might appear to refute the Freudian thesis. However, the Freudian response to any such putative counter-example is likely to be that the culture in question has succeeded in developing ways of fostering those psychic forces which effectively inhibit or redirect the aggressive instinct. In this way, the Freudian can cling to his claim that the instinct is always present, however it may be dealt with, and the claim then begins to appear unfalsifiable by any empirical evidence. It seems, after all, that one's acceptance or rejection of the view that human beings are innately aggressive will simply reflect one's own individual temperament. The optimists among us will hold that human beings are basically good, the pessimists will hold that human beings are basically bad, and each view will be nothing better than an act of faith.

I do not, however, think that our situation, when we try to assess Freud's claim, is quite as desperate as this. In the first place, we can examine the arguments which Freud himself offers. These, we find, involve a generalized appeal to experience.

Homo homini lupus (Man is a wolf to man). Who, in the face of all his experience of life and of history, will have the courage to dispute this assertion? . . . Anyone who calls to mind the atrocities committed during the racial migrations or the invasions of the Huns, or by the people known as Mongols under Jenghiz Khan and Tamerlane, or at the capture of Jerusalem by the pious Crusaders, or even, indeed, the horrors of the recent World War—anyone who calls these things to mind will have to bow humbly before the truth of this view. (*CD* V.8.)

Now of course, what these examples by themselves show is not that human beings are innately aggressive, but that throughout history human beings have acted aggressively. The question then remains how we are to *explain* these instances of aggressive behaviour. One thing which we might do therefore (though I certainly cannot do it here) is to examine each of these examples, and consider whether the ruthless cruelty exhibited there can be explained by specific features of the historical situation. To the extent that they can be so explained, Freud's hypothesis of an innate aggressive instinct becomes that much less plausible. To take another example, the atrocities of the Nazis could be added to Freud's list, and would probably be seen by Freudians as further evidence of the death instinct. (Freud's own pessimism in *CD*, published in 1930, was partly fuelled by his forebodings about the rise of Nazism.) Yet there have been plenty of attempts to explain Nazism without recourse to a theory of aggressive instincts, in terms of the specifics of German society in the 1930s—by reference, for example, to the insecurities of a newly urbanized and industrialized society, and especially the insecurities of a vulnerable lower middle class which had experienced the Depression and which lacked the cohesive social identity of either the upper classes or the working class. The success of such explanations would be clearly relevant to our assessment of Freud's claim.

Beyond that, we could consider not just particular explanations of particular cases but also, more generally, what kind of explanation would in principle be appropriate to such behaviour. Here my earlier remarks about the concept of 'instinct' again become relevant. Is 'aggression' the kind of thing which could in principle be properly classed as an 'instinct'? If by aggression we simply meant something like 'discharge of violent energy', then it might be plausible to call it an instinct. Aggression in this sense could be exhibited not just in wars, massacres, and other forms of violence directed against other human beings, but in attacking any task with gusto, pushing oneself hard in physical exercise, and so forth. Now, since aggression in this sense can cover a very wide range of different physical activities, I am inclined to think that, for reasons previously stated, the term 'instinct' is inappropriate. Nevertheless, it could plausibly be claimed that human beings have an innate need to engage in some kind of 'aggressive' activity in this sense.

The cases where we can most appropriately talk about an

'aggressive instinct' in animal behaviour are cases where a quite specific physical stimulus triggers off a quite specific physical response. An example would be an animal's attacking any other animal of the same species which intrudes within certain territorial limits. Here, both the situation and the behaviour can be specified in precise physical terms, and it therefore seems legitimate to describe such behaviour as 'instinctive'.

Now, the trouble with Freud's notion of aggression is that it does not fit into either of these two categories. On the one hand, it is more specific than simply 'discharge of violent energy', for essential to aggression in Freud's sense is a hostility to other human beings. On the other hand, it is more general than any precise physical response of the kind I considered in the example of territorial aggressiveness. 'Aggression' in Freud's sense covers a wide and complex range of hostile actions towards others, not provoked by any precisely defined stimuli. What locates Freud's 'aggression' between these two categories is its connection with certain kinds of *emotional attitudes and beliefs*. Freudian aggression characteristically involves attitudes of hatred, or hostility, or vindictiveness towards others, desires to see others suffer, beliefs that one has been wronged by them, or that they are a threat to oneself, or that they are inferior, and so forth. It is these kinds of beliefs and attitudes which make Freudian aggression more specific than mere 'energetic activity', and more general than animal instincts. The having of such beliefs and attitudes presupposes a background of a human language and a human culture. Consequently aggression in Freud's sense, defined by its distinctive motivational character, does not seem to be the kind of behaviour which could be described as 'instinctive'.

If destructively aggressive behaviour is not instinctive, there seems to be no good reason for regarding it as innate and inevitable. If it is, on the contrary, the kind of behaviour which falls into the category of conceptually intelligible behaviour, behaviour which is not just a physical reaction, but is a *meaningful* response to a situation, then it has to be understood and explained in terms of the situation which evokes it and to which it is appropriate. At this point I find useful a distinction which Fromm makes between two kinds of hate, which he refers to as rational 'reactive' hate and irrational 'character-conditioned' hate. The former he defines as 'a person's reaction to a threat to his own or another person's freedom, life, or ideas' (*Man For Himself* p. 214). It has, he says, 'an important biological function: it is the affective equivalent of action serving the protection of life; it comes into existence as a reaction to vital threats, and it ceases to exist when the threat has been removed'. Character-conditioned hate, on the other hand, is 'a continuous readiness to hate, lingering within the person who *is* hostile rather than reacting with hate to a stimulus from without'. It 'can be actualised by the same kind of realistic threat which arouses reactive hate; but often it is a gratuitous hate, using every opportunity to be expressed, rationalized as reactive hate'. Fromm argues that the destructiveness of character-conditioned hate stems from the frustration of basic needs, needs for the realization of one's productive potentialities. 'If life's tendency to grow, to be lived, is thwarted, the energy thus blocked undergoes a process of *change* and is transformed into life-destructive energy. *Destructiveness is the outcome of unlived life*' (Ibid. p. 216). Corresponding to these two forms of aggressive behaviour, then, there would be two kinds of explanation. Behaviour which is an expression of reactive hate would be explained by describing the situation to which it is a response (for example, one might explain why a person hates his employer by showing how the employer exploits him). Behaviour which is an expression of character-conditioned hate would be explained by indicating the deep-rooted frustrations in the person's life which give rise to this character trait. Both kinds of explanation would thus explain the behaviour in terms of specific situations which produce it, and would thereby undercut the view that a tendency to aggressive behaviour is a permanent and inescapable feature of human nature. Now of course, there is no guarantee that Fromm's classification of the two kinds of hate is complete, nor is there any guarantee that all character-conditioned hate can be explained by the frustration of basic needs. Nevertheless, it is clear from experience that the two kinds of explanation have a very wide application, and it is at least plausible that all aggressive behaviour can be explained in one or other of these two ways. This, taken together with my earlier argument that aggressive behaviour is not the kind of behaviour which could in principle count as an instinct, seems to me to amount to a strong case against Freud's claim that aggression is a permanent and inescapable feature of human behaviour.

If this is so, it further follows that there are no good grounds for regarding the morality of the super-ego as an inescapable necessity. Freud, we saw, was committed to the inevitability of the super-ego because he regarded it as an unavoidable means of combating the destructive instinct and making social life possible. Employing Fromm's dichotomy, we can say that the aggression stemming from reactive hate does not need to be combated in this way, since it is a positive and necessary phenomenon. Character-conditioned hate, on the other hand, though it is indeed negative and destructive, is effectively eliminated not by repression, but by the satisfaction of the basic needs whose frustration has given rise to it. If it can be eliminated in this way, the super-ego and its moral inhibitions would cease to be necessary.

What would this mean in practice? What would it be for one's actions not to be governed by an alienated morality? It might be thought that the contrast is with a way of life taking the form of a pure spontaneity, where all actions flow directly from immediate impulses and inclinations. This idea seems to emerge in the work of Wilhelm Reich, another dissident Freudian. Reich rejects, as I have done, Freud's theory of an independent aggressive instinct. He retains Freud's view of the centrality of the sexual instinct. He therefore argues that aggressive and antisocial tendencies arise only as a result of the repression of the sexual instinct, that they would cease to exist with the achievement of genital gratification, and that their regulation by the compulsive morality of the super-ego would cease to be necessary. He says:

Someone who represses his sexuality develops his own particular forms of moral and aesthetic self-protection . . . If, in the course of restructuring, he recognizes not only the necessity but also the indispensability of genital gratification, the moral straitjacket drops off along with the damming up of his instinctual needs . . . The formerly indispensable mechanism of self-control . . . disappears because vital energies are withdrawn from the antisocial impulses. There is scarcely anything left to be controlled. The healthy person is virtually without compulsive morality, but neither does he have any impulses that would require a restraining morality. Any residual antisocial impulses are easily controlled if the basic genital needs are gratified . . . The organism regulates itself.[3]

This seems to me to be simplistic. It is simplistic in its assumption that genital gratification is the only thing necessary for the elimination of compulsive morality. More relevantly to the present argument, it is simplistic in its assumption that the elimination of compulsive morality could mean the elimination of restraint. Reich vastly underestimates the extent of conflict in people's lives. The complexity of people's needs and desires, and the complexity of people's relationships to one another, make it inevitable that, in the best of worlds, situations will occur where one set of considerations comes into conflict with another. Difficult choices then have to be made. And the very fact that the choice is difficult means that adhering to the chosen course will involve a difficult task of restraining one's conflicting inclinations. One has to stick to one's commitment when the going gets tough, when one feels the attraction of the alternatives, and is inclined to give up. Nevertheless this kind of restraint can be distinguished from the restraints of an alienated morality. Non-moralistic restraint may involve great sacrifices, but the sacrifices are made for the sake of a cause to which one is fully and authentically committed. In an important sense, however great the sacrifices, one feels oneself affirmed in them. They are not undertaken in the name of a Kantian duty which stands opposed to one's inclinations; rather, they coincide with one's own deepest inclinations. One may, for example, be willing to sacrifice even one's own life for a person one loves, but the sacrifice is made because one's love for the other is an integral part of one's own life and one's own self; in that sense it is not imposed by duty, but it is a form of self-affirmation. Similar things could be said about not only devotion to other individuals but also devotion to a social group or a political cause. (My earlier remarks, in

Chapter 8, about the range of morally significant social relations, are relevant here.)

The question then arises: if a non-alienated morality still involves some notion of restraint, can it also retain a non-alienated notion of 'conscience'? Fromm thinks that it can. He distinguishes between 'authoritarian conscience', which is the Freudian super-ego, and what he calls 'humanistic conscience'.

Humanistic conscience is not the internalized voice of an authority whom we are eager to please and afraid of displeasing; it is our own voice, present in every human being and independent of external sanctions and rewards . . . Humanistic conscience is the reaction of our total personality to its proper functioning or dysfunctioning; . . . the expression of our true selves. (*Man For Himself* pp. 158–9.)

Fromm is clearly trying to set out a non-alienated notion of conscience. Nevertheless, I feel that the very language of conscience as an 'inner voice' militates against this. Fromm speaks of the humanistic conscience as something which we 'hear', which we can 'listen to' or 'become deaf to', which makes 'demands' on us, and which we sometimes 'act against'. Thus the very idea of conscience seems to be inseparable from the idea of a split between 'me' and 'my conscience', with the latter issuing commands which I have to obey. The same is true, I think, of the concept of guilt, which I take to be tied up with that of conscience; the actions which conscience forbids are those for which one feels guilt when one has performed them, and this guilt is the sense of having acted against one's conscience. It is significant that Fromm retains this tie between his 'humanistic conscience' and the sense of guilt (e.g. ibid., pp. 162, 165–6, 171), for I regard guilt as being, like conscience, essentially a phenomenon of alienation.

This is brought out incidentally by Freud in a passage in his account of the super-ego. Freud traces back the origin of the super-ego to a supposed event at the dawn of human history, when human beings lived in extended family groups ruled over by a patriarchal father, and when the sons banded together to slay their father and usurp his power. The bizarre quality of Freud's excursion into prehistory need not detain us. What is interesting is the way in which Freud describes the event.

> But if the human sense of guilt goes back to the killing of the primal father, that was after all a case of 'remorse' . . . This remorse was the result of the primordial ambivalence of feeling towards the father. His sons hated him, but they loved him, too. After their hatred had been satisfied by their act of aggression, their love came to the fore in their remorse for the dead. It set up the super-ego by identification with the father; it gave that agency the father's power, as though as a punishment for the deed of aggression they had carried out against him, and it created the restrictions which were intended to prevent a repetition of the deed. And since the inclination to aggressiveness against the father was repeated in the following generations, the sense of guilt, too, persisted . . . (*CD* VII.13).

What emerges here is a distinction between the remorse which is an expression of the sons' love for the father they have slain, prior to the creation of the super-ego, and the subsequent sense of guilt which is a sense of having offended against the super-ego. This remorse arising out of love, which Freud allows to the prehistorical sons, seems to disappear from his account of contemporary humanity. It is, however, a point of great importance. Contemporary human beings are also capable of love, and of other kinds of commitment to and concern for one another, and are therefore capable of feeling remorse when they violate or betray those relationships. I suggest that we can usefully distinguish between *remorse*, defined as our sense of having injured other human beings, for whom we at the same time feel an authentic concern, and *guilt*, defined as the sense of offending against one's own conscience or super-ego. (This is a stipulative definition, since in ordinary usage 'guilt' and 'remorse' are often used interchangeably.) The difference between the two is apparent in a vivid example which Skillen provides:

> A child hits and hurts her friend who stands howling, and the parent or teacher turns on the offending child and scolds her, ignoring meanwhile the victim's distress. The punishment actually teaches the offending child to ignore the direct impact of her actions and to focus, not on the good or harm that is the action's direct upshot, but on herself as the condemned, as the punished.[4]

In terms of my definitions, the child is being taught to feel guilt rather than remorse. And I am suggesting that 'conscience' and 'guilt', as I have defined it, belong within the context of an alienated morality, whereas the feeling of remorse is embedded in our actual experience of interpersonal relations and belongs within a 'morality' (if we want to call it that) which emphasizes such relations.

I believe, then, that Freudian theory further substantiates the critique of morality as traditionally conceived. The account of morality which I considered in my discussion of Marx, stressing its alienated character, is given a psychological grounding by Freud. This Freud does in spite of himself, for his cultural pessimism prevents him from recognizing as dispensable the kind of morality whose irrationality he so effectively reveals. By questioning Freud's theory of instincts, and thereby questioning his cultural pessimism, we are able to take his critique of morality to its natural conclusion. The problem is, then, to offer a more adequate theory of the good life and rational action, free from the limitations of traditional morality.

Notes

1   Freud himself acknowledges that 'a better term for a stimulus of instinctual origin is a *need*' (*Instincts and their Vicissitudes*).
2   I take the list from Fromm's *The Sane Society* Ch. 3.
3   Wilhelm Reich: *The Sexual Revolution* (London, 1951), pp. 6–7.
4   *Ruling Illusions*, p. 161.

11 Ethics and Rationality

Reading: No one text or author provides background reading for this chapter. Some important short pieces of writing to which I shall refer are:

Bertrand Russell: *Religion and Science* (London, 1935), Ch. IX 'Science and Ethics'.

C. L. Stevenson: 'The Emotive Meaning of Ethical Terms' and (briefer but clearer) 'The Nature of Ethical Disagreement', both included in Stevenson's *Facts and Values* (New Haven, 1963).

Philippa Foot: 'Moral Beliefs', in *Theories of Ethics*, ed. Philippa Foot (London, 1967).

J. R. Searle: 'How to Derive "Ought" from "Is" ', in Foot: *Theories of Ethics*.

All these pieces are widely anthologized. Complete books to which I shall also refer are:

R. M. Hare: *The Language of Morals* (London, 1952);
G. J. Warnock: *The Object of Morality* (London, 1971).

I have previously asserted that the classical tradition of ethical theory has been more effectively continued by Marxian and Freudian thought than by the work of twentieth-century academic philosophers. Nevertheless, it would be absurd to suggest that the latter have had nothing of value to offer. Important issues have been raised and debated, and the most important of these has also been central to the present book. I have examined various substantive ethical theories, but in doing so I have also raised the meta-ethical question: can a rational justification be given for any one particular view about how human beings ought to live? A discussion of this question will enable us to look at the work of some contemporary philosophers, and at the same time serve to draw together various strands of this book.

Ethical Subjectivism

I mentioned in my Introduction the preoccupation with meta-ethics on the part of contemporary academic philosophers.

This has not been an exclusive tendency, but it has certainly been the dominant one within ethical philosophy as pursued and studied in British and American universities since 1900. Philosophers have been concerned especially with questions about the meaning and logical status of moral and practical beliefs, and the terms of the argument have been largely set by the view known as 'ethical subjectivism'. A clear statement of this position was Bertrand Russell's chapter on 'Science and Ethics' in his 1935 book *Religion and Science*. He defined ethical subjectivism as the doctrine that

> if two men differ about values, there is not a disagreement as to any kind of truth, but a difference of taste. . . . The chief ground for adopting this view is the complete impossibility of finding any arguments to prove that this or that has intrinsic value. . . . Since no way can be even imagined for deciding a difference as to values, the conclusion is forced upon us that the difference is one of tastes, not one as to any objective truth (pp. 237–8).

Russell's subjectivism was developed further by other philosophers such as A. J. Ayer and Charles Stevenson into the theory which came to be known as *emotivism*. What these philosophers emphasized especially was the theory of meaning which they held to be needed for a correct understanding of the nature of ethical judgements and other value-judgements. They distinguished between *descriptive* meaning and *emotive* meaning. Linguistic utterances have descriptive meaning when their function is to state facts, and a condition of their having such meaning is that they should be empirically verifiable. Now, although these philosophers wanted to link ethical judgements with feelings and attitudes, their claim was not that such judgements *describe* or *state facts about* feelings and attitudes. The primary kind of meaning which ethical utterances have is not descriptive meaning, they said, but *emotive* meaning. This emotive meaning has two components. The first is a tendency to *express* the speaker's own feelings. The second is a tendency to *induce* the same feelings in others. These are the two main functions which ethical judgements perform. Thus the statement, 'Drunken driving costs lives', has descriptive meaning. It states a fact which can be verified (or falsified) by compiling statistics correlating drunken driving with fatal road accidents. The assertion, 'Drunken driving is wrong', does not, on the other hand, state any fact about drunken driving, nor does it state any fact about the speaker's attitude to drunken driving. It does not, for example, *state* that the speaker disapproves of drunken driving. What it does is to *express* the speaker's disapproval of drunken driving. And it is also intended to evoke the same feeling of disapproval in those to whom it is addressed. Thus Ayer and Stevenson would agree with Russell that such an assertion cannot be true or false. It cannot be true or false, because its function is not to state a fact. Its function is to express and evoke feelings, and an expression or evocation of a feeling is not the sort of thing which can be true or false.

Emotivism was widely objected to on the grounds that it presented the making of ethical judgements as more of an emotional affair than it really is. Ethical judgements, it was said, may be but are not necessarily delivered with emotional fervour. My view that drunken driving is wrong may be an entirely calm and dispassionate one. And I may not be trying to evoke feelings in others. I may, for example, be addressing someone who already shares the same views. Such objections, however, are not entirely fair to the theory. In the first place, the theory defines the emotive meaning of an ethical judgement as its *tending to*, or *being fitted to*, express and evoke feelings, rather than its actually doing so on each particular occasion when the judgement is uttered. Secondly, the theory uses the notion of 'emotions' or 'feelings' in a very wide sense. The feelings which ethical judgements express are not necessarily impassioned ones. Characteristically they would be feelings of approval or disapproval, liking or disliking, and the use of the word 'attitudes', as an equivalent to 'feelings' or 'emotions', probably conveys more accurately the intent of the theory.

At any rate, many philosophers who saw an important element of truth in the emotivist theory were led to try to reformulate that element in terms which avoided the emphasis on emotions. The most influential and successful of these attempts was that of R. M. Hare, whose book *The Language of Morals* was published in 1952. What the emotive theory is right to point to, according to Hare, is the *practical* character of moral judgements. This consists in the fact that moral language, like other kinds of evaluative language, is essentially *action-guiding*. It guides people's actions not, as the emotivists would have it, by working on people's emotions and thereby inducing them to act in a certain way, but simply by being addressed to people as rational agents and *telling* them what to do. Moral judgements thus function very much like imperatives. Judgements such as 'Drunken driving is wrong', or 'You ought not to drink and drive', entail the imperative 'Do not drink and drive'. Similarly the action-guiding force of the word 'good' can be characterized by saying that its function is to commend things and thereby to guide people's choices. To take first a nonmoral example, if someone wants an apple and is told, 'This is a good apple', that judgement entails the imperative, 'Choose this apple'. Similarly, in the moral case, the judgement 'The good life is one which is inspired by love and guided by knowledge' entails the imperative 'Choose a life inspired by love and guided by knowledge'. The main difference between moral judgements and imperatives is that the former are *universal*. Whereas imperatives are typically addressed to a particular individual or group of individuals, moral judgements are at least implicitly addressed to everyone. The judgement 'You ought not to drink and drive' commits the speaker to asserting that everyone in relevantly similar circumstances (including the speaker himself) ought not to drink and drive.

Hare says that moral judgements are addressed to people as rational agents. How then does reason enter in? According to Hare, the role of reason is to derive moral judgements from other, more general moral judgements. In this respect too, moral judgements are like imperatives, for an imperative can be derived logically from a more general imperative. Thus the imperative, 'Do not drive your car', is entailed by the imperative, 'Do not drive your car when you have been drinking', in conjunction with the factual statement, 'You have been drinking'. The entailment can be set out formally as a syllogism:

Do not drive your car when you have been drinking.
You have been drinking.
∴ Do not drive your car.

A precisely analogous syllogism can be constructed employing moral judgements rather than imperatives:

You ought not to drive your car when you have been drinking.
You have been drinking.
∴ You ought not to drive your car.

The moral judgement which serves as a reason here may in turn be derived from a more general principle, and so on. Eventually, however, the chain of reasons will come to an end, when we reach some moral principle which is so general that no further reason for it can be given. The premiss of our previous syllogism, for example, could be derived as the conclusion of another syllogism:

You ought not to do what costs lives.
Driving your car when you have been drinking costs lives.
∴ You ought not to drive your car when you have been drinking.

The principle, 'You ought not to do what costs lives', is so general and basic that one may decide that no further reason can be given for adopting it. At that point, according to Hare, one must simply choose. Some people will choose to adopt the principle. It may be that other people, taking full account of everything that follows from the principle, will choose not to adopt it. If that is so, neither party can describe the other as mistaken. Because it is a matter not of ascertaining facts, but of choosing one's basic values, the choice must be an individual commitment.

Hare's insistence on the *practical* character of moral judgements should remind us of Hume's similar insistence. Hume, we saw, puts this in psychological terms. Reason, he says, is wholly inactive. Only our sentiments or passions can move us to action. Since moral judgements are intended to lead to action, they must accordingly have their origin in sentiment rather than reason. Hare translates Hume's claim into the vocabulary of logic rather than psychology. In place of the distinction between 'reason' and 'sentiment', he offers the distinction between the 'descriptive' and 'prescriptive' functions of language, and he claims that the primary function of moral language is prescriptive. Hence he agrees with Hume on the impossibility of deriving an 'ought' from an 'is'. No moral or other evaluative conclusion can be deduced from purely descriptive premisses. The evaluative conclusion would have to perform a quite different logical function from the descriptive premisses, and therefore it cannot be entailed by those premisses. No set of facts can by itself commit us to a choice of values.

The attempt to derive values from facts is the hallmark of ethical naturalism. Naturalism, as I have defined it previously, is the view that ethical conclusions can be established on the basis of facts about the nature of human beings and the world in which they live. The attempt to reach ethical conclusions in this way is, according to Hare and others, a logical error, and, following G. E. Moore, they have referred to it as 'the naturalistic fallacy'.[1] Is naturalism, then, inescapably fallacious? The overall tendency of this book has been towards the defence of naturalism. I have been suggesting that whatever is of value in the theories I have discussed can be worked into a broadly naturalistic ethics. That suggestion must now confront the thoroughgoing critique of naturalism mounted by twentieth-century philosophers.

The Revival of Naturalism

As a matter of fact, ethical naturalism underwent something of a revival in the 1950s and 1960s, and it is probably true to say that academic philosophers are now fairly evenly divided between some form of naturalism and some form of subjectivism in ethics.[2] I want to look briefly at two influential articles which helped to revive the cause of naturalism. The first of these is an article entitled 'Moral Beliefs' by Philippa Foot, one of Hare's Oxford colleagues, which was published in 1958. Foot there questions Hare's idea that moral judgements have some special 'commendatory' or 'action-guiding' force. The practical significance of moral judgements is, she says, more satisfactorily accounted for not by assimilating them to imperatives but by seeing them as providing *reasons* for acting. The question, then, is whether statements of fact can ever by themselves provide reasons for acting. If they can, then we need no longer maintain, as Hare does, a dichotomy between statements of fact and moral judgements or other value-judgements.

Foot then argues that some statements of fact can provide reasons for acting. Consider, she says, the concept of 'injury'. An injury can be defined in factual terms as any damage to a physical limb or organ which interferes with its performance of its function—which prevents the eyes from being used for seeing, the hands for holding or manipulating, the legs for walking, and so forth. Given this definition, injury is, according to Foot, something which any person has a reason to avoid. In general, she says, a person is given a reason for acting if he or she is shown that the action is necessary for something he or she wants. But if a person wants anything at all, he or she must necessarily need the effective use of limbs and physical organs. Without these a person cannot act effectively in the world to satisfy his or her wants. Therefore, just in virtue of the facts of the human constitution, injury is something which any human being has a reason to avoid. Foot is claiming, in effect, that there are basic and universal human needs which can be identified objectively. And like Plato, she is taking the case of physical health and physical functioning as a paradigm of objective practical reasoning.

The concept of 'injury' is one whose practical significance derives not from any special kind of linguistic meaning which the concept has, but from the facts of what injury consists in. Can the same be said of moral concepts? Foot suggests that the concepts of the virtues are definitively moral concepts. A morally good person is one who possesses the virtues of prudence, courage, temperance, and justice (a list which appears to derive from Plato). Foot then attempts to show that the concepts of the virtues are reason-giving in essentially the same way as the concept of injury. The virtues are qualities which any human being has a reason to want. This is clear enough in the case of prudence, courage, and temperance, for any human being will need to be able to act with foresight, to resist the temptations of immediate pleasures, and to stand firm against fear and danger. Justice is more problematic. Justice in the wide sense Foot defines as the virtue which covers all our obligations to other people. Therefore it might seem that justice is not something we are bound to want but that, on the contrary, as Plato's Thrasymachus would claim, the person who is inhibited by considerations of justice will be less likely to achieve what he wants. Nevertheless, Foot claims, the facts tell against Thrasymachus. One could live effectively without justice only if one could live quite independently of other people, never needing their help or co-operation, and escaping their detection whenever one wronged them. Since the facts of the human condition are not like this, justice is something which all human beings need to possess in their dealings with their fellows.

Foot's references to Plato should remind us of problems raised in earlier chapters, when we consider Plato's and Aristotle's attempts to link the virtues with happiness. What Foot offers is an *instrumental* vindication of justice in terms of self-interest. It is the kind of justification offered in the *Republic* by Glaucon rather than by Socrates. And the difficulties with this approach are the difficulties which I stated in Chapter 4. If one cultivates justice as a means of gaining other people's goodwill and inducing them to reciprocate, it is not really justice (that is, respect for other people's rights and interests as such) that is being cultivated, but only a semblance of justice. Moreover, it is not clear that this kind of argument will justify even that much. If one conceives of one's interests in this way, and then asks what kind of policy towards other people will most effectively maximize those interests, the answer may well be that one should cultivate a reputation for justice, while being prepared to act unjustly towards others when one can get away with it and escape detection.

There are, then, difficulties for Foot's argument. At this point one might be tempted to try another way of linking the virtues with human needs and interests—the way which is followed, for example, by G. J. Warnock in his book *The*

Object of Morality. Like Foot, Warnock makes the virtues central to morality. His own preferred list of virtues is 'non-maleficence', 'beneficence', 'fairness', and 'non-deception'. Like Foot, he tries to justify them in terms of their conduciveness to the satisfaction of human wants, needs, and interests. But the wants, needs, and interests which they serve are those of people in general, rather than the agent's in particular. According to Warnock, the human condition is such that, given people's limited sympathies, things are inclined to 'go badly'. The purpose of cultivating the moral virtues is to ameliorate the human condition, by counteracting people's limited sympathies and thereby making things go better. Warnock's factual claim is reminiscent of Hume's assertion that the virtues are qualities useful or agreeable either to their possessor or to others. That last phrase—'or to others'—is the important addition which makes the claim more defensible than Foot's position. It is more plausible to claim that if people in general cultivate the virtues, people in general will be better off, than to claim that if a particular individual cultivates the virtues, he or she will be better off. But this gain in plausibility is achieved only at the cost of leaving it much less clear why any particular individual has any reason to acquire the virtues. If there is no guarantee that *I* shall be any better off for doing so, if all I can be sure of is that it will contribute to human betterment in general, why should I be virtuous? Warnock's answer is that some people just do happen to want to help better the human condition. But this leaves us with the question, 'What if they don't?' For it would seem that to someone who takes no such interest in the betterment of the human condition, Warnock's account offers no reason at all for being virtuous.[3] It is clear, then, that the attempt to link morality with human interests raises starkly, as it did in earlier chapters, the problem of egoism and altruism. And whichever justification of the virtues is offered, Foot's or Warnock's, the egoistic or the altruistic justification, there seem to be major difficulties.

Foot has subsequently abandoned her position. She no longer thinks that her attempted justification of the virtues, or at any rate of justice, is either possible or necessary. She now says that moral considerations do not, in fact, give reasons to every human being. They constitute reasons for acting only if one already has some commitment to the moral point of view, or to some particular moral value.[4] Though she does not say so, this seems to me to amount to the abandonment of the attempt at formulating an objectivist ethics. In my view, however, there is no need for her, or for us, to abandon that attempt. What we should look for, rather, and what would enable us to escape from the impasse represented by Foot's and Warnock's difficulties, is a much wider and more thorough theory of human needs. I have uncovered, in the course of this book, various sources for such a theory, and I shall return to the question shortly.

I turn now to a second article which contributed to the revival of naturalism, John Searle's 1964 paper 'How to Derive "Ought" from "Is" '. Whereas Foot attempted to break down the dichotomy of facts and values by attending to facts about human needs, wants, and interests, Searle attempted to do so by focusing on facts about human institutions. Institutional facts, he claimed, do have evaluative implications. Consider the institution of promising. Within that institution it is just a fact that if someone has promised to do something, he or she has undertaken an obligation to do it. That is what promising *is*. Hence we can construct an argument of the following form.

> Jones uttered the words, 'I hereby promise to pay you, Smith, five dollars.'
> ∴ Jones promised to pay Smith five dollars.
> ∴ Jones placed himself under (undertook) an obligation to pay Smith five dollars.
> ∴ Jones is under an obligation to pay Smith five dollars.
> ∴ Jones ought to pay Smith five dollars.

Each of these statements follows from the previous one in conjunction with additional straightforwardly factual premises (e.g. that no one has released Jones from his obligation). But the initial statement is undeniably factual, and the conclusion is undeniably an 'ought', an evaluative judgement. So it seems that anyone who accepts the factual premisses must accept the evaluative conclusion. The conclusion follows from the premisses because the rule, 'To make a promise is to undertake an obligation', is, according to Searle, a constitutive rule of the institution of promising. It serves to define the institution, and someone who does not recognize the rule cannot understand what promising is. Searle suggests that analogous constitutive rules define the institutions of property, marriage, language, punishment, and so on, and generate ethical principles in the same way.

Searle's opponents, such as Hare, retort that the derivation of 'He ought . . .' from 'He said, "I promise. . ." ', will have a very different significance depending on whether one views it from inside or from outside the institution. Someone who simply reports it as an external observer, in the manner of a cultural anthropologist, will mean by it only, 'This is what they (the participants in the institution) *call* "promising", this is what they *call* "placing oneself under an obligation".' So long as he speaks from outside the institution, he will not report the 'ought' as a full-blooded 'ought', by which he himself would be bound. The 'ought' applies only to the participants in the institution, and therefore one is bound by it only if one is committed to the institution. According to philosophers such as Hare, one is committed to the institution only if one chooses to be, and the choice is itself an ethical choice; therefore the 'ought' will follow from the 'is' only by way of such an ethical choice, that is, only if one accepts the institution and thereby accepts the substantive ethical principle which is its constitutive rule.

I believe that this objection is valid up to a point. It does indeed make a crucial difference whether one is committed to the institution. The believer in free love, or in sharing all things in common, cannot be shown that he ought to respect monogamous fidelity or property rights by being shown that this is a constitutive rule of the institution of marriage or private property, for it is just this rule and this institution that he questions. If he is not committed to the institution, it is entirely rational for him to reject the corresponding ethical principle. The question is, then: what is it to be committed to a social institution? Hare and others seem to think that this is simply a matter of individual choice, as though one could stand outside all social institutions, survey them all and take one's pick. This, as we saw in Chapter 8, is a false picture. Any human individual exists within, and is formed by, a context not only of social institutions but of social relations generally. Thus, though one can in principle criticize any specific social institution, one cannot detach oneself from all social relations in order to make some sort of socially unencumbered autonomous choice. Moreover, one may criticize a particular institution and regard it as ideally needing to be abolished or replaced, while nevertheless continuing to participate in that institution, and having a commitment to it in its existing form. One might, for instance, regard the contemporary nuclear family as a radically imperfect institution, but one might nevertheless live within such a family, and one's family relationships might constitute one's own deepest commitments. To understand how and why people come to be committed to institutions, as I suggested in Chapter 8, we have to look at the more basic pre-institutional social relations which underlie them. For example, one's commitment to a particular country as a political institution, perhaps despite deep criticisms of it, may be grounded in one's ties to a place, to a language, to a culture, to a way of life—ties which one cannot just choose. Searle's theory of the ethically constitutive rules of social institutions thus needs to be located within a broader account of social relations and their ethical significance. But Searle is right in this, that the facts about the social relations in which people stand to one another are not ethically neutral. They are, at the same time, facts about the ethical commitments and responsibilities which serve to define those relations, and one cannot understand the social relations without understanding their ethical implications.

Both Foot and Searle point us in directions in which we need to look for the components of a naturalistic ethics. Each, however, is too limited. We have to develop a more comprehensive theory of human needs, and a more comprehensive theory of social relations. The historical tradition I have surveyed, from Plato and Aristotle to Marx and Freud and the neo-Freudians, can help to provide the materials for such a theory, and for a naturalistic ethics richer in content than any yet developed by contemporary ethical philosophers.

Components of a Naturalistic Ethics

A book of this nature is not the place to develop such a theory in detail. What I do want to do, however, is to look back over the tradition I have followed from Plato and Aristotle, and gather together the material which would go to the making of an adequate and objective theory of the human good.

In placing considerations of human good and human harm at the centre of such a theory, we are already pre-supposing a certain ethical perspective. We are presupposing what I would want to call a 'humanistic world-view', in contrast to a 'religious world-view'. The contrast here is between a perspective in which 'man is the highest being for man',[5] and one in which man occupies a subordinate position in the universe, owing submission to forces or purposes which transcend him. A religious world-view may be based on a relatively specific belief in a god or gods. It may be grounded in a more generalized sense of the insignificance of human projects and aspirations, a sense that human beings inhabit a world which evades their final understanding or control and which is ultimately a realm of mystery. The view of the world that we are dealing with here is one which rests on fundamental attitudes of reverence and awe. It is this which leads to an ethics stressing not *mastery* of the world to serve human aims, but the *conformity* of human beings to a pre-given status or purpose.

In contrast, a humanistic world-view will insist on the centrality of human concerns and purposes. This may be tempered by a respect for other living species, such that the environment as we shape it should be one we can share with them, rather than one in which we are prepared to exter-minate any other species which do not serve human purposes. But respect for other species is not the same as a fundamental submission to any non-human power or powers. A humanistic world-view will therefore conflict with certain kinds of religious perspective—for example, with a 'natural law' ethic of pre-ordained purposes to which human beings have to conform, or with a Buddhist or Christian asceticism, aiming at a negation of self and a release from the 'tyranny' of desire. In its practical implications, however, it can harmonize with certain other kinds of religious perspective, such as one built around the idea of a divine creator whose primary concern is for the well-being of his human creatures, and who wishes their own actions to be guided by that same concern.

Difficult philosophical questions arise as to how one might decide between these competing world-views, and what kinds of reasons could be given in support of one or the other. I cannot hope to deal effectively with these problems here, and will not attempt to do so.[6] Suppose, however, we assume a humanistic world-view as our starting-point. What then will be the nature of those 'human concerns' which are to be given the central place? As I suggested at the end of the last section, it seems to me that the two basic components of a naturalistic ethics would have to be (a) human needs, and (b) social relations. I will look at each of these in turn.

We can, to begin with, agree with Foot on the objective character of *physical* needs. Human beings, if they are to act effectively at all, need the effective use of their limbs and organs; they need physical health, they need to avoid injury, they need food and drink, clothing, and shelter. Any human being has good reason to aim at the satisfaction of these needs. So basic are they that writers on ethics tend not to think of them as having an ethical significance at all, and to assume that ethics involves more elevated concerns. But any other and 'higher' needs which may take their place within a naturalistic ethics must be seen as continuous with these basic physical needs, and must presuppose the satisfaction of the latter. Human beings must first of all eat and drink, acquire clothing and shelter, in order to engage in any of the other activities which make life worthwhile. It is true that, for the sake of another person or a cause, one may sacrifice one's own physical well-being, or even one's life. But it *is* a *sacrifice*. What is sacrificed is itself something of great value, and the sacrifice will be rational only if there are other things which matter to one even more than one's own life. Only from some non-humanist perspective can the martyr's sacrifice be seen as some kind of release from the limited confines of human life, and thus as no real sacrifice at all.

The most elementary and basic human needs, then, are these physical needs. But they are certainly not the only ones, and I have already remarked that we require a fuller theory of needs than Foot and others can offer. Looking back now over earlier chapters, we can list some of the other kinds of needs. We found in Plato and Aristotle the idea that human beings need to achieve the kind of psychic harmony which consists in a proper relation between reason and the emotions. I argued that it is Aristotle who offers the better account of this, as a relation in which the emotions are neither repressed by reason, nor simply overcome it, but rather are themselves rational, sensitively attuned, and appropriate to the circumstances. In Kant we encountered the idea (not, indeed, expressed by him in the vocabulary of 'needs') that human beings need to be treated as persons, as rational and autonomous beings capable of choosing for themselves and pursuing their own projects and aspirations. Mill's doctrine of 'higher pleasures' identified the needs of human beings to employ their rational and intellectual faculties. Bradley introduced the concept of 'self-realization', and I suggested that this concept pointed especially to the human needs for coherence, for a sense of identity, and for positive activity. Marx helped to fill out this concept of self-realization with his account of the need for meaningful unalienated work, and of the centrality of work in human life. Freud focused our attention on the need for sexual fulfilment, and in turning then to the deficiencies of Freud's view of human nature, we looked at Fromm's neo-Freudian discussion of the needs for relatedness, for transcendence and creativeness, for rootedness, for a sense of identity and individuality, and for a frame of orientation and devotion.

Adding all these together would produce a rather untidy list. It is clear that there is a good deal of overlap between these various needs, and some of them are perhaps to be seen simply as more specific versions of others. We could perhaps try to introduce some order into the list. One possibility, for example, would be to reduce these various needs to three basic ones: the need for a proper relation between reason and the emotions; the need for meaningful work and activity; and the need for supportive, affectionate, and co-operative relations with others. We could then fit into the picture the more abstractly described psychological needs, such as the need for a sense of identity, and the need for one's life to have a unity, by suggesting not that they are additional to these three, but rather that these three represent the relatively concrete ways in which the more abstract needs are satisfied. It would, however, be a mistake to look for any uniquely correct way of classifying human needs, for there is none to be found. The needs which I have surveyed are all intimately connected with one another, and there is a relative arbitrariness about how exactly we divide them up and categorize them.

More important is the question: what entitles us to describe them all as needs? Given the diversity of human desires and inclinations, what grounds are there for saying that any human being will necessarily need these things? Can we ascribe to these needs an objective status? A basis for doing so which we have encountered frequently in this book is the analogy with physical health. Just as physical needs are prerequisites of physical health, understood as the proper functioning of the various organs of the body, so it can be argued that other kinds of needs, which are not purely physical, are in a comparable sense prerequisites of mental health, understood as that harmony of the personality which enables a person to function effectively. To the extent that people's fundamental needs are unsatisfied, their lives will be empty and frustrated, and their actions are more likely to be irrational, dominated by unconscious motives and compensations, by fantasies, and by compulsive drives. To that extent, they will be less able to function effectively —and to function effectively is something which all human beings need to do, whatever the particular aims and objects to which they may be devoted.

This, then, will be one important basis for the claim that such needs have an objective status. Something more, however, is required. There is surely more to the idea of a good human life than merely being able to function effectively. If a person's needs are satisfied only to the extent that enables him or her to cope, to get by without debilitating mental conflicts, that seems to constitute only a bare minimum. A fuller and more adequate picture of the good life would surely have to involve the notion of a life of happiness and fulfilment, a life that is rich, and rewarding, and deeply satisfying. What I want now to suggest is that those needs which have to be satisfied in order for one to be able to function effectively are the same needs whose fuller satisfaction makes for a richly happy life. The satisfaction of them up to a certain level enables one to cope; the more complete satisfaction of them produces positive enjoyment. There is no *a priori* reason why this should be so. It could have been otherwise. It could have been the case that, once our basic needs were satisfied to the point that enabled us to achieve some kind of mental equilibrium, further satisfaction of them produced no added bonus of happiness, and that people's positive enjoyments were found elsewhere. It does, however, seem to be a brute fact of human experience that the two kinds of satisfaction are directly linked. Human beings need their emotional life to be in touch with reality, they need to engage in activities which are not totally mindless and mechanical, they need a basic degree of supportive recognition from other people and they need these things just in order to stay sane. But it is also the case that the richest enjoyments and satisfactions of human life are to be found in the further meeting of these same needs—in work which uses to the full one's creative capacities, and in the life of the emotions, and the many different kinds of human love and solidarity.

I have said that there is no *a priori* reason why there should be this continuity between the conditions of effective functioning and the conditions of happiness. We can nevertheless provide a plausible empirical explanation of an evolutionary kind as to why this should be so. Clearly the conditions which make for human survival and effective psychological functioning are more likely to be satisfied if they are also the conditions which make for positive enjoyment. Accordingly, it is not at all surprising that the human species should have developed in such a way that the two coincide.

The notions of happiness and related concepts thus provide a second test of the objectivity of human needs. Notice that this claim is compatible with the undeniable fact of the diversity of aims and objects which human beings pursue. Certainly, not all people find happiness in the same specific kinds of activities, and this has led some philosophers to deny that there can be any objective answer to the question of what constitutes a good life. Warnock, for example, suggests that in so far as morality has an objective content, this cannot provide any answer to the question of how one should live, if this is taken to be a question about the goals one should pursue, or the general character one's life should have.

For is there any goal in life at all of which one could say, quite in general, that 'one'—that is, anyone and everyone—should aim at achieving it? . . . The goals appropriate to a 'man of action' are not, surely, to be recommended to the contemplative scholar, the dedicated artist, the religious recluse . . . (*The Object of Morality* pp. 90-2.)

Nevertheless, though aptitudes and enthusiasms may differ, there are, I think, certain general psychological features which any activity would have to possess, if it were to occupy a central position in a worthwhile and fulfilling life. The man of action, the contemplative scholar, and the dedicated artist may indeed be engaged in activities which at one level are very different, but in order to find those activities fully satisfying, they will need to experience them as activities which are demanding and make full use of their abilities, which offer scope for creativity and initiative, and so on.

In suggesting that basic and objective human needs are to be defined, in part, as those needs the satisfaction of which would make for human happiness, I may seem to be tending in the direction of utilitarianism. It is true that the position I am adopting has affinities with what I have previously identified as the positive strand in Mill's theory. It is the Mill who talks of 'higher pleasures', and the fully human life, rather than the Mill who aspires after a quantifiable hedonistic calculus, with whom I would align myself. I have previously explained the contrast between the two (Chapter 7, p. 143), and there is an aspect of the contrast which I must especially reiterate now. In linking 'needs' with 'happiness', we must not suppose that all human needs are therefore at bottom the same, a need for some single homogeneous commodity which is 'happiness'. Happiness is, as Mill says in a more enlightened moment, 'not an abstract idea, but a concrete whole' (*Utilitarianism* IV.6), and the basic human needs are different 'elements' or 'ingredients' occupying a place within this whole. Their variety is irreducible.

The realm of 'needs', then, is one of the two principal components of an adequate naturalistic ethics. It would be characteristic of a certain kind of naturalism to stop at this point, and to suppose that the concept of 'needs', or related concepts of 'wants' or 'interests', can provide its whole content. This, however, makes for an excessively goal-directed conception of ethics, and rests ultimately on an impoverished theory of human nature. Quite simply, it is not the case that the only things which *matter* to human beings are states to be brought about, satisfactions to be achieved. In general terms, I want to suggest, the other fundamental category of human concerns is that of the commitments and loyalties which are involved in social relations, and it is these that must form the second principal component of a naturalistic ethics. The traditional distinction between 'teleological' and 'deontological' conceptions of ethics reflects the distinction between these two fundamental kinds of considerations, 'needs' and 'social relations', which can function as reasons for human actions. Both are essential components of an adequate theory.

I have indicated in Chapter 8 what I take to be the range of ethically significant social relations, and have stressed how important it is to do justice to the whole of this range. Short-term person-to-person relations of trust and reliance, such as are involved in promising or communicating; more long-term person-to-person relations of friendship or sexual love, or parent–child relations; larger-scale attachments to a place or a culture, to a class or a society, to an economic enterprise or a political movement—all of these have their place in the gamut of human relationships, and all of them engender their own characteristic kinds of commitments and responsibilities.

I want to stress not only the irreducible variety within the two categories of 'needs' and 'social relations', but also the irreducibility of each category to the other. Certainly 'needs' and 'social relations' are connected, for I have indicated that people's needs include needs for certain kinds of relationships. Nevertheless, it is important that people's reasons for acting in particular ways derive in part from the relations in which they *actually* stand to one another, *whether or not* those actually existing relations coincide with the kinds of relations people ideally need to achieve. Hence, though we need certain kinds of social relations, the ethical category of 'social relations' cannot be incorporated within that of 'needs'.

Given that the various components of a naturalistic ethics are irreducibly diverse, they are also incommensurable. That is to say, there is no single scale on which they can all be measured and weighed against one another, in cases of practical conflict. Consider an example. Suppose that my involvement in my work conflicts with my commitments to my children. Suppose that I am fortunate enough to be doing work which is genuinely satisfying and which matters a great deal to me, to the extent that it could be said that this work is one of the basic things which I live for and which gives point to my life. But suppose that the demands which it makes on me are leading me to neglect my children, by spending less time with them, and becoming increasingly distant from them. I have to make some kind of choice. How am I to resolve this conflict? How am I to weigh the demands of my work against my commitment to my children? There is no single scale on which they could both be measured, as different qualities of some common unit (such as units of 'happiness'). We may then seem drawn to the conclusion that there is no 'right answer' in such cases, and it is, I think, the experience of incommensurable conflicts of this kind that gives ethical subjectivism its plausibility. All we can do in such cases, it may seem, is to choose, in non-rational fashion.

However, such a conclusion would, I think, be too simple. It fails to do justice to the way in which the process of deciding what to do in such cases is a process of *discovery*. It is a matter of *finding out* that one set of considerations is more important than another. Now, it is true that there is no way of *describing* this relative importance other than by specifying what it leads one to do. Compare a similar example used by Sartre, of a young man living in Nazi-occupied France, who has to decide whether to join the Resistance or to remain at home with his mother, who 'lives only for him'. Sartre asks:

How does one estimate the strength of a feeling? The value of his feeling for his mother was determined precisely by the fact that he was standing by her. I may say that I love a certain friend enough to sacrifice such or such a sum of money for him, but I cannot prove that unless I have done it. I may say, 'I love my mother enough to remain with her,' if actually I have remained with her. I can only estimate the strength of this affection if I have performed an action by which it is defined and ratified. But if I then appeal to this affection to justify my action, I find myself drawn into a vicious circle.[7]

Sartre concludes that the decision which resolves such a dilemma is a *creative* act. If the young man decides to stay with his mother, he thereby *makes* it the case that his devotion to her is more important than his devotion to the cause of the Resistance. Similarly, Sartre would say that if I decide to devote more time to my work or to my children, I thereby make it the case that one or the other is more important. Now what is true here is that there is no way of specifying how important a certain consideration is, other than by specifying what it will outweigh in practice. I cannot say *how* important my commitment to my children is except by saying something like, 'It is so important as to require that I give less time to my work.' But still, the fact that it is so important is an independent fact in its own right, distinct from the fact that I may be led to act accordingly. This can be seen from the consideration that in such cases my decision may sometimes turn out to be mistaken. I might decide to give less time to my work and more to my children, and subsequently discover, from the resentments which I find myself harbouring against my children, that the decision which I made was the wrong one and that I had wrongly estimated the importance of my work. What I have actually been led to do will then have failed to reflect the real importance of the competing considerations. Thus the degree of their relative importance is an objective truth, to be discovered.

What the example also brings out is the *personal* character of the decision. When I discover the relative importance of the competing considerations, I discover something about myself. The relative importance of my work and my children is their importance for *me*, and it says something about the nature of my life. For someone else, a different kind of person living a different kind of life, they might have a different importance, without its needing to be the case that either of us is mistaken. This again may seem to support subjectivism. Nevertheless, we need to reiterate that in making this decision of relative importance, I am discovering a *fact*, albeit a fact that has this personal dimension. Moreover, despite the personal element, not just anything goes. The relative importance of work and children may be different for different people, but the conflict is a difficult one just because both considerations are, by their very nature, the sorts of considerations which are bound to be of very great importance. From the fact that, in such a case, different people might, with equal rationality, give different importance to the two, it does not follow that one could rationally give absolutely any importance to absolutely anything. It does not follow, as Hume once claimed in a celebrated sentence, that 'it is not contrary to reason to prefer the destruction of the whole world to the scratching of my finger.'[8] The scratching of one's finger is, by its very nature, in itself a *minor* injury (I am ignoring possible further complications such as that it might lead to blood-poisoning). As a matter of objective fact it is not substantially incapacitating in the way in which a major injury would be, and no personal idiosyncrasies can give it an importance which, by its nature, it simply does not have. Thus, though the weighing of conflicting considerations may involve an inescapably personal element, it does so only within certain limits. The limits are set by the objective facts as to what is and what is not, in general, important to human life. And when I claim that the two important components of a defensible naturalistic ethics are 'needs' and 'social relations', I claim that this is an objective fact.

My discussion in this section raises many further questions, which I should have to deal with if I were offering a fully worked-out theory, and not just a sketch. As it is, I shall not attempt either to state or resolve them. One question, however, presents itself inexorably, both because of its intrinsic importance and because it has been a central theme of this book. I have already alluded to the question of the connection between 'needs' and 'social relations'. Is it the case, perhaps, that facts about human needs provide reasons for cultivating certain kinds of relations with others? In particular, can it be claimed that the development of altruistic relations with others—relations which involve one in a concern for other people's needs and interests— will constitute a greater satisfaction of one's own needs?

The question of altruism and its justification is, as we have seen, a central problem for any naturalistic ethics. Are there any objectively good reasons why we should, in general, be concerned for other people's needs and interests, and not merely for our own? It is to that question in its various aspects that I now finally return.

Rationality and Altruism

Are there good reasons for acting altruistically? No single simple answer is possible, but once again we can draw on all the writers we have considered. We shall then arrive at an answer more satisfactory than any one of their theories taken by itself.

The first thing to be said is that, in so far as there are reasons for acting altruistically, they are reasons which can be effective only with someone who is already in some degree capable of responding to other people's feelings. They are reasons which presupposes a capacity to be moved by other people's needs, and joys, and sufferings. They presuppose, in other words, what Hume calls 'sympathy', or 'humanity', or 'fellow-feeling'. If someone lacked sympathy totally, they could not be induced to feel it by any set of reasons, for, to such a person, the reasons would be incomprehensible.

Hume, we saw, thinks that sympathy is something universal to all human beings. I suggested that there is a good deal of plausibility in Hume's claim; this at least can be said, that anyone who was incapable of being moved by other people's joys and sufferings would be regarded as pathologically defective. Drawing on Bradley as well as Hume, we can also suggest that the capacity for sympathy is not just a brute psychological fact about human emotions. It is intimately tied up with the social nature of human existence. Human beings cannot grow and develop, except by interacting with others, acquiring the habits and customs, the language and ideas of their community. In so doing they learn to share the feelings of others.

As Hume was aware, people may feel sympathy yet not be moved actively to help and care for others. However, where this rudimentary capacity for sympathy does exist, people can then be given reasons for exhibiting such active concern. These reasons cannot conjure up altruism out of nowhere, but they are reasons for cultivating it and extending it. Recalling our discussion of Plato and Aristotle, we can say that they are reasons which appeal to the agent's own needs and happiness, and that they are reasons which assert not just the instrumental value of altruistic behaviour, but its intrinsically rewarding character. The relevant facts of experience are that a life shared with others, not self-enclosed but developing and extending outwards, to find new interests in the activities of others, and thereby creating relations of mutual recognition and support with other people, is to that extent a richer and more satisfying life. These are not reasons for subordinating one's own interests and concerns quite generally to those of other people. Nor are they reasons for adopting, in a quite general way, the utilitarian stance of treating one's own interests as no more important than those of any other human being. But they are reasons for fostering certain kinds of relationships with people, and a feature of those relationships will be that one will sometimes sacrifice one's own interests for those of others.

We also need to recall from Chapter 4 the distinction

between two levels of reason-giving. Reasons which appeal to the agent's own needs and happiness may be reasons for living a certain kind of life, and creating certain kinds of relations. But someone who is committed to such a life and to such relations may, on particular occasions, care for other people, not because this satisfies his or her own needs, but out of a wholly disinterested concern for others. Other people's needs and interests have then become reasons in their own right.

In Chapter 5, in connection with Hume and rule-utilitarianism, we looked again at the idea of a two-tier system of moral justification. We saw that the problem for any such system is: can the two tiers really be kept separate? In the present case, what enables us to maintain the distinction between the two levels of reasons is, I think, the concept of *commitment*. If one is genuinely committed to attitudes of concern for others, and thus committed to particular relationships with others, these attitudes and these relationships will have acquired their own independent force and momentum. Such a commitment may then override one's own interests on particular occasions.

However, it also has to be said that the sacrificing of one's own interests need not be a sacrificing of oneself to something external. We have learned from Bradley that relations with others are not purely external to the self. My commitment to my friends or my children, to a person whom I love or a social movement in which I believe, may be a part of my own deepest being, so that when I devote myself to them, my overriding experience is not of sacrificing myself but of fulfilling myself.

Of course people do sacrifice themselves in unfulfilling ways. They do act in opposition not only to their own inclinations but to their own deepest needs, because they conceive it to be their moral duty to do so. We have learned from Marx and from Freud the sorts of social and psychological mechanisms that are involved here. We have seen how this kind of compulsive or alienated morality can come into being, and have seen it to be an essentially irrational phenomenon, involving the disguised and distorted internalization of an external authority.

So far we have identified, as positive reasons for acting altruistically, reasons which appeal to the agent's own needs and satisfactions. Now these are in themselves only reasons for developing *some* altruistic relations with others. It is quite possible for such relations to coexist in one and the same person with a ruthless disregard for others' interests elsewhere. An example would be a violent criminal, or an unprincipled careerist, who is motivated by a genuine concern to do his best for the family to whom he is devoted. Less spectacularly, most of us, most of the time, combine a concern for some people with a thoughtless lack of concern for others. Are there then any good reasons why one ought to show concern for *everyone's* interests?

Hume, at this point, would invoke the need to correct our variable sentiments by means of general standards. In order to make communication more effective, he says, we abstract from the particularities of our own situation, and apply to all cases the same impersonal standards. I have previously suggested that, as a claim about the requirements of practical convenience, Hume's point is unconvincing. As so often with Hume, however, what he presents as a psychological claim can be restated as a point of logic. The reason for adopting an impersonal standpoint is a matter, not of convenience, but of *consistency*.

It is important to understand what arguments from consistency can and cannot do. I have noted previously, in Chapter 6, the attempt to construct a complete argument for altruism entirely out of the requirement of consistency. The attempt is based on the idea that anyone who attaches practical importance to his own interests must, if he is to be consistent, attach the same importance to everyone else's interests. This argument, however, will not work. I could pursue my own interests and, without any inconsistency, completely disregard other people's interests. My own interests would weigh with me, not just because they are interests, but because they are *mine*. Consistent egoism is perfectly possible.

Suppose, however, that someone is already committed to an altruisitic concern for *some* people. This means that he or she treats the very fact of their being in need as a reason for trying to meet that need. If, in the case of certain other people, he or she *fails* to treat their needs as reasons for exhibiting concern, it can be said that he or she is inconsistent. Consider a woman whose child is ill, and who feels a desperate pity for her child, and wants to do all she can to help him recover. One thing that is important here, as I have said previously, is that it is *her* child. She stands in a quite special relationship to this particular child, and the nature of that relationship is the reason for the quite special kind of devotion she shows. But a part of that very devotion is that she *pities* the child, that she is moved to action by the fact of the child's suffering. She responds *to the suffering*, and it is the fact of the suffering, as well as the nature of the relationship, that weighs with her. Therefore, it could appropriately be said, 'Here are other sick children, suffering in just the same way that your child suffered; do not they too deserve pity, and if you can do something to help them too, should you not do so?'

This is not to say that, in order to be consistent, one would have to give the *same* weight to the needs and interests of everyone. As I have said, special relationships (such as the parent–child relation) are reasons for *special* concern, and this follows from the very nature of the relationship. But we can say that consistency requires that one should give *some* weight to the suffering of *anyone* whom one is in a position to help, just on the grounds that that person is suffering.

In this way, then, we can go beyond Bradley's stress on specific social relationships, to the universalistic humanitarianism of Kant and Mill. Note that, to fill out the content of this universalism, we need to draw on *both* Kant *and* Mill. Following Mill, we can say that a concern for other human beings must, in part, take the form of a concern to promote their happiness and prevent their suffering. Following Kant, however, we can also say that we owe to other human beings a respect for their autonomy as persons, and that this respect cannot be interpreted in purely utilitarian terms. It may require that, in particular circumstances, we accord others the freedom to make their own choices, even at what we take to be the cost of their own happiness.

The consistency argument can, then, establish that we

ought, as far as possible, to take account of the needs and interests of everyone. It does not, however, establish *how much importance* we ought to attach to different people's needs and interests. To establish that, we have to look again at specific kinds of social relations. We have seen that some kinds of social relations may require us to give special importance to particular individuals. We have special loyalties to our children, our friends, and so on, over and above the concern which we owe to all human beings. In other contexts, it may be appropriate to attach *equal* importance to *everyone's* interests. This requirement of equality, however, is itself specific to certain kinds of social relations, for I would suggest that it is within a co-operative community, where persons all share in a joint enterprise, that principles of equality become appropriate. In short—as Aristotle, Hegel, and Marx would all agree—the study of ethics inevitably leads us on to the study of social and political philosophy. In lieu of that study, I can here offer only the bald reminder that human beings are social beings. That, however, is enough; it enables us, at least, to give some account of the place of altruism in a naturalistic theory of ethics.

Notes

1 G. E. Moore: *Principia Ethica* (Cambridge, 1930), especially Ch. 1. Moore himself employs the phrase 'naturalistic fallacy' against the background of a very different theory. He maintains that the term 'good' denotes an objective property of which we can have direct knowledge. It is, however, he says, a unique and unanalysable non-natural property, and hence its existence cannot be deduced from the existence of any natural (i.e. empirical) property. Any such supposed deduction would be an example of the naturalistic fallacy.

2 Recent examples of the defence and the rejection of subjectivism are, respectively, J. L. Mackie: *Ethics: Inventing Right and Wrong* (Harmondsworth, 1977), and Renford Bambrough: *Moral Scepticism and Moral Knowledge* (London, 1979).

3 Warnock does at this point invoke also a kind of 'universalizability' argument. He says: '. . . moral reasons really are reasons, and could not rationally be denied to be so. . . . A man who will suffer if he acts in a certain way has a reason for not so acting. . . . But if *his* consequential suffering is a reason for *him* not to act in a certain way, then consequential suffering is a reason against courses of action; for the suffering of other persons is not *different*, merely in not being his, from his; what makes my sufferings rationally relevant to practical questions is that they are sufferings, and not that they are mine'

(p. 163). This is an attempt to generate *impartiality* out of *consistency*, of the kind which I have criticized in Chapter 6.

4 Her self-criticisms can be found in *Theories of Ethics*, p. 9, and in *Virtues and Vices* (Oxford, 1978), pp. xi–xiv, 130–1, and 161–7.

5 Karl Marx: *Towards a Critique of Hegel's Philosophy of Right: Introduction*, in *Selected Writings*, ed. McLellan, p. 69.

6 For an attempt to deal with the problems, see my article 'On Seeing Things Differently' in *Radical Philosophy* 1, reprinted in *The Philosophy of Society*, ed. Rodger Beehler and Alan R. Drengson (London, 1978). I now think that the article concedes too much to relativism; in particular, I would now withdraw the words 'and equally valid' on p. 11 (Beehler and Drengson, p. 335). But I remain committed to the broad lines of the attempt to do justice to both the objective, and the personal character of the choice between ethical world-views.

7 Jean-Paul Sartre: *Existentialism and Humanism*, trans. Philip Mairet (London, 1948), p. 37.

8 David Hume: *A Treatise of Human Nature* Book II, Part III, Section 3.

Index